THE ART OF ANT

LONDON SCHOOL OF ECONOMICS MONOGRAPHS ON SOCIAL ANTHROPOLOGY

Managing Editor: Charles Stafford

The Monographs on Social Anthropology were established in 1940 and aim to publish results of modern anthropological research of primary interest to specialists.

The continuation of the series was made possible by a grant in aid from the Wenner-Gren Foundation for Anthropological Research, and more recently by a further grant from the Governors of the London School of Economics and Political Science. Income from sales is returned to a revolving fund to assist further publications.

The Monographs are under the direction of an Editorial Board associated with the Department of Anthropology of the London School of Economics and Political Science.

THE ART OF ANTHROPOLOGY

ESSAYS AND DIAGRAMS

ALFRED GELL

Edited by Eric Hirsch

LONDON SCHOOL OF ECONOMICS MONOGRAPHS ON SOCIAL ANTHROPOLOGY

Volume 67

Oxford • New York

Reprinted in 2006 by

Berg
Editorial Offices:
1st Floor, Angel Court, 81 St Clements Street, Oxford OX4 1AW, UK
175 Fifth Avenue, New York, NY 10010, USA

First published in 1999 by

The Athlone Press
London, UK

Berg is an imprint of Oxford International Publishers Ltd.

ISBN-13 978 1 84520 484 6 (Paper)
ISBN-10 1 84520 484 0

www.bergpublishers.com

CONTENTS

LIST OF PLATES

FOREWORD

Eric Hirsch, Department of Human Sciences, Brunel University

Alfred Gell's wife, Simeran, has recently recounted the day in October 1996 when Alfred learned that he had about six months to live:[1]

> He had a life-long loathing of base emotionalism into which he classed self-pity, and he spurned all dogmas premised upon faith – demanding a suspension of rationality and selfhood – as a degradation of humanity. To his own catastrophic news he consequently responded with a rational and cool, almost indifferent, fatalism and devoted himself to alleviating the agony of his family and friends as best he could, and to preparing us for what was to come.

The next day he sat down to finish the book *Art and Agency: An Anthropological Theory*, which he had begun earlier in the year. Having worked at a steady pace for about ten days, and having finished the last chapter of that book, he then began work on the paper which forms the last piece of this collection. It was delivered as the Frazer Memorial Lecture in Cambridge on 22 November 1996. In December, he turned his hand to this collection of essays, a project which had previously been urged upon him by colleagues at the London School of Economics. He planned to provide no Introduction to the collection, and the circumstances in which one was subsequently written are worth mentioning as they inform some of its style and content.

During the first of many visits to Alfred, I suggested to him that an Introduction would be useful in providing a unifying framework with which readers could approach his work. Alfred was initially reluctant, because he thought such a project would – indeed should –

be of little interest since he could think of 'nothing more boring' for readers than his reflections on himself and on his own writings. He was never one for taking himself too seriously, and he would, one knows, be urging his readers to abstain from doing so as well. Nevertheless, I persisted, and eventually in late December Alfred began to write an Introduction, a draft of which was finished within a few days. It is difficult to know why he overcame his initial reluctance, but Simeran feels Alfred had begun to adopt a semi-detached observer's perspective on himself, and he approached this particular task – which called for a bird's-eye view of his involvement with anthropology – as just another opportunity for engaging his intellect.

The Introduction which follows is a response by Alfred to the question of what unites the various papers written at different times throughout his career. And his response is characteristically modest and witty: all the papers were performances delivered for the benefit of departmental seminars. Indeed, in an earlier incomplete draft, he described the 'spirit of comedy' which he found so attractive in the discipline of anthropology.[2] These themes are not banal, although they might at first seem so, and they belie the serious intellectual conundrums with which Alfred engaged. In any case, he hoped to make elaborations on various points in the Introduction but was by then too exhausted to resume work upon it. We agreed that the best way forward would be if I questioned him on aspects of his work, using his draft text as the basis for our discussions, and then recorded his responses on tape. We met three times for this purpose in January 1997, and transcripts of some of our conversations are included in the Introduction.

I have left out most of the material concerning Alfred's period at boarding school, something we explored in our discussions because it provided an insight into what Alfred termed the 'collegiate conviviality' that shaped his predilection for 'seminar culture'. It was at boarding school (together with Stephen Hugh-Jones and Jonathan Oppenheimer, friends and students of anthropology with whom he maintained very close ties until his death) that Alfred developed his interest and skill in the practice of wit as a medium of social communication. Upon reflection he came to see his preference for the performative dimensions of seminar culture as an outgrowth of these displays of wit which were honed and refined during his youth. In one interview, he spoke of being part of an 'intellectual elite' of his school:

But it was not an intellectual elite founded on how much you knew, or how well you were doing in exams, or being a swot and reading books – nothing like that. It was an intellectual elite founded on wit, the ability to make people laugh. I seem to remember we even used to give one another marks out of ten for making witty remarks and jokes. That's what our self-esteem was based on. It was a form of mild verbal aggression, a sort of verbal competition, one-upmanship, the desire to be top dog. If X says something, then you can cap it with some other funny thing, continually: what Boswell describes as 'the flow of spirits', and he was a great one for squelching the opposition with some witty remark. I think I probably carried a lot of that sort of adolescent competition to, in some ways, be wittier than the next person into the academic work that I do. The aim is to write a paper which is essentially wittier than somebody else's paper.

A book which impressed me a great deal when I read it was Koestler's book on wit and science,[3] in which he argues that humour arises through the clash of two contradictory frames of reference, or paradigms. New knowledge is always subversive of old knowledge because it involves this clash of what he calls frames of reference. I think that in so far as I had a method, I modelled it on Koestler's notion of the conflict of frames of reference, so that the aim was to be productively witty. I realize that it's very dangerous to talk about wit because it implies that one possesses it. I can afford to take that risk.

The boarding school period of Alfred's life is of particular interest to me because it helps account for a fundamental tension in his anthropological persona. As Chris Fuller noted in his obituary of Alfred (*The Independent*, 1 Feb. 1997, p.18): '[i]n many ways he was a romantic, but he was also adamantly rationalist'. While I concur with this, I think there is also another equally powerful tension present. As Alfred's student and later colleague, I was always struck by his powerful intellectual capacities and insights and his equally powerful refusal to develop a 'Gellian' school or system of thought to rival some of his other intellectually ambitious colleagues. The tendency is there in his book *The Anthropology of Time*[4] and in *Art and Agency*,[5] but once the exercise is complete, Alfred moves on to the next topic of interest, to the next intellectual performance. In hearing him speak about his youthful interest in common-room wit and humour, and in particular his fondness for the Victorian novelist

George Meredith (mentioning to me that *The Egoist* was one of his favourite pieces of literature (see *Anthropology Today* obituary, April 1997: 21–23)), the penny dropped, so to speak. For the first time I clearly understood the tension between the very serious anthropological scholar and the man always intent on never taking himself or his work too seriously. Alfred was as 'ambitious' in *this* quest as some of his other colleagues were in their 'seriousness'.

To do justice to Alfred Gell's formative years is beyond the scope of this Foreword, and would require study of numerous other sources: correspondence with his parents from boarding school; travel journals as an undergraduate; fieldnotes from New Guinea and India; notebooks from the mid-1970s to the time of his death in which he sketched his ideas for books and papers; computer disks from the 1980s onwards; a video made before his death in which he recounts his experiences among the Umeda; a series of tapes which record his early childhood experiences, and so on. Simeran Gell hopes to write a memoir of Alfred based on this material and to contextualize these life experiences properly, as well as to incorporate hitherto unpublished papers.

In our discussions, Alfred and I were aware that time was pressing and we confined ourselves to the essays chosen by him for inclusion in this volume. Given his wide-ranging and eclectic interests, he had nevertheless selected those essays which best exemplified the anthropological themes that had most recently engaged him: exchange and consumption, art and language, and tribal India.[6] Our discussions were held during the last several weeks of his life, during which time his clarity of thought, as well as courage and dignity, were remarkable. The last meeting was on the 23 January 1997, and before leaving his house I returned to the room where Alfred was resting. He spoke as if he knew there could be no further discussion: 'Eric, I am really no more use to you'. Several days later he died.

There is a final matter to note and that is the title of this volume. Alfred pointed out that he was 'hopeless' with titles and finally opted for a rather simple one: *Essays and Diagrams*. Simeran and I discussed this and finally decided on a longer one – *The Art of Anthropology: Essays and Diagrams* – which in its slight ambiguity highlights both Alfred's passion for art and his distinctively artistic approach to the practice of anthropology itself. Its provenance, however, is Marilyn Strathern's address at the memorial ceremony held at the London School of Economics on the 13 March 1997. There she read the obituary she had drafted for *The Times*, but which was not published (she drily remarked this was because it had not been sent with an accompanying 'Strathernogram' – see Chapter 1):

> He was important for social anthropology because of his skill in showing the myriad ways in which anthropology knew more than it realised. Who else would have lit with such finesse on body tattoo in Polynesia as a route to speculating on political structure (*Wrapping in Images*, 1993)? Nothing was too small – or too large for that matter – for investigation. Sometimes his sheer originality broke through as sheer mischief, like the working title for the critique of the idea of 'art' he was completing as he died – 'The anthropology of art' indeed!

Encouraged by this passage, we felt that Alfred would have approved of our title – *The Art of Anthropology* – as one which conveys his talent for creative mischief, and for productive wit.

Notes

1 Alfred died from cancer on 28 January 1997.
2 The draft Introduction by Gell reads as follows:

> Reflecting on the genesis of the essays published for the first time or reprinted in this volume, I find that I am drawn, inexorably, towards a new, and possibly difficult theme: namely, comedy, and its status as an anthropological muse. I do not claim, far from it, that anthropology is 'essentially' a comic discipline – anthropology has no 'essence' and is far too diverse a field ever to be pigeon-holed in such a way. Most of anthropology is serious, technical, even tragic or impassioned. I do not decry seriousness; in fact, I am impressed by it more often than not. But the purpose of this introduction is not to discuss anthropology as a whole; it is only to discuss the particular perspective I have on it – a perspective founded on my character and education, acquired before I ever opened an anthropology book, still less wrote one. And I must observe that, for me, the attraction of anthropology has never been its passionate, tragic, or even serious nature, but its potential for comedy. If I had been a novelist, I would have tried to write comic novels. If I had been a journalist, I would have written comic journalism for the Sunday supplements and magazines. But, quite contingently, I became an anthropologist, so the spirit of comedy, which the very act of writing summons up whenever I try to put words on paper, had to express itself in the peculiar form of a series of academic texts. I do not suppose that this has been any great loss to light literature or journalism in my lifetime; in fact, I think I was lucky to have found a genre of writing to which my particular literary proclivities were quite well suited. Readers

of this book, and my others, can make up their own minds about that.

Does it make sense to describe any anthropological text as embodying the spirit of comedy, and if so, what is this spirit? Of course, I do not expect readers to laugh out loud while perusing my pieces, though I can occasionally make audiences laugh at seminars and lectures, as any teacher of anthropology who cares to be liked learns to do. There is a distinction to be drawn between 'comic writing' and out-and-out 'humour' of the best journalistic kind (e.g. Michael Frayn). Comedy does not aspire to produce laughter so much as a sense of amusement. This gentle emotion has, however, far-reaching literary and scientific implications which are worth exploring more fully than is commonly done, especially in 'serious' academic subjects like anthropology.

I do not think that I am the only anthropological writer who tries – no, not 'tries' but is impelled – to evoke the comic spirit. In fact, I think that this spirit has been present from the beginning, and was one of the factors which made anthropology 'possible' as an innovative, distinctively twentieth-century, discipline. Consider the much discussed issue of 'Malinowski's style'. There could be no disputing that Malinowski's literary gifts launched our subject in its modern form. Prolonged fieldwork and superior linguistic ability would have availed him nothing had he written boringly. But, as we know, besides meticulous fieldwork, Malinowski read and wrote obsessively in three languages, setting each against the other, and perfected a wonderful, urbane English prose which took the (educated) world by storm. Malinowski's name is coupled, in literary terms, with that of Conrad, because of the perhaps superficial fact of shared Polish expatriate identity. Conrad's novels, however, are much more tragic in tone than anything that is to be found in Malinowski's public, as opposed to private, writings. Malinowski's public writing is indisputably comic (just re-read *Argonauts* or *Crime and Custom* or even *Coral Gardens* with this in mind). Malinowski's personality, so far as one can discover, was quite unlike Conrad's (he did not suffer from depression, for instance) and the tone of his ethnographies is light, even sunny, which is why they are still so readable. I am certain that Malinowski read Meredith and Dickens and Trollope, Gogol and Balzac, as well as Frazer and Conrad, and that the effects of these comic novelists on his eventual output were just as profound. Malinowski's themes are the social comedy of 'exchange' and the intellectual comedy of 'magic', contained within the broader comic frame of the expatriate polyglot Pole versus the rooted, self-assured, Trobrianders who (unlike their scribe) think they inhabit the centre of the world and can control it with a word or gesture. Both Pole and Trobriander are comic figures. Dangerous though it may be to assert this in the current climate, we are undoubtedly being asked, by Malinowski, to be amused by the Trobrianders, just as we are invited to be amused by the characters in George Meredith's *The Egoist* or any of the best comic novels. Which is not to say that the Trobrianders are being pilloried, or are not also being presented as admirable, even heroic, human beings. They certainly are, and this is one pivot of Malinowski's comedy, just as the implicit 'heroism' of the anti-hero Oblomov is a hidden pivot of Goncharov's comedy, in a cruder, more obvious, way. But I have to insist on my dangerous point, which is, that it is possible to write anthropology which, to an extent, finds in the Other a source of amusement, of comedy. And it was the discovery of the right tone in which to communicate this amusement – which Malinowski reserved for his public writings – which propelled anthropology out of the nineteenth-century 'scholarship' and into the twentieth-century during which it developed, above all, as literature. This 'tone' is very hard to define; without actually being racist and colonialist, it has absorbed racism and colonialism as an inescapable, historical, given. The comic anthropologist (Malinowski) knows that he is on the wrong side of the ledger, morally speaking; and that he can produce only text, not historical change (especially not the undoing of the past). Given that, the comedy of manners unfolds brightly over a darkened backcloth, part of which is the historical identity of the scribe: his intrusive tent, his writing implements and cameras, his wealth, his access to white society and lands beyond the seas where everything is different. The comic tone relies on the fact that the western reader (the only intended reader) knows all this and knows that the anthropologist is kicking against the pricks of world history in advance of Pauline 'conversion' to the 'natives' point of view' – which can never be definitively adopted, either.

The worst that can be said of the comic tone is that it is not 'activist' in the modern (or really, post-1968) sense, that is, Malinowski does not denounce colonialism, but simply writes colonialism in a way sympathetic to both parties to that unequal relation. Come to that, I have never denounced colonialism myself, and would never dream of doing so, not just because I descend from a line of colonial officals, soldiers and missionaries, but also because I consider such literary gestures futile in the absence of some practical activity. Writing anthropological comedies is not going to set the world to rights: it is just going to amuse some readers, initially and predominantly western-educated readers, in a certain way. The moral ledger remains just in the same one-down situation as before, but since I do not aspire – nor do I think Malinowski much aspired – to live 'morally', that fact has simply to be accepted.

3 *The Act of Creation* (London: Hutchinson, 1964).
4 Oxford: Berg, 1992.
5 Oxford: Clarendon, 1998.
6 There are plans for a second volume of Alfred's essays, all of which have been published elsewhere. Simeran and I discussed the possibility of incorporating some of these in the present volume. In the end, however, we felt it was appropriate to leave Alfred's present selection and its ordering in the manner he envisioned.

ACKNOWLEDGEMENTS

The editing of this volume was sustained throughout by the tremendous support of Simeran Gell. To her and Rohan Gell I offer many thanks and a deep sense of appreciation. An early draft of the Introduction benefited from the comments of Stephen Hugh-Jones and Chris Pinney. I am most grateful to both of them, as well as to Jonathan Oppenheimer, for their help and interest. Marilyn Strathern provided extremely helpful editorial assistance with Chapter 1.

The taped conversations with Alfred were transcribed by Louise Byrne, whose work greatly facilitated the subsequent editing. Funds to enable the transcription were kindly made available by the Department of Anthropology, London School of Economics, and in particular the Head of Department at the time, Jonathan Parry.

PERMISSIONS

Chapter 3, 'The market-wheel: symbolic aspects of an Indian tribal market', originally appeared in *Man* (vol 17: 470–91, 1982), and is reprinted here by permission of the Royal Anthropological Institute.

Chapter 4, 'Style and meaning in Umeda dance', originally appeared in P. Spencer (ed), *Society and the dance: the social anthropology of process and performance* (1985), and is reprinted here by permission of Cambridge University Press.

Chapter 5, 'The technology of enchantment and the enchantment of technology', originally appeared in J. Coote & A. Shelton (eds), *Anthropology, art and aesthetics* (1992), and is reprinted here by permission of Oxford University Press.

Chapter 6, 'Vogel's net: traps as artworks and artworks as traps', originally appeared in *Journal of material culture* (vol 1[1]: 15–38, 1996), and is reprinted here by permission of Sage Publications.

Chapter 7, 'On Coote's "Marvels of Everyday Vision"', originally appeared in *Social analysis: journal of cultural and social practice* (vol 38: 18–30, 1985), and is reprinted here by permission of *Social analysis*.

Chapter 8, 'The language of the forest: landscape and phonological iconism in Umeda', originally appeared in E. Hirsch & M. O'Hanlon (eds), *The anthropology of landscape* (1995), and is reprinted here by permission of Oxford University Press.

Chapter 9, 'Exalting the king and obstructing the state: a political interpretation of royal ritual in Bastar District, Central India', the Frazer Lecture 1996, originally appeared in *The Journal of the Royal Anthropological Institute* (vol 3: 433–50, 1997) and is reprinted here by permission of the Royal Anthropological Institute.

INTRODUCTION

NOTES ON SEMINAR CULTURE AND SOME OTHER INFLUENCES[1]

All the essays collected in this volume began life as texts intended to be delivered out loud to audiences, mostly at seminars. They are not really essays for reading so much as scripts to be performed. I have been lucky enough to spend my entire anthropological career in departments large enough to support weekly 'Anthropological Theory' seminar series, with outside and departmental speakers, reasonably sized audiences of anthropology teachers and postgraduate students, and so on. I have also often been invited to speak at similar seminars in other departments of anthropology. My interest in my subject has been largely sustained by the existence of such weekly seminar series, in which I have always participated eagerly both as a member of the audience (entitled to question the speaker) and as a speaker myself.

The British-style (anthropology) seminar is a peculiar institution with rules of its own. A regular weekly (term-time) event, the 'ideal' seminar usually brings together some 20 or more participants, around a table, under the chairmanship of an experienced teacher and seminar leader. The chairman introduces, and generally gives moral support to, the speaker, while the audience undertake the role of critics, and may, indeed, ask extremely hostile-sounding questions. In a good seminar, there are usually three or four expert seminar practitioners, who can be relied on to give the speaker something of a grilling. The questioning goes on for an hour, allowing time for the more junior members of the seminar to intervene as well and acquire the interrogatory skills of their seniors. However, the seminar is not as unfriendly an occasion as it sometimes seems to visitors unused to its conventions. There is an implicit rule that really severe questioning is reserved for speakers who have shown, in the course of their papers, either that they possess the dialectical skill to handle even the most destructive questioning, or, on rare occasions, that they are so bumptious and thick-skulled that they are unlikely to comprehend the devastating nature of the questioning they receive. The mild, tentative, paper from an inexperienced speaker will not be dealt with harshly. Meanwhile, the skilled dialectician relishes the cut and thrust of debate, and exploits the opportunity afforded by hostile questioning to produce additional extemporized displays of wit, turning the questions back on the questioners and making fun of their positions. As the question period draws to a close, the skilled speaker elaborates the main points of the paper in a series of improvisations on themes suggested by the audience. Adrenalin flows copiously through the speaker's bloodstream by this time – now the hard questioning has been overcome – and unusual freedom of expression may be attained. The audience are enjoying themselves too. But the chairman must close the seminar once the time allotted for its duration is over, since, like Cinderella's ball, seminar bonhomie has a fixed temporal compass, which cannot exceed *two hours*, even by a second. At this point, the chairman thanks the speaker, conducts him to a place of refreshment, where adrenalin is tempered with alcohol, and happy, animated conversations ensue.

The point is that the seminar is a social occasion, a game, an exchange, an ordeal, an initiation. To one of a naturally social disposition, to hear a paper in a seminar is intrinsically much more interesting than to read the same paper in cold blood, because one's social proclivities are excited as well as one's strictly academic or intellectual interests. I confess to being a social animal of this type. Consequently, it is much more exciting for me to write a paper for presentation at a seminar than it is to write for an imaginary reader, as one does when writing a book. Books do not give anything like the feedback that one gets from seminars.

It will readily be seen from this (idealized) description that an anthropology department without a weekly seminar series is like a body without a heart. It is in the seminar context that departmental solidarity, if it is to accrue at all, must be forged. This has institutional implications that I cannot pursue here. It will also be apparent that a seminar series without a supply of speakers whose papers generate the quintessential feeling of *bonhomie* is also doomed. Fortunately, I can report that at the seminars in which I have participated there have always been enough good papers presented to keep the ideal alive, and often very much more than enough – at times, even a cornucopia of such papers. British social anthropology may have its disadvantages (poor pay, threatened cuts, lack of jobs for good students, and so on) but at least in the larger centres *seminar culture* has thrived since I have been on the scene, and seems set to continue. Visiting American anthropologists have often commented to me on how lucky we are in this one respect, if no other.

Why am I pursuing this theme? Because it is important to emphasize something about the context in which most of the following papers were written, that is, as contributions to 'seminar culture', not as 'publications'. Seminar culture is what really defines my academic *métier*, rather than membership of a rather nebulous 'profession'. Of course, no sooner are these words out, than I realize how elitist and self-indulgent they must sound. Is the writing of anthropological papers really a matter of social exchange among a particular set of seminar-goers? Is providing 'entertainment' for this crew the service for which I have been paid a salary all these years? Well, I can claim to have done other things as well (conducted researches, taught students, published books, and so on), but I still think of seminar culture as somehow more central to my true interest than anything else I have done. Leaving aside the question of whether there is any 'point' to academic activities of the kind I have pursued (is there any 'point' to the activities of a stockbroker? or an airline pilot?), I may as well be honest about what these activities are. And the concept of 'seminar culture' does serve to define their focus. But the notion of an academic *habitus* founded on social exchange, 'entertainment value', and productive of *bonhomie* and solidarity, seems sufficiently heterodox (from the accepted Bourdieuian perspective) to demand a more elaborate and detailed defence.

Let me recount my apprenticeship as a seminar practitioner. I was introduced to seminar-giving by Meyer Fortes (*c*.1966). He had the excellent idea of teaching the Cambridge third-year anthropology students by means of a two-hour seminar, during which the students had to give papers of at least half an hour's duration, if not three-quarters of an hour. I had to give my presentation on M. Meggit's 'Walbiri Kinship'[2] – an exceptionally complicated book about Walbiri aborigines having to marry their mothers' mothers' mothers' mothers' brother's daughter's daughter's daughter, or some such. This was quite a trial, but Fortes was a most sympathetic seminar chairman, and moreover, my audience consisted of fellow students with whom I had basically solidary relations anyway. Since I knew that my audience would be bored unless I took great care over my presentation and made it as interesting as possible, I took enormous pains over it – no doubt to the detriment of my eventual exam performance, since, in typical Cambridge fashion, there was nothing about the Walbiri marriage system, or anything like it, on the exam paper. In the event, I was thrilled to the core by the experience of expounding the 'mothers' mothers' mothers' mothers' brother's daughter's daughter's daughter' to my peers. As a rather shy boy, a bit lost in 'fast' Cambridge undergraduate society, I found that I seemed to possess a distinct edge when it came to this particular (very specialized) form of public speaking, and that I could get an audience not just to respect my intelligence in this context, but also to like me personally. So I spent a great deal of my remaining term at Cambridge, when I should have been revising, writing my very own 'seminar' paper, even though there was no seminar before which I could, as a mere undergraduate, present my work. This paper, my Opus 1, dealt with Don Juan 'mythology' in Lévi-Straussian fashion. It was actually also designed as an offering to Edmund Leach, whom I worshipped from afar but who was not my supervisor and with whom I had no personal relationship. I sent my paper to him and received copious and encouraging comments. But how I wished instead to read it to him myself, in the company of his elect! – but that was not to be.

My supervisor during my last year at Cambridge was Andrew Strathern, who was responsible for encouraging me to become a Melanesianist, and who conspired with my subsequent PhD supervisor at the London School of Economics (LSE), Anthony Forge, to obtain for me a Social Science Research Council (SSRC) studentship. But although I greatly liked, and learnt a great deal, from Andrew Strathern, I have to say that Leach was probably the anthropologist who influenced me most during my initial stages. My undergraduate view of anthropology was simple and dualistic. Lévi-Strauss was God, Leach was his vicar on earth, and Meyer Fortes, I am ashamed to say, was the functionalist Satan, whom we structuralists spurned and derided, and his side-kick was Dr Jack Goody, from whose lectures, supposedly filled with calumnies against structuralism, we absented ourselves lest we be contaminated. I know that this all sounds very silly now – we were puzzled, in fact, to see that Leach and Fortes appeared to be good friends despite arguing so fiercely in print – but this is how the callow undergraduate mind works.

I had to wait until I was recruited (by Anthony Forge) to the LSE anthropology department before I could savour seminar culture to the full. Not only was the teaching for the M.Phil conducted in the 'seminar' format, with the presentation of long papers (i.e. 20–30 minutes) before the assembled class, but we were also admitted to the famous 'Friday Seminar' which had been going, non-stop, since Malinowski's day. This seminar was run by Raymond Firth in a most excitingly autocratic fashion; all those in attendance were assumed to be able to comment intelligently, and would be asked to do so if the chairman saw fit. Since I never knew when Raymond might ask 'Well, what do *you* think, Mr Gell?' it was absolutely necessary to pay attention both to the paper and to the subsequent discussion, on pain of possible public humiliation. I still retain the ability to listen to an hour's paper and 50 minutes of discussion without lapses of concentration, as a result of this early, invaluable, training.

I must have shone during the M.Phil mini-seminars, because I was invited to give a paper to the grown-up Friday Seminar even before I left for the field in 1969. For me, this was an absolutely epochal event, and I never worked harder than on the preparation of my paper for this occasion, which concerned Melanesian 'Big-Man' politics. It was not that I simply wanted to avoid a fiasco; I was much more ambitious than that. My aim was to seduce my audience, to make them admire me just as if I had been a débutante dancer going on stage. My presentation of self had to captivate just as much as my words. (I may say that at this period I was a fumbling, oh-so-British lover, so perhaps there was a large element of sexual compensation at work.) Anyway, I was in luck. My paper went swimmingly, and even won a prize, the very first Firth Prize for the best postgraduate paper of the year. While it was gratifying to get a prize, what I yearned to repeat was the actual performance itself, the dawning realization that the thing had *struck home* .

This seminar, and some later ones I gave as a PhD student, while writing up my dissertation, were of very great importance to me in that while I never believed that I was better at 'anthropology' than my more intelligent age-mates, I always prided myself on giving better performances in the specific 'seminar' setting. So, since then, I have concentrated on working towards particular 'performances', rather than concentrating, as perhaps I should have done, on the development of anthropological theory in a more general sense. What I have always wanted to produce was the 'ideal' seminar paper for reading out loud (rather than some specific advance in anthropological knowledge). This performative or dramaturgical notion of anthropological 'text' contrasts, of course, with the American one – the framework underlying 'Writing Culture' – which is much more print-dominated. Of course, I do not claim to have produced this 'ideal' performance, only to have attempted it.

But it would be disingenuous on my part to claim that I did not have theoretical ambitions and inspirations as well. I have already mentioned the hero-worshipping attitude I had towards Edmund Leach while I was an undergraduate. The papers 'Rethinking anthropology',[3] 'Genesis as myth' and 'The legitimation of Solomon',[4] provided the model for my literary activity from the start. People complain about Leach's scratchy prose style; but I hear Leach's authentic and unforgettable drawl behind his printed words, and the whole text comes alive. Leach's style has the supreme virtue of allowing his wit, his sheer cleverness, to emerge fully; the absence of shading, delicacy and embellishment only contribute to this central purpose. I, on the other hand, was more interested than Leach in prose as a literary medium. Partly, this came from my early and assiduous reading of Lévi-Strauss, a much more refined prose stylist than Leach. Having passed French A-level, I was not dependent on translations – of which there were few to be found in the 1960s. I struggled through *Les Structures Élémentaires de la Parente*[5] and *La Pensée Sauvage*[6] when I ought to have been reading Fortes, Goody and Evans-Pritchard, to my eventual detriment in the exams. I still think that Lévi-Strauss is the greatest of anthropologists, and that he will never be overtaken, however long our discipline remains in existence – his only rival being Malinowski, a taste for whom I acquired only later. Lévi-Strauss' urbane and convoluted style inspired me greatly, and it is fair to say that at the outset of my career I wanted to produce 'Leachian' displays of hard-hitting anthropological wit, wrapped up in Lévi-Straussian gravitas and mellifluousness.

By the time I had finished my postgraduate studies at the LSE, though, I had broadened my range of influences considerably. For one thing, as soon as I left Cambridge, I finally got round to reading Fortes, particularly his work on the developmental cycle of the domestic group. At this time I also discovered phenomenology, or, to be more precise, phenomenological social theory and psychological theory. My guides were Alfred Schutz and Maurice Merleau-Ponty, whose works I took with me to New Guinea when I went into the field in 1969. I made a very thorough study of Schutz's collected papers, and *The Phenomenology of Perception*,[7] not least because I had little else to read and much time on my hands, immured in my mosquito-net. Exactly why I became interested in phenomenology is rather a puzzle to me. I came across Schutz by chance in the LSE library on a browsing expedition, while Merleau-Ponty, unless I am much mistaken, I first read because *La Pensée Sauvage* is dedicated to him and his name has such a fascinating ring to it.

I wrote my monograph on the Umedas in 1972–3. This was presented as a 'structural analysis' in the Leach/Lévi-Strauss mode, and seemed very fashionable when it came out, but only for a little while, because 'sixties structuralism' was already in decline. I like to believe that the attention *Metamorphosis of the Cassowaries*[8] received from other anthropologists was due to its literary ingenuity rather than its theoretical message, which was really quite out of tune with the times.

I was somewhat at a loss then how to proceed during the 1970s, which I spent in wonderfully relaxing circumstances in the Australian National University (ANU). Resurgent Marxism was in the air; but I had no left-wing leanings and I never believed that anthropology was a force to set the world to rights or undo the effects of colonialism. I could hardly present myself as a fire-breathing anti-colonialist given that my ancestors were all colonial officials, soldiers, and even missionaries and bishops. I never had the slightest feeling that I could be 'engaged' or 'committed' or identify with the subjects of anthropology, if only because my middle-class income – even an academic salary – was so much greater, and cost me so much less sweat to obtain, than the incomes of Umedas or, later, Muria Gonds. I have never understood how bourgeois like myself can consider themselves the class allies of third world peasants, since it seems to me that we are all just walking, breathing examples of the results of their exploitation. All that people like me can do in the third world is watch and listen sympathetically, and maybe form a few personal relationships which, in the nature of things, are without significance so far as the wider historical relationships between nations are concerned. The business of bourgeois anthropologists like me is only to produce texts – or give seminars – directed towards a reception of other anthropologists and interested (metropolitan) parties. Possibly, I am totally wrong about all this, though of course I have the support of Lévi-Strauss in *The View from Afar*.[9]

Because the anthropological Marxism of the 1970s repelled me, before I read Bourdieu[10] and was reconciled, I was forced, more or less, to spend the decade interesting myself in non-anthropological studies, particularly philosophy and psychology. It was at this time that I conceived the idea of writing an anthropology of time, a project on which I squandered an inordinate amount of—time. The

whole effort would have been wasted but for the fact that my manuscript, which had been rejected by Cambridge University Press in
1984, was, some years later, taken up by Bruce Kapferer and published in much revised form by Berg (1992). But truth to tell, the
whole period between 1977, when I returned from studying the
Muria, and 1984, when I began to work on 'art' was something of a
wilderness period. The most important influence on my theoretical
outlook during this period was Bourdieu. Only on the surface am I a
Bourdieu critic.[11] Actually, I read Bourdieu obsessively, and with
unstinted admiration for his dialectical skill. I think of Bourdieu as
just as much one of my masters as Leach, Lévi-Strauss, and the
phenomenologists Schutz, Merleau-Ponty and Husserl.

Meanwhile, seminar culture sustained me and I sustained seminar
culture. In Australia, and later at the LSE (from 1980 onwards) I
produced about one seminar paper every year, most of which went
down pretty well and some of which are reprinted here. Of these, the
most important to my subsequent development was 'The technology
of enchantment and the enchantment of technology' (Chapter 5)
which, although it only appeared in print in 1992, was actually written in 1984, in the depth of my 'wilderness' period, just after my
'Time' book had been rejected. For the purposes of this paper (and
inspired by Annette Weiner, Nancy Munn and Shirley Campbell)[12] I
started to read Malinowski properly, especially *Coral Gardens*[13]
which I had not even opened before. I think that I became very much
influenced by Malinowski stylistically, following this immersion, and
that my writing became simpler and more expressive as a result –
anyone who thinks this is an odd thing to say about Malinowski
should just try reading him. Malinowski was a supreme literary
stylist whose elegant texts (along with Evans-Pritchard's) should be
imitated by every anthropological beginner.

From the mid-1980s most of my work has been concerned with
the anthropology – or sociology, it's the same thing – of art. I was
destined to write about art for two reasons. Anthony Forge, my
supervisor and long-time patron, was the leading theorist of the
anthropology of art of his day. Although I now take positions which
are, in many ways, opposed to my teacher's, I acquired from him the
conviction that the study of art raises some of the most interesting
problems in anthropology. Secondly, I was destined to write about
art because of my own personal predilection for 'art' as an activity
which gives me pleasure. I have always drawn and painted (both
my parents are skilled artists)[14] so for me the graphic channel of

expression is as natural – in fact, rather more natural – than writing. *Metamorphosis of the Cassowaries* is dominated by this mode of expression, and is really an 'art' book as much as a 'ritual' book. The same could be said of my subsequent monograph on Polynesian tattooing.[15] When I write, I see pictures in my head and I write accordingly; the diagrams come first and the text later. There are many 'diagram based' papers in the present collection (e.g. Chapters 1, 3, 4 and 8). Extensive use of pictures and diagrams is also part of effective seminar culture, since giving the audience something to look at, as well as to listen to, makes it far easier to ensure their concentration over the full hour. The anthropological seminar, as practised by me, often has close relations with that other performance genre, 'the illustrated talk' (e.g. Chapter 6) normally associated with art history and other visual disciplines.

(NB: the following comments on individual chapters are compiled from Alfred Gell's notes, and from his conversations with Eric Hirsch.)

In fact, Chapter 1, the essay on 'Strathernograms', began life as a lecture (part of a 'Melanesia' course) and only later became a seminar paper, delivered at the LSE Friday Seminar in 1995.[16] It derives from my determination to come to grips, finally and definitively, with Marilyn Strathern's famous, but difficult, book[17] with which I had been struggling more or less since it came out, but especially in the summer of 1993–4. I do not think that I have ever written anything which demanded more intellectual effort on my part. Understanding Strathern, whose mind works very differently from mine, was like doing fieldwork all over again, but fieldwork on a text rather than on that vague entity, a 'culture'. The Strathernograms themselves are, so to speak, the genealogical diagrams which seem to me to underlie this text, and I hope that they are as explanatory for others as they are for me. I am glad to say that Marilyn Strathern herself read a draft of this essay and was kind enough to grant it her *imprimatur*, so I am confident that I have not totally traduced her ideas, even though I have, of course, been very selective in my presentation of them.

When I was struggling during my first year as an undergraduate when I first tried to read Les Structures Elémentaires de la Parente, *I seem to remember that the diagrams in Lévi-Strauss were one of the few bits that I could understand. I found that I could understand Lévi-Strauss if I paid close attention to the diagrams, and reconstructed the meaning of the text on the basis of the diagrams. So I was always very diagram conscious, and I've always* appreciated *really good* diagrams. *For example, the diagrams in Robin Fox's book* Kinship and Marriage[18] *are* superb *pieces of clear graphic expression. The diagrams in Lévi-Strauss are sometimes quite ambiguous as to their meaning, but nonetheless they are always extremely thought-provoking. The diagrams in Fortes are very interesting. There are innumerable diagrams in Leach's* Rethinking Anthropology, *many of which have a very, very clarifying* effect *on the text. It would be hard to imagine* Rethinking Anthropology *devoid of its diagrams. It wouldn't be a meaningful text at all. And also, I was very interested in myth, and myth analysis is an intrinsically diagrammatic procedure.*

Myth analysis is done by converting the myth into some form of matrix and the form of these matrices is essentially diagrammatical, iconic. So you make an iconic representation of the myth and when you've subjected it to various transformations, you look for an existing myth which conforms to the transformations which you've made. That was something that I found very productive as an intellectual technique. Other people's minds don't work like this. I know perfectly well that other people occasionally think of putting in a diagram to clarify what they are trying to say at certain points, but I didn't. I sort of perceive – not always, obviously – but I often perceive by means of some image or diagram, particularly when doing things in a more structuralist mode.

[EH: In your essays on 'How to read a map',[19] and 'The market wheel,'[20] you argue that artifactual maps, these particular diagrams which are used routinely in our culture, are actually at a formal level not so very different from the maps people the world over carry around in their heads in an intuitive way.]

It is said that 95 per cent of the information which we make use of is originally derived from visual sources. Yet anthropology as a business consists of the production of texts in propositional form. There is a basic contradiction here in the sense that anthropology is a very wordy business, yet the subject-matter of anthropology is – not always, but often – cognition or peoples' thought processes, or how people perceive and understand the world. If one wanted to know how X perceived and understood the world, one would have to know what they had seen and what they had made of what they had seen, rather than what they had thought in words and what they were prepared to express in propositional form. This was the point that has been made by Maurice Bloch[21] among others. And I think that this is true. When I am writing papers I generally start with an image, even in those papers which don't have any diagram as such. For example, the 'Swing's paper'[22] starts with an image of somebody being swung. The fact that one constructs a paper out of a seam of life which is imaginable primarily as a visual image – or in the case of 'the language of the forest' (Chapter 8) as a movement – is significant. If the diagrammatic method has anything to be said in its favour it is that it tends to keep closer to the actual ecological characteristic of human cognition, which is that it doesn't proceed propositionally, let's say, as a set of verbal propositions but as a series of images which are supplemented and overlaid by further images and so on and so forth – something which has, for example, been emphasized by Roy Wagner. I habitually think in terms of images, and of bringing images to things, and in terms of graphs, such as 'Strathernograms'. It seems to me that whenever Strathern-type social relations are made manifest, they are made manifest as images of some kind or another, or they often are manifest in this way.

Chapter 2, 'Inter-Tribal Commodity Barter and Reproductive Gift Exchange in Old Melanesia', was written in early 1989 (before I even read *Gender of the Gift*) for a seminar series held in Cambridge. It represents my own particular take on Melanesian gift exchange, which is quite different from Strathern's. I would still stand by the arguments that I advance here. It was not written to refute Strathern, but simply from a different, independent, point of view. The purpose of this essay is to criticize the unthinking Mauss-ism which still prevails in many discussions of 'the gift', and which certainly did prevail in 1989. I admit to a certain mischief-making intent as well, since I was brought up to believe that if there was one thing to which brideprice could not be compared, that was commercial exchange, that is, barter. But it has always seemed to me that bride-price and barter are highly similar, though perhaps not quite the same in all respects. This mischief-making was directed at my friend and one-time collaborator Chris Gregory, whose work[23] I nonetheless much admire and which has influenced me a great deal.

Mauss is connected in the western mind – because he intended that it should be so – with forms of exchange which are ethical as opposed to forms of exchange which are unethical. And commercial exchange has been treated as unethical. Now I objected to this for various reasons, one of which is that in India I had studied not a world of merchant communities but people who worked in markets and were traders, and I didn't think that these people were any more unethical than anyone else. I was concerned that many Indian scholars thought that anybody who lent money in the village, merely by virtue of so doing, was a more wicked person than somebody who had any other alternative occupation that the village might provide, such as building a cart, or doing something else.

But I hadn't been asked [in the essay on inter-tribal barter] to defend commercial exchange. I'd been asked to write about barter, so I took it the other way round and instead showed elements of commercial exchange in the very type of 'altruistic', reproductive, ceremonial exchange relationships which were usually considered Maussian and therefore ethical. I was also slightly peeved by the rise of political correctness. I didn't like the implication being made that some people – maybe in Papua New Guinea itself – were morally inferior because they engaged in commercial and barter types of exchange, and those who didn't were morally superior. I thought that was ridiculous.

Chapter 3, 'The Market Wheel: Symbolic Aspects of an Indian Tribal Market' was written while I was at the ANU, and was presented at seminars there and in Sydney in 1978–9. The main influence is actually Geertz, whose paper on the cockfight I took as my model, as so many others have done. I include it both because it reveals my 'diagrammatic' method of procedure, and also because it is an early example of 'consumption' anthropology as well as a 'market' study. Perhaps also it expresses an originally Fortesian idea that social relations can be read spatially as well as conceptually, that is, from the layout of people and things 'on the ground'.

Simeran went to do fieldwork in India among the Muria [in 1977–8], and I went along as the spouse. I'd asked for a research grant to study time among these people, but since I couldn't provide any satisfactory answer to the question 'If you study people's time, what do you study?', the ANU had wisely not given me a grant. Not having any grant, I had nothing in particular to study, so I could choose myself. I must say, it was a very, very nice fieldwork indeed, not having any research grant, not having any research project. And so I collected material on the markets simply because the market was one of the most interesting social occasions which happened every week, and it was really wonderful. I loved the market, and I liked the traders and the hustle and bustle of it all – very beautiful it was, exotic.

[EH: It almost sounds as if you're going to the other extreme, making commercial trade Maussian?]

Well, yes, you could say so. Of course the paper on the 'Market wheel' – which was written long before the paper on Melanesian barter – was written in the 1970s and is a product of its period. But I think it's quite a nice paper of the period. One thing you cannot possibly do is make out that I'm being theoretically consistent between the 1980s and the 1970s because I'm not. But this market paper is about the diagrammatic method. That's what I came back from the field with – a mapping of the market, and what people went into the market to sell and what they came away with, which was always subtly different. I don't know how phenomenological you could say that was, but not very. And it really wasn't against interpretation. It wasn't against Mauss. It certainly wasn't against Geertz either. It was very pro-Geertz. I was in a mellow mood. It wasn't against anybody.

I'd always been interested in the idea of layers or levels. The market has a centre and you then get a circle around it, and then another round around the first round and so on. That's obviously related to the model of the limbum palms which you find in Metamorphosis of the Cassowaries *where you get the white interior, then the red marginal area and then the green, and then the black. This kind of 'spheres within spheres within spheres' has always been interesting for me to think about. But in this paper, the important thing is the diagram. From diagrams one can extract unexpected relations that are not intuitive. For example, when you see a tribal market – it looks like a higgledy-piggledy arrangement of stalls. When you make a map of it, on the other hand, you discover that you have in fact got this terribly neat map of social relations. So that's the production of the counter-intuitive redescription of the world. I thought, if you line up all the goldsmiths, then the less important jewellers, and then the important high-value commodities like tobacco, and then the lower-value commodities, and then the groceries, and then the bulk groceries, and so on, what you've actually got is a map of* value, *a scheme of* value *governing the society as a whole. And it just came to me like that – in a flash!*

Chapter 4, 'Style and Meaning in Umeda Dance', introduces the study of art as a system of transformations, which is still a very basic theme of mine. Only here it is not plastic art that is at issue but Umeda choreography. Once again, this whole paper is based on a graphic technique (for representing dance movements taken from cine-film) which I worked out laboriously on a film-editing machine in the basement of the School of Oriental and African Studies. The 'dance studies' community dislike this paper because it does not use one of the conventional dance notations, such as Laban notation. This has never worried me in the slightest. I developed my graphic technique because it allowed the use of coordinate transformations, in the D'Arcy Thompson[24] manner, which none of the other dance notations permit. I had to represent dance movements this way in order to say what I wanted to say about them, dance 'experts' notwithstanding.

This paper was written because I had something I specifically wanted to say, namely, that you could see each dance step within a certain genre as a transformation – let's say that you could break down a dance step into a certain number of variables, treat those variables independently, and put them together again in a different configuration. And then you'd have transformed that version of that dance. This idea of transformation plays a large part in Metamorphosis of the Cassowaries. *I think the bit of* Metamorphosis *which probably gave me the most happiness when I was writing was the analysis of the fringes of the masks, because it's so simple. I felt that that sort of transformational analysis was an extremely powerful weapon analytically.*

It can provide you with strong arguments very fast that X is connected to Y, and that some relationship exists. My frustration with Laban notation or the other one (they quarrel with one another incessantly about which of these two systems they should use[25]) was that there was no way of making these transformational relationships immediately visually pertinent, even though they are pertinent. One can see a parodied ballerina-type walk, and a really over the top ballerina-type walk as two versions of the same thing. In fact they could be part of an innumerable series of gradations of the same sort of thing, and with Laban notation you can't say that easily. You have to use little arrows and you'd have to have somebody specially standing over you to teach you for a year. And that means that dance studies have always belonged in the ghetto because basically you have to have such a lot of technical training before you can do dance anthropology that the barriers to entry to the dance anthropology field are such as to make it extremely unlikely that anybody with any anthropological skills worth mentioning

The transformation of mask-types (drawn by A. Gell)

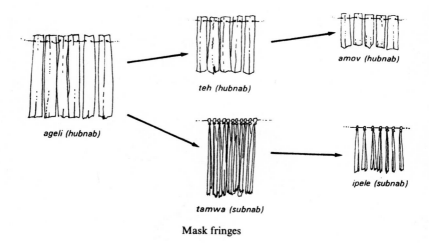

amov (hubnab)

teh (hubnab)

ageli (hubnab)

ipele (subnab)

tamwa (subnab)

Mask fringes

would accept those barriers. Where in an ideal world one could have a better notation transcription system, we don't live in that world, and until we start living in some kind of ramshackle simulacrum of that world, people in anthropology will never find anything of much interest about dance, about technical aspects of the anthropology of dance.

In a way [this article] is about the way I was introduced into anthropology by Edmund Leach, because one thing you'll notice with the mask analysis and the dance analysis is that they can be done on this rubber sheeting. Leach had this idea that you could put social structure on rubber sheeting and twist it around. Well, it's that idea basically. I think that idea (which comes in Rethinking Anthropology*) had a very, very powerful long-term effect on me, so that whenever I come across bodies of data which do seem to be susceptible to being shown as a series of twistings and stretchings on rubber, I automatically do so.*

Chapter 5, 'The Technology of Enchantment and the Enchantment of Technology', is perhaps the most popular and widely read of the articles I have published, so I need say little about it except that the idea came to me in a flash. The paper took five days to write and eight years to publish – so that I could use it as my seminar warhorse for an extended period. I came to know it virtually by heart. The only point I might need to underline, however, is that I am not actually a Philistine, or a promoter of philistinism, as some have apparently supposed. I merely advocate 'methodological philistin-

Plate 1   During field work among the Umeda, photographed by an Umeda, 1969

Plate 2   In Canberra, during the years
at the Australian National University,
1976

Plate 3 During the last months, with
his wife Simeran and son Rohan,
October 1996

Plate 4   Alfred during field work with the Muria

Plate 5   Alfred Gell in 1996

ism' as an analytic device, so as to wrest the anthropological study of artworks away from the soggy embrace of philosophical aesthetics. I, personally, am a practising aesthete, never happier than ooh-ing and aah-ing before the great masterpieces of art.

During my undergraduate and postgraduate years the great issue in anthropology, as in many cases even nowadays, was considered to be meaning. It was the high period of semiotic anthropology. Barthes' Elements of Semiology[26] *was very widely disseminated and the great advantage – in the study of art – was that art objects could be treated like texts in that they had a solid physical existence as objects, and that they were part of intersubjective experience. And because of their objective physical existence and their not belonging to a natural language but to the world of things, it seemed probable to people like Anthony Forge[27] that art objects would provide a kind of royal road into a kind of meaning more basic, more fundamental, than linguistic meaning because they were not so dependent on the special features of linguistic codes in their horrid grammaticalness. Language is so fiendishly complicated, has so many rules and is so evanescent, whereas there is something solid and elemental about art objects. So it seemed that art objects could provide a very good experimental animal, as it were, for discussions of meaning, so long as one assumes that art objects* had *meaning, and it seemed a very natural assumption to make that they* had *meaning, and that the production and circulation of art objects were social acts, and moreover that social acts by definition were considered to be likely to have meaning.*

As you can see from my later works, I am not convinced – I do not think that meaning is an essential property possessed by works of art. Meaning was Anthony Forge's problem. It was my problem to the extent that I was taught by Anthony and I was introduced to the subject via the study of meaning. Anyone can see that Metamorphosis *is about meaning. But I do not see things in those terms any more. When I wrote the 'Swings' paper'[28] I abandoned the semiotic model in favour of a more psychological, non-linguistic view of religious vertigo which represented me trying to get away from these sorts of formative ideas which I'd spent so much time on before. And 'The Technology of Enchantment' paper was important in that it carried further the process of emancipating me from the notion of socio-linguistic models of meaning.*

If you do things semiotically, you have this embedding problem – exactly how is the semiotic system embedded in social practice? I thought that by thinking of enchantment as a form of social technol-

ogy, I'd find a way of both preserving the absolutely significant aspect of the work of art as something which has a powerful cognitive effect on the spectator as well as something which is produced by very potent cognitions of the maker. But I had a way of linking that side of the equation to the social efficacy of art – the fact that we produce and consume art in ways which very often do not seem to be in the self-interest of the immediate agent or patient, and the Bourdieuian idea of the social system as a self-propelled, self-sufficient set of social relations, which are mediated by cognitive performances of whose ultimate long-term significance the agent may not be self-aware.

Chapter 6, 'Vogel's Net: Traps as Artworks and Artworks as Traps', is a recent paper which derives from an interest in Duchamp and conceptual art which I have maintained since the 1970s when I first studied Duchamp's notes for 'The Bride stripped Bare by Her Bachelors Even' as part of my 'Time' project. It has always seemed to me a pity that the anthropology of art has only joined forces with 'modern' art in the most stupid, reactionary way: that is, because the anthropology of art is supposedly about 'primitive' art. This paper makes a plea for the material culture of non-western people to be seen as advanced and witty – like Duchamp's art – rather than primitive and barbarous.

This paper has got a number of themes in it – the nature of the art work, the trap, and what's wrong with the anthropology of art. Now what's wrong with the anthropology of art is that it has finally come to a definition of the art object which is basically a nineteenth-century one, and which does not take into account that most significant twentieth-century art has been surrealist or conceptualist, the most important of all being the work of Duchamp from 1912 onwards. It seems an invidious distinction to draw, to allow ourselves to have an art which consists purely of a kind of witty reframing or reperceiving of objects which surround us in everyday life, like urinals or traps, or what other things are there, and the famous bicycle wheels, Duchampian objects, ready-mades . . . [allowing this] to be art for us because we are so advanced and technically sophisticated. Whereas for 'them', they've got to make do with a definition of art in which the only things that can be art are things which would be, if produced by our civilization, of low quality, that is, things like any statue of a saint which if commissioned today is going to be a poor piece of art. There is no way historically that it can be anything except a pretty, rubbishy piece of ecclesiastical art produced by an artist too timorous to actually pursue a career in proper art, and who instead opts for provincial security as a provider of chunky images of saints for country churchyards and things like that.

Whereas I argue that art – in so far as art is that which intellectually fascinates us and disturbs us – exists in all possible societies. That's art number one. Art number two is however defined as art by virtue of the number of aesthetic criteria which are met by aesthetically pleasing artworks and not met by urinals and sharks and things like that. So I argue that if we look at the actual artifacts produced by non-western cultures, they do see these artifacts in ways which are entirely similar to the kind of tricksy ways in which the same sort of artworks might be viewed by westerners.

This paper pivots on a passage in Pascal Boyer's account of his conversations with an African philosopher of a particular rural cult among the Fang who tells him that every different animal has to have its own kind of trap. With a deer you just make a hidden place in the ground and fill it with thorns, but the chimpanzee is too clever for that. He'll see your hole in the ground however well concealed it is. You need a clever trap for a clever animal. So what you make is a deadfall type of trap which is moved by a very, very thin string, so that the chimpanzee walks by, and its arm gets caught by the string, and he looks at it and thinks 'strange piece of grass' and he carefully takes his arm out of the piece of grass and he thinks, 'hm, I'll just give it a little tug, just to see' and then—bang! So the traps in the forest are full of this kind of hidden wisdom which comes from the knowledge of psychological dispositions and behaviour of the Other. The Fang philosopher concludes that in fact sacred knowledge is a trap too, in the sense that if you have too much of it, it can endanger you as well as allowing you to endanger other people. Anyway, what I end up saying is that something like intentional complexity can be embodied in objects in a way which is, to a certain degree, capable of transcending cultural boundaries.

[EH: The recurring theme in a lot of your papers is—]

The theme that they're not so damned different from us as you think.

Chapter 7, 'On Coote's "Marvels of Everyday Vision"', was originally presented at the 1993 ASA Decennial in Oxford in a session organized by Jimmy Weiner entitled '"Too many meanings": a critique of the anthropology of aesthetics'.

Coote supports E.H. Gombrich[29] in saying that all *people everywhere have a basic aesthetic which is part of their culture, which is culturally distinct. So depending on what culture you belong to, your aesthetic predilections will be different. Once you've got some aesthetic you've got* some *set of preferences, and if you've got* some *set of preferences, you've got some set of objects in your world which are these priceless objects of everyday vision, which are objects which are valued not necessarily because they are artifacts which have been well made, but are valued as things which have been well made by God, like display oxen of the Sudan. Every boy has his ox which he oils and polishes and makes much of. Well, Coote's argument is that the anthropology of art has been held back because it's been too preoccupied with art objects, and what we ought to be concerned with are aesthetically valued objects, whether or not they are artifacts. And I take a different view, saying that this universal visual aesthetic is a myth one could never show. One would always have to have some way of showing that somebody had a visual preference for this kind of thing. Now they could just show it in their behaviour, so that it would always turn out that the oxen in their flock were spotted and with long horns. But it's hard to imagine that somebody could both make sure that all their ox were spotted and long horned, and not be able to* say *that the reason why they chose those oxen was because they were spotted and long horned, that is, so that it would be a piece of verbal culture as well.*

Essentially this paper is about reformulating the anthropology of art by rejecting the notion of an aesthetic work of art, by looking at the work of art as something more pragmatic and something which emerges out of a context of social interaction in whatever form you like. But it does also involve value, which means that one can't have a purely means–end notion of the work of art, one has to create complexity, one has to create fascination from somewhere. You know we can't just put a thing in the art gallery and just have it be there and then we'll all go away and have lunch! It has got to fascinate and that means it has to have certain cognitive properties, a certain appeal *to other minds, which I would distinguish very strongly from beauty, as in conventional aesthetics. Indeed, it's got nothing necessarily to do with beauty, but it does often have something to do with power or fascination. So in the Coote paper, what I show is that Coote says that the Dinka don't have art objects, they just have these oxen which walk around and look very smart. But I'm saying that the reason why the Dinka have these oxen is because these oxen are the basis of a form of social competition between young men of an explicitly aesthetic kind, that is, sung poetry, and so consequently it's not that they think that the oxen are beautiful and then write poems about them. They write poems, they compete with one another. Basically if you are a 19-year-old Nuer, you're in a competitive situation* 100 *per cent of the time. You don't have an emotion recollected in tranquillity while you're thinking about your ox, and how nice it is. You're out there* competing *and it's quite clear from the ethnographies that that's what they all do. So that 'beauty' is created by social competition rather than the other way round.*

Chapter 8, 'The Language of the Forest: Landscape and Phonological Iconism in Umeda', was originally presented at a conference on 'The Anthropology of the Landscape', organized by Eric Hirsch and myself at the LSE in 1989. I include it because it deals with one of my most enduring hobby-horses, i.e. the iconic characteristics of language. And this paper is based on a diagram – one of my most baroque ones – originally devised for a paper in *Canberra Anthropology* (1979).

I've always been on the side of the 'language is not arbitrary' position. Well, first of all, because it is counter-intuitive. They're the underdogs, the people who say that language is not arbitrary. And of course, I'm a natural supporter of the underdog, partly because it's in my nature, and also because it was generally subversive to structural linguistics – take for example the Harris and Chomsky[30] type of structural linguistics – which looked very imposing but appeared to me to be very little to do with the way people communicate in actual situations. Whereas what Malinowski in his appendix to Coral Gardens *says concerning the embedded nature of language, and the fact that language is not arbitrary at all because it's absolutely suffused into the texture of social interaction, was much more appealing to me than the Saussurian view of language that obviously constitutes a particular view of linguistics as a science. That is to say, I'm a natural linguistic functionalist and a post-linguistic structuralist, even though I use linguistic structuralism as a model in* Metamorphosis of the Cassowaries *for the interpretation of symbolic systems. Structural linguistics is an excellent way of approaching the interpretation of symbolic forms, but it's a very much less feasible way of discussing 'language as she is spoke' in real life. Linguistic interaction – now that's a rather complicated question.*

[EH: Does this paper connect back to your 'The Umeda language poem?'[31]]

No, it's like this: 'The Umeda language poem' was written in 1977 and it presents a problem of this one particular language which has this very peculiar characteristic which languages should not have, namely of the sound of the word being connected with the meaning. But in the end it's all very well showing that this is the case, which I can do, or I think I can do up to a point, and make certain, perhaps, helpful assumptions. That's all very well, but then that raises the question: How on earth could this happen? Why should some languages be like that and not others?[32] So although they relate to the same problem, they were two completely different papers. One is not an expansion of the other. The one answers the question which was left dangling unanswered in the other one. So I don't develop any idea which I have in the 1977 paper into the later paper simply because I give a descriptive model of Umeda as a language which has this high degree of linguistic iconism. That's just a recapitulated description and it doesn't recapitulate any theoretical proposition.

Chapter 9, 'Exalting the King and Obstructing the State: A Political Interpretation of Royal Ritual in Bastar District, Central India', was delivered as the Frazer Memorial Lecture on 22 November 1996 in Cambridge.

In 1977–8, when Simeran and I were visiting Jagdalpur during our first fieldwork, we were enquiring about the 'tribe' called the Halbas, from this man who was said to be an expert on Halbas, but who turned out to be a great gossip – an old retired schoolmaster of the type you find in provincial towns. We'd been hearing, in the village, stories about this great massacre and the death of the Raja of Bastar in 1966, which was then slightly more than a decade past. It's still a relatively current event. He told us about this shooting in the palace yard, and said that the Raja was going to hold up his hand – like this – to quell the people and send them away, and that the police, out of malice, shot him on the grounds that he was calling the people to rise up. The first bullet went through his hand. This is unlikely to have been historical fact, I somehow feel. Nonetheless, I was very intrigued from that moment onwards about the idea of a Raja of Bastar and his death and why it caused so much panic in the countryside as it did. Everybody killed all their goats, pigs and chickens, and pigs just never came back. People said the soldiers had fanned out among the villages and selected and shot people whom they believed had been in the courtyard during the time of the killing of the Raja because they didn't want them to be able to testify later to the number of people who'd been killed. I thought perhaps one day I'll live long enough to write a history of Bastar for myself which would certainly be an exciting thing to do. In fact it would be not just exciting, it would be very impossible to do because the whole question of the history of Bastar is so political – white foreigners poking their nose into Congress affairs in Bastar is certainly not on at the moment. Then I found a description somewhere of Bastar Dasara ceremonies. I picked up on the idea of the abduction of the Raja and his stealing away, and how similar that was to the 1876 riot, and so on and so forth.

So what I was really working towards, I suppose, was something like a Sahlinesian picture of history in which history is people replaying the categories which had been handed down to them from the distant past. And it just seemed to me such an interesting, neat example of all that happening. Every year the South Asian Anthropologists Group holds a conference. So I wrote a draft which formed the basis of that paper to give at the 1993 conference. But I never intended to publish it as that. I was going to sit on it as I usually do with my papers, but then this Frazer lecture offer came in, so I thought, ah that'll do nicely for that one – it was connected with Frazer. The paper obviously fits in with the sort of slight historicizing tendency which you can find in my admiration for Sahlins.[33] And it also provides me with an opportunity to do something which I really like to do – which is to take the piss out of these development people, particularly in India, who think that the poor downtrodden tribals have got anything to thank them for. In India most of the petty government officials are pretty much corrupt. But they all nonetheless think that because they have got a bit of education that gives them the right to rip off ordinary country folk and despise them at the same time. They don't do it in the name of self-interest, which would be quite reasonable in my view. They do it in the name of 'development' and 'progress'. So I've always been very much against development and progress, and this gave me an opportunity to be against 'development' and 'progress'.

Postscript (a collation selected from the interview material):

Overall, what I'm interested in is producing something which is counter-intuitive – all that I ever wanted to do was to produce articles and papers which would make people sit up – and to do that the last thing that one wants really to be interested in is some Big Subject. For example, the landscape paper (Chapter 8) makes use of cognitive psychology, and it makes use of a rather antiquated cognitive psychology of Kohler, and of the example of Manuma and Tekete. But what is very interesting is the fact that everybody knows which one of those two figures is Manumo and which one is Tekete. It also makes use of cognitive linguistics in the work on American sign language. But these things are just made use of. I'm never going to open another book on sign language! I'm not interested in sign language. Sign language is just an ingredient plucked off the shelf for the single purpose of producing a result which will have interest in the context in which it is presented, and the context in which it is presented is to provide an answer to a very specific puzzle – not one of the great puzzles of world – as to why the Umeda, of all people, might be the ones to have a language in which there were an usually large number of linguistic iconisms.

And so I haven't put in this cognitive psychology because *I'm interested in cognitive psychology. I'm interested in everything! I'm interested in the entire contents of the* Scientific American *every time it comes out. I read the ones about the sensory equipment of spiders and the ones about escalating health care costs in America, and so on and so forth. You give me the* Scientific American: *I read the whole bloody thing! I'm not more interested in one bit of it than I am in another and my interest in science and indeed the arts or anything else is simply that they provide a series of ingredients which can be combined – with luck – by means of pattern-building intuitions, to provide some kind of particular counter-intuitive or apparently counter-intuitive solution to some kind of problem which can be stated in a fairly restricted sort of way. Other anthropologists think of themselves as contributing to some ongoing march of science. That's maybe why other anthropologists are greater anthropologists than I am, because they actually believe in science and progress and cumulativeness. Whereas I am actually one of nature's genuine postmodernists, always was, from the very beginning. I mean, I was a postmodernist before postmodernism had ever been invented, in the sense that I wasn't really interested in actually, as it were, 'advancing the subject' in any particular way. All that I was interested in doing was producing a certain* frisson, *a certain artistic effect which could be achieved by taking a random collection of objects which could be made to fit together in an interesting way. You know, like a bird decorating its nest with an arrangement of little pieces of tissue paper, a leaf, a flower.*

The article on traps (Chapter 6) is a case in point. I am sort of semi-interested in the issue between [Arthur] Danto and his philosophical critics. But I'm not a philosophical aesthetician. Nothing for me fundamentally hangs on the outcome of that. But what I want to be able to do is to produce an essay which allows me to combine Danto, the extraordinarily metropolitan New York Philosophy of Art Professor, with the Pygmy theory of why chimpanzees are too clever for their own good. It's the possibility of creating these conjunctions and unexpected connections that interests me.

What is interesting is what is counter-intuitive. Let's say it's part of knowledge to discover that if you're poor, your life expectancy is lower. It's a true fact. If somebody should go out there and prove it, one might say anybody would have bloody expected it – so of course. If, on the other hand, one finds some section of the poor class, who contrary to expectation actually appear to live longer than a lot of rich people, then you've made a counter-intuitive discovery, and it's intrinsically more interesting. So the pursuit of the counter-intuitive is always more interesting.

Lévi-Strauss is a great master of the counter-intuitive. When you read the myths in Lévi-Strauss, frankly they are a mess. These myths are arbitrary tales in which absolutely anything appears to be able to happen and probably will. Just to speak of the structural study of myths is a contradiction in terms, because if there is one thing that doesn't obviously have a structure, it's some silly story about somebody climbing up the top of some tree and falling out and marrying a jaguar who was his mother's brother. But Lévi-Strauss manages like a magician through manipulation of the data to turn what is apparently arbitrary into something which is very, very orderly. And so the secret of – the magic of – Lévi-Strauss is this: not only that he makes it all very orderly, but that he also makes it productive. Let's say you get to the end of one elaborate paragraph of Lévi-Strauss in which he shows that everything is an inversion of everything else, and then the next paragraph starts 'Nor is this all', and then he produces the whole trick all over again in some other dimension! And it's that kind of conjuring with our feelings about reality and order and so on which makes Lévi-Strauss such a genius. Now it's that which I intended to produce.

Seminar culture obviously depends heavily on the pursuit of the counter-intuitive, in that it's saying the counter-intuitive proposition which is going to make people sit up and listen. Well, some people are so boring and some people are so hide-bound that they don't like counter-intuitive propositions. They make them feel nervous. However, the fact that one has encountered them shouldn't make one generalize. But on the whole the interesting members of the audience will be interested by some form of counter-intuitive argument, the demonstration of order where only chaos seems to reign at the level of ethnography.

The expression of the counter-intuitive is very neatly bound up with diagrams – as, for example, in the expression of the idea 'One relation is contained within another relation' (see Chapter 1). If I just say that as a proposition, you can say 'Oh yes, sure, right, what the hell do you mean?' But if you find the diagrammatic form in which one can express that idea, then something which appears to be, well, extremely puzzling, can be made cognitively accessible – which again is something counter-intuitive.

What I'm trying to do is to have a series of experiments with ideas which are really for their own sake. I don't want to teach by propounding a doctrine. What I want to teach is by providing examples of a particular kind of intellectual performance and getting others to do likewise. But it was as an exemplary stylist that I actually wanted to make my mark on the world. I was trying to do a series of tricks, to get the machine to work – like an inventor for whom, you know, today it's the perfect mousetrap, tomorrow the perpetual motion machine.

Notes

1. To distinguish the written Introduction (by Alfred Gell) from that based on interview material (with Eric Hirsch) the latter has been set in italics. All the notes in this chapter have been provided by the editor.
2. *Desert People: A Study of the Walbiri Aborigines of Central Australia*, (Chicago: University of Chicago Press, 1962).
3. Chapter 1 of the volume with the same title published in 1961 by Athlone, London.
4. The last two essays were published by Leach in *Genesis as Myth and Other Essays*, (Jonathan Cape, 1969).
5. Paris: Presses Universitaires de France, 1949.
6. Paris: Plon, 1962.
7. London: Routledge & Kegan Paul, 1962.
8. London: Athlone, 1975.
9. Oxford: Blackwell, 1985.
10. For example, *Outline of a Theory of Practice* (Cambridge: Cambridge University Press, 1977).
11 See A. Gell: 'How to read a map: remarks on the practical logic of navigation', *Man*, (n.s.) 20: 271–86.; *The Anthropology of Time: Cultural Constructions of Temporal Maps and Images* (Oxford, Berg, 1992) chapters 26–9.
12. In this chapter Weiner's work is not referred to, but see *Women of Value, Men of Renown: New Perspectives in Trobriand Exchange* (Austin, TX: University of Texas Press, 1976).
13. London: Allen & Unwin, 1935.
14. *Both my parents drew. My mother was a draughtswoman trained in the art of doing the drawings that go with archaeological expeditions and my*

father was an amateur artist, and so the materials were always present in our house. When I was a small child, I entertained myself by drawing mostly, as many small children do. I don't say I was a brilliant child artist but I would produce huge series of pictures. We had comics, and one week the comic started a big story about how some Vikings landed on a piece of rural Sussex. And there they are stampeding through the countryside wearing their hats with horns, with wings coming out, and their chain mail. On the basis of this, I was inspired to produce hundreds of pictures of Viking feats, as a child. Then when I started doing anthropology, we did archaeology, anthropology and physical anthropology, as well. And of course both archaeology and physical anthropology involved drawing skulls and stones. The first book of anthropology that I studied was Habitat, Economy and Society *(7th edition, London: Methuen, 1949) by Darryl Forde, and I copied out all the pictures in it. When I got to study anthropology properly, I became equally fascinated with kinship diagrams – and not merely by the* realistic representations of pictures of reindeer in their harnesses and things like that, which I'd copied out of 'H, E & S'.

15. *Wrapping in Images: Tatooing in Polynesia* (Oxford: Clarendon, 1993).
16. This is the only previously unpublished paper in the present collection.
17. *The Gender of the Gift: Problems with Women and Problems with Society in Melanesia* (Berkeley, CA: University of California Press).
18. *Kinship and Marriage: An Anthropological Perspective* (Harmondsworth: Penguin, 1967).
19 See note 10.
20. 'The market wheel: symbolic aspects of an Indian tribal market', *Man*, 17 (1982): 470–91.
21. For example, 'What goes without saying: the conceptualization of Zafimaniry society' in A. Kuper (ed.) *Conceptualizing Society* (London: Routledge, 1992).
22. 'The gods at play: vertigo and possession in Muria religion', *Man* (n.s.) 15 (1980): 219–48.
23. For example, *Gifts and Commodities* (London: Academic, 1982).
24. *On Growth and Form* (Cambridge: Cambridge University Press, 1942).
25. See page 140 below.
26 London: Jonathan Cape, 1967.
27. For example, see Forge's edited volume *Primitive Art and Society* (London: Oxford University Press, 1973).
28. See note 22.
29. *Art and Illusion: A Study in the Psychology of Pictorial Representation*, 5th edn (Oxford: Phaidon, 1977).
30. For example, Z. Harris, *Structural Linguistics* (Chicago: University of Chicago Press, 1960); N. Chomsky, *Aspects of the Theory of Syntax* (Cambridge, MA: MIT Press, 1965).
31. *Canberra Anthropology*, 2 (1979): 44–62.
32. *It comes in this bit of prose from 'The Umeda language poem' (Canberra* Anthropolgy, *2: 60), namely: 'these are alchemical flowers which open only in waters which are perfectly still'. In other words, I say that linguistic iconism would occur everywhere if there were no historical change. But that's not really a very likely proposition.*

How can one say that people are historyless, and how could one ever know that they were historyless? Umeda people had lots of history but it was all linguistic. So I didn't have an answer – that was a fact. I just had this beautiful sentence, though. Its a particularly beautiful sentence. Well, I was very proud of it at the time.

The common speech of the people is poetic speech in that it utilizes a language already imbued with everything a poet might wish to put there . . . . But it is only in very special circumstances that language as a whole, rather than the specialized production of linguistic virtuosi, incorporates a coherent poetic aesthetic. These are like alchemical flowers which open only in waters that are perfectly still: a language only begins to assume the crystalline geometry of an all-embracing iconism when the cultural and historical contexts within which the language develops have assumed a degree of extreme stability over a long period of time.

And of course nobody knows what alchemical flowers are. But you know those chemistry experiments where the thing crystallizes under water, and very quickly it seems to grow, and then it suddenly solidifies – like that. Those were called alchemical flowers, but they only do it in still water.

33. For example, *Islands of History* (Chicago: University of Chicago Press, 1985).

CHAPTER I

STRATHERNOGRAMS, OR, THE SEMIOTICS OF MIXED METAPHORS

Marilyn Strathern is one of today's best-known and most influential anthropologists, but there is reason to doubt whether her work is always well understood. Her writings are conducive to scholarly abuse, that is, citation for effect rather than sense, and the picking-out of little snippets of ideas from here and there, without any real reference to the structure of the argument from which these snippets are drawn. The secondary literature on Strathern is beginning to mount up; with special issues of anthropology periodicals being devoted to her, and theses being written about her. But to the best of my knowledge there are no summaries or digests of her ideas to which a student can turn for guidance, as they very easily can find summaries of the ideas of Geertz or Malinowski or Lévi-Strauss. One reason for this is that there are three distinct but intertwined aspects to her academic persona: there is Strathern the contemporary cultural critic concerned explicitly with feminism and rather less explicitly with postmodernism; secondly there is Strathern the meta-anthropologist, concerned with knowledge practices and the author of an anthropology of anthropology; and finally there is Strathern the straight anthropologist, an activity in which she has a formidable track record. When Strathern gets written about, it is Strathern the feminist or Strathern the postmodernist or Strathern the meta-anthropologist who gets written about, not Strathern the straight anthropologist. Some of the things which have been written about Strathern are very good: the published critiques by Margaret Jolly (1992) and Lisette Josephides (1991) spring to mind, and especially an unpublished thesis by Huen (1993). These works, though, are all essentially cartographic, trying to situate Strathern in the context of the intellectual field, the map of knowledge. What the enquiring student is not going to get from them is some clue as to how to make sense of fieldwork data, that is, how to anthropologize in the Strathernian way, rather than how to identify Strathern's position in the intellectual firmament. I think this is a pity, and that something should be done to codify and operationalize the interpretative strategies she brings to bear on ethnography, so that everybody can put them into practice, if they so wish. The key text for this purpose is GG (*The Gender of the Gift* (Berkeley, CA: University of California Press, 1988)) and, moreover, GG read in a particular way. Actually GG contains long passages which are about feminism and meta-anthropological problems. I am not concerned with feminism, since no male can be expected to discuss feminism without dissimulation. I also leave aside meta-anthropology, though I have always shared what I take to be her view of the very hybrid character of ethnographies as literary texts. I am also not going to say anything about Strathern's more recent work on English kinship and new reproductive technology. My quarry in this presentation of her ideas is Strathern the Melanesianist, the interpreter of Melanesian social and symbolic practices.

The *Gender of the Gift*, her anthropological *magnum opus*, is an infernally difficult book to read, as it must also have been to write. Paradoxically, the reason why it is difficult is not that it is rambling or incoherent, but because it is systematic and rigorous, requiring one to keep numerous different ideas going in one's head simultaneously. After a page and a half, saturation point is reached and mental indicators reading 'OVERLOAD – CONDITION RED!!' flash on, making progress slow and painful. What's the problem? I thought at one time it was her writing style, and that something could be done by dividing each sentence in half, then attaching the first half of each sentence to the preceding one, and the second half to the succeeding one, and in that way one could produce a series of sentences each of which was on one topic, rather than each being precariously suspended between two topics, as I felt was usually the case. But I have since changed my mind; it is not the manner in which she writes, but the content of what she says, that is difficult to understand.

But I do have one criticism of Strathern's presentation of her ideas in GG. The anthropological ideas she is interested in exploring are, if not pictorial, then frequently formal, but she hardly ever uses graphics to express them. Until Strathern herself provided me with irrefutible evidence to the contrary, I imagined that she was one of those people (of whom there are many) who panic when asked to draw something. Actually, Strathern can, and does, draw for pleasure, but not for public consumption. Drawing happens not to be her mode of anthropological communication; and this is no doubt compounded by the fact that, just at present, anthropology is going through a non-diagrammatic phase, after the excesses of diagram-making which marked the heyday of structuralism. Lévi-Strauss, Leach, and also, I would say, Fortes, were masters of graphic means of expression in anthropology. But today's anthropology comes from the very un-diagrammatic mind of Clifford Geertz, and the intellectual icons of the day are such dreadfully verbal authors as Derrida, Ricoeur, Heidegger and so on, none of whom ever drew anything, or, probably, wanted to. We are in a moment of verbalism, in which the graphic impulse is checked on ideological grounds, because graphics are associated with science, high-tech, and particularly, engineering (Leach's original discipline) and engineering is, from the standpoint of the cultural studies mind-set, Disciplinary Enemy No. 1.

I do not think that Strathern participates in this anti-formalism; she is far far closer to Lévi-Strauss than to deconstruction, appearances notwithstanding. Moreover, her closest anthropological ally, Roy Wagner, uses graphics extensively, and it is also worth noticing that Bourdieu, another creator of contemporary anthropology, uses diagrams and graphics very effectively as well.

The virtual absence of a diagrammatic channel of communication in GG is particularly puzzling in that, as one reads this text, images of forms, relations and transformations continually materialize before the mind's eye, and one has the strongest impression that while Strathern was writing, she likewise spent a lot of the time seeing forms, relations, and so on, in her mind's eye (as well as scenes from Melanesian life). Indeed, she has since told me that she does use a series of diagrams as schemata in the process of writing, but that she eliminates them subsequently since the text has to stand by itself (pers. comm.). She also remarks that diagrams can give a spurious logic to texts which are, in fact, discursively incoherent, a point which is well taken. In this essay, I want to supply the missing graphic channel of expression to the argument of GG. Of course, Strathern's point about coherent-looking diagrams accompanying incoherent texts should not apply here. The text of GG is certainly not incoherent, difficult though it may be.

My aim is to attain graphic coherence, doing justice to Strathern's textual coherence; though of course I am also writing an expository text of my own, which has to be coherent as well. In fact, I see my task as somewhat akin to the making of a TV adaptation of some long and complicated novel, with a view to assisting the dissemination of the text in a more easily assimilated (verbal/visual) format than the original. I can only record that, in practice, I have found this task as intellectually demanding as any that I have attempted as an anthropologist. Meanwhile, I am uneasily aware that many students of anthropology are even more put off by diagrams than they are by difficult, abstract, texts. I once had to teach kinship theory to a clever student who blandly informed me that she did not even bother to glance at the (to my mind, ultra-clear) diagrams in Robin Fox's *Kinship and Marriage* because they were too horrible and difficult-looking. For such individuals, perhaps, my text alone may be of some use, but I am not sanguine about this. Seriously diagram-averse persons might save time by simply turning directly to Strathern's text.

First let me outline what I believe is the theoretical stance taken in GG. I think it is fair to say that GG is written from an idealist standpoint: that is, it describes a world in which the real is an idea, or a system of ideas, signs, and so on, rather than a collection of objects about which we, or the Melanesians, have ideas, or of which our ideas can be taken to be representations. Idealism is an old and respectable philosophical doctrine, but Strathern is not a philosopher and she is not advancing her idealism as a solution to philosophical problems. Idealism is, in her work, a heuristic for dealing with the problems of ethnographic analysis, so she offers no defence of idealistic ontology or epistemology as such. However, I think it is useful to think of Strathern as an idealist, and I was encouraged somewhat in this belief by hearing Henrietta Moore, in a lecture, refer to Baudrillard as a proponent of 'idealist semiotics'. The Strathern of GG seems to me to be on quite a parallel track to Baudrillard, despite the fact she is dealing with the conventionally archaic (Melanesia) and he is dealing with the conventionally hyper-modern (TV ads).

There are two aspects to Strathern's idealism. Firstly, she describes the world as an array of signs. The perceptible world is the vehicle of meanings. Meanings, however, do not originate in the perceptible world, but in the code or system which encompasses the perceptible world, which is culturally produced and reproduced. Thus material things and bodies are not isolable things-in-themselves, but exist only in so far as they convey, or encipher, meaning deriving from the code. Because of this they have, in themselves, no fixed identities or essences as real entities, but can assume limitless identities according to their shifting articulation to the code. Secondly, and deriving from this, I detect a specific idealist thesis underlying GG, which concerns the concept of relations, which plays a basic role in Strathern's scheme. Idealists hold that all relations are 'internal', that is, participate in a system/code; and that there are no 'external' relations, that is, relations between objects which are theoretically independent of one another. In realist ontology, the world consists of a collection of things which exist independently of one another and which enter into external (e.g) causal relations. These objects can have internal relations, in the sense that the front cover of a book is internally related to the back cover of the same book, but the relation between one book and another book is treated as an external relation. In idealist philosophy (notably Bradley's) it is argued that it is mistaken to assume that one can divide relations into external and internal in this way, and that all relations between objects, or between objects and subjects are internal (like our front and back covers of a book), and in particular, the relation between the perceiver and the thing perceived is an internal relation, whereas for realism it is an external relation. The whole of GG is about various types of internal relations, particularly ones which seem counter-intuitive from a western point of view. In the frame of reference of GG, the contrast I have just alluded to between 'internal' and 'external' relations, coincides with the opposition between 'gifts' – which participate in, and generate, 'internal relations', and 'commodities' which participate in and generate 'external relations'. In Melanesia, 'the gift' prevails: in the West, the commodity economy.

GG is not a philosophic defence of idealism, however, but a text in which idealism is deployed as an interpretative heuristic. The book is constructed around an imaginary opposition between 'Melanesia' which is represented (as representing itself) in idealist terms, versus 'the west' which seeks to represent itself in 'realist' terms. It would be just as possible to represent the west's own self-representations from an idealist standpoint (as the Baudrillard example shows, and perhaps also Strathern's own work on modernity) but the architecture of GG depends on this contrast being maintained. Conversely, it is possible to interpret Melanesian ethnography on the assumption that Melanesians think about certain (ostensible) 'gift' transactions in 'commodity' terms; indeed I have myself published an essay precisely along these lines (see Chapter 2). However, if the latter path is chosen, it is not possible to arrive at any of the insights provided by

GG, whatever else may be achieved thereby. And since the insights of GG, not some alternative work written from a different point of view, are at issue here, we can resist the temptation to enter into what would, in any case, be a very empty debate.

The 'Melanesia' of Strathern's discourse (or mine) is not a 'real' place, which either idealists or realists could visit for the purposes of finding proof-positive of their own views and refutations of their opponents'. The 'Melanesia' of GG is not the actual nation states of Papua New Guinea, the Solomon Islands, Vanuatu, and so on, but a manner of speaking, or more precisely the site of certain problems of expression and understanding, peculiar to the cultural project of anthropology, which is (almost) exclusively a 'western' project, like it or not. It is important to underline the fact that 'Melanesia' stands for an intellectual project rather than a geographic entity because the methodological usefulness of Strathern's interpretative technique is not restricted to (geographic) Melanesia, as opposed to Africa, America, Asia or anywhere else. It has got nothing intrinsic to do with the totally artificial and internally discontinuous ethnographic area which happens, for mostly rather bad reasons, to have been christened 'Melanesia'. Perhaps the best way to think about Strathern's Melanesia, especially for those who feel rather resistant to postmodernist relativism on other grounds, is to think of Melanesia as the anthropological equivalent of Abbot's Flatland: that is, the setting for a sustained thought experiment. As Strathern pointed out to me (pers. comm.) neither realists nor idealists can obtain visas for Flatland, yet both may take profitable if imaginary trips there.

Though 'Melanesia' as the site for thinking through the consequences of idealist interpretative strategies is a mythical place, the detailed working-out of Strathern's scheme is undoubtedly carried on in terms of ethnographic particulars derived from the regional literature of Melanesian anthropology. A world consisting exclusively of signs and internal relations is imaginable anywhere, but the particular signs and relations discussed in GG are drawn from this literature, so I will respect this constraint in giving the following general conspectus of the system 'M' which you can take to stand for Melanesia or Marilyn, as you wish.

The system 'M' is founded on the following premisses.

In M the concept of a relation, specifically, an internal relation, does the work that the concept of the thing/person does in anti-M, the world as understood by realist ontology. The ultimate constituents of the world of M are relations rather than things/persons. The perceptible entities which would be thought of as self-sufficient 'things' or 'people' in anti-M are in M only indices or cyphers of relations, which are regarded as ontologically basic, whereas their sign-vehicles have, so to speak only a secondary status.

What is a 'relation'? Strathern does not tell us this, but, on her behalf, I assert that a relation is a connection between two terms. The number 5 is such a term, when it is related to the number 4, another term, by the relation > (is larger than). Terms are not things, just as the numbers 5 and 4 in the preceding sentence were not things. Terms are not self-sufficient in internal relations (relations in the number series are self-evidently internal) but are constituted out of the relationships into which they enter, as the numbers in the number series are. There would be no 4 without 5, and 3, and so on. Similarly, there would be no mothers without children, because a mother only attains that identity by virtue of a relationship she has with her child. But it is not the visible, physical, woman who is the term in the relation she has with her child (also a term). A woman is a mother not because she physically exists, has arms and legs and other functioning biological organs, and not necessarily because she has physically given birth. Not only are there many non-biological forms of motherhood (by adoption, for instance) but there is also no logically necessary reason why parturition, as such, should result in the particular relationship we think of as being a mother. The social world is pervaded by relations which seem to be like this, that is, relating *relata* (or terms) which are identifiable only in and through the relationship itself, as with mothers and children. The idea we have to grasp is that relationships in the social world are not between visible entities, such as mothers and children, but between terms within the code. The here-present mothers and children are regarded as signifiers, encyphering the relations between mothers-as-terms and children-as-terms. Terms are, in other words, ideal entities, not perceptible appearances of objects in the physical world.

I think that one can justifiably criticize Strathern for not doing enough to elucidate the concept of relationship, as I have just done, and in particular for saying so much about relationships without introducing the logically essential concept of terms, i.e., what relationships relate. She took all this for granted. In what follows, relationships are necessarily between terms, and terms are treated as constituted out of the relationships in which they participate.

The system M is an account of the social world based on the premiss that the social world consists of relationships between terms, and is thus ideal, and that the perceptible world consists of appearances which encypher the social world. That could be said of any social world, but in the system M there are two huge constraints, which govern the working-out of this entirely general idea: the first constraint is that all relations between terms in M are exchange relations, and the second constraint is that all terms of relations in M are gendered. Hence the title of the book from which I am drawing all this, the *Gender of the Gift.*

Now let me start constructing a graphic system to represent the system M. The graphic convention I use is that TERMS are placed in square or rectangular boxes, and RELATIONS in circles or ovals.

Thus a relation, in its simplest form is depicted as in Fig. 1.1. All

Figure 1.1

the relations and relationship-sets I am going to discuss are dyadic, as in Fig. 1.1; thus the triangular relationship A⊗B⊗C would be treated as A⊗B + A⊗C + B⊗C as in Fig. 1.2, and the reflexive or re-

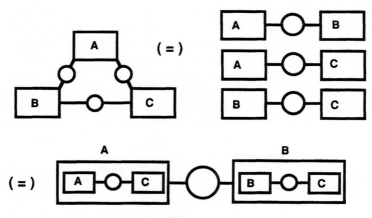

Figure 1.2

entrant relationship A⊗A would be treated as a dyadic relation A⊗A' as in Fig. 1.3. This means that all of the following diagrams have an

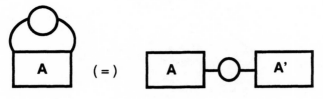

Figure 1.3

identical format, as in Fig. 1.1. However, there is a third graphic element which needs to be introduced. Relationships are only accessible in so far as they have sign-vehicles in the sensible world, which reveal their presence. Terms and relationships are impalpable, ideal significations, which are encountered only in so far as there is something palpable which cyphers them. These one may call APPEARANCES and in the graphic system I use all appearances are placed in lozenges. If something appears in a lozenge it is implied that there is a real-world 'thing', functioning as a sign-vehicle, corresponding to it, and secondly that the real-world thing so singled-out cyphers a relation. It might be thought that the introduction of 'appearances' is an underhand means of reintroducing the 'real world' and 'real things/persons' into the ghostly landscape of semiotic idealism, but this is not really so. The status of appearances in the system M is exclusively that of signifiers, and signifiers are produced not by the self-sufficient workings of the objective world, but by the aesthetic which deciphers them as signifying this or that relationship between ideal terms. Thus, just as it is the ideal system of language, not physics, physiology or accoustics, which constitutes the sound-shape DOG, or CHIEN or HUND or whatever, as a signifier of dogs, so we must imagine that all appearances have this kind of secondary, or relative, status. The addition of appearances, indicated by lozenges, completes the elementary graphic module which one can use to expound the system M as in Fig. 1.4.

The appearance which cyphers a particular relation could be described using Eliot's memorable phrase as the 'objective correlative' of the underlying relation, what makes it an object which can be accessible to a subject. Strathern refers to the revelation or making apparent of relations in appearances as 'objectification'. Objectification is conventional, and is guided by what she refers to as an 'aesthetic', that is, a system of social conventions as to which appearances indicate which relations between which terms. I do not know whether Strathern explicitly had in mind the use of the term

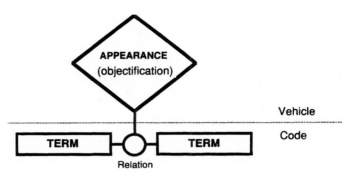

Figure 1.4

'aesthetic' in Kantian philosophy, specifically the concept of transcendental aesthetic in the *Critique of Pure Reason*, but in any case the convergent usage is appropriate, because Strathern's is one more addition to the long and distinguished lineage of sociological/ cultural/anthropological reworkings of the *Critique*, her immediate predecessors in this enterprise having been Durkheim and Lévi-Strauss. Strathern's aesthetics are only secondarily and in a derivative sense to do with beauty, essentially; however, they have to do with the metaphysical project of deriving the world of appearances from, or at any rate, via, the Idea.

Let me now apply our graphic conventions to the elucidation of the most primordial relationship system which Melanesian ethnography provides, namely, the ceremonial exchange of pigs between exchange partners. One could try to represent pig exchange visually as in Fig. 1.5. But such a visualization would fail to do the transaction justice on a number of counts. First of all, what is shown is only a snap-shot of a 'relation' which persists over time, not just for the duration of the hand-over event. And even a cine record which followed through the events over time could not make transparent the actual relations between people and pigs, and people and people via pigs, which are involved here. What all well-instructed readers of the Maussian literature on gift exchange know is that, in giving a pig as a gift to his exchange partner, the donor gives something of 'himself' (his person) to his partner, in the form (appearance) of a pig. And no amount of sketching, photography or cinematography is going to bring this to light. The relations between donors and recipients at ceremonial exchanges are invisible, notwithstanding the visibility of the events themselves. The events, and the human and non-human

Figure 1.5

entities involved in the events, objectify the salient relations. So an abstract representation is the only satisfactory alternative.

What the system M provides is a means of working backwards and forwards between the visible and the invisible. The visible world consists of a series of discrete appearances (sign-vehicles, pigs, humans, artefacts etc.) between which there are no truly visible relations, but only underlying, invisible, connections given by the code. What I want to do now is to use the graphic conventions so far introduced to visualize the invisible, that is, the relations which the visible components of the scene cypher.

The ostensible participants in pig exchanges are men and pigs. Very approximately, one can indicate the concept of 'a man' in the system M by means of Fig. 1.6. Human beings of either gender are sign-vehicles of the exchange relations which connect them to others; thus a man is, *inter alia*, a sign-vehicle of the relationship of exchange between his parents and numerous other relatives. Which

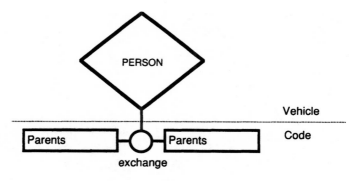

Figure 1.6

of the very numerous exchange relationships any one visible person might at any time evoke is a complicated contextual matter, so it would be unprofitable to pursue this particular example. To make things easier, it is more useful to concentrate on the pig which is being handed over in Fig. 1.5. Of what terms and relations is this creature the appearance or objectification?

Even a pig is a complex sign, objectifying more than one relationship. So far I have not discussed the polysemous characteristic of objectifications and explained how this is dealt with in M. The principle adopted is that a unique objectification (a particular pig) objectifies a cluster of relationships which are themselves related. Thus we cannot envisage a situation in which X (object, sign-vehicle) objectifies, so to speak, two separate sets of relations which are only arbitrarily related via their shared objectification, X, as in Fig. 1.7. There will be a further relationship between the multiple relationships which one object objectifies. How to represent (or imagine) this? To my mind, the key feature of M is the treatment given to

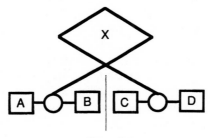

Figure 1.7

'relations between relations'. As I understand it, Strathern proceeds by nesting, or including, relations of a more subordinate order within relations of more encompassing order, that is, the principle governing the relations between relations is hierarchy. As I noted earlier, in her exposition Strathern does not introduce an explicit concept of the terms of relations, and consequently one is never very clear as to how a relationship of lower order can be contained within a relation of higher order. Using graphics, on the other hand, we can give a very explicit representation of exactly how a relation can be included within another relation. There is only one logically satisfactory way to conceptualize this, and that is to assume that a subordinate relation is included in a superordinate one by being nested within one term of the superordinate relation, as in Fig. 1.8 (a nested R).

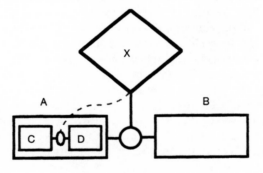

Figure 1.8

One can assist comprehension by drawing a dotted line between the subordinate or included relationship and the objectification, in addition to the line joining the objectification to the superordinate relation, but this is logically superfluous; it is automatically implied that if the relation A⊗B is objectified in X, then so is any relation which is included in the terms A or B, such as the relation C⊗D, in Fig. 1.8. But the principle which ensures that relations between relations are hierarchical has a further consequence which is interpretatively crucial: namely, that the subordinate relation C⊗D is only accessible through A⊗B, and that, in consequence, C⊗D is occluded or, to use Strathern's word, 'eclipsed' by A⊗B. (Parenthetically, it may be pointed out that Strathern's term 'eclipsing' is almost synonymous with the term used by Roy Wagner for similiar symbolic operations on relations, that is, 'obviation'. The difference is that 'obviation' carries a stronger implication that the imposition of one set of relations gets rid of the preceding set, while 'eclipsing' implies that the prior set of relations are still implicit, though latent, in the succeeding ones.)

Now let us consider our pig. As I mentioned at the outset, the system M is governed by two constraints, the twin pillars of Melanesian-ness, namely that all objectifications objectify exchanges, and that all exchanges are between gendered terms. This must apply to such very Melanesian objects as pigs, so let us see how.

Pigs objectify the process through which they are (re)produced via gendered exchanges. Strathern does not discuss pig reproduction, but in order to expound her ideas I will consider the biological reproduction of Melanesian pigs first of all, placing the word biological within the very heavy scare-quotes which have to be used in this connection, for pigs as much as for people. Melanesian pigs are reproduced via the activites of sows and boars. Sows and boars must be understood to exchange with one another, and that they have done so is signified by the appearance of piglets. Sows and boars clearly do not engage in Maussian gift exchange with one another, even in New Guinea, so in what sense may they be said to 'exchange' (Fig. 1.9)? Clearly, for the 'Melanesian' constraint that 'all objectifi-cations objectify exchange relations' to work, a great many transac-tions not normally included under the rubric of 'exchange' will have to be included, including those which go on between sows and boars. These are exchanges in which there is no 'gift' – no *mediatory object*. We are, however, perfectly familiar with the idea that *services* (i.e. kinds of 'work') may be exchanged. Thus an accountant might

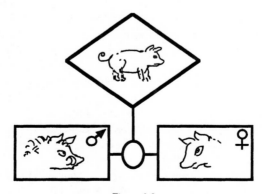

Figure 1.9

help a professional golfer with his tax returns, in exchange for some useful advice on improving his swing. In general, the sociological phenomenon known as 'the division of labour' can be seen as a complex exchange system, particularly in non-monetary economies such as those prevailing in traditional Melanesia. Strathern calls services, directly or indirectly rendered, 'unmediated exchanges' and is thus able to treat the division of labour and the service economy as an exchange system, in addition to the Maussian gift economy, which includes all transactions mediated by gift objects, which are distinguished as 'mediated' exchanges, (cf. Fig. 1.10, unmediated exchange).

What boars and sows exchange is the gendered reproductive capacities; the capacity of the boar to act the boar in relation to the sow's reciprocal capacity to act the sow. A boar with no sow to exchange with is not a boar, because his boar-capacity is only activated by an exchange with sow-capacity, and vice versa.

In terms of biological origins, a pig objectifies the gendered exchange between its pig parents, namely, the division of reproductive labour in pigdom. But a pig used in a ceremonial exchange, though always ultimately a biological pig, is not seen primarily in this way at all, but as a human, rather than a porcine, product. Piglets must grow reasonably big before they can be honourably exchanged, and that requires nurture in a human domestic milieu, and extra feeding usually on produce deriving from sweet-potato

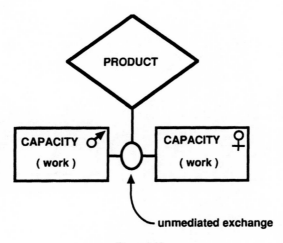

Figure 1.10

gardens. In other words, exchange pigs objectify human-gendered exchange relationships more saliently than porcine-gendered exchange relationships. According to Strathern, pigs objectify the unmediated exchange of domestic services between men and women in their roles as husbands and wives. The wives herd the pigs, harvest and prepare their food, while the husbands provide (and defend) the land on which the pig's food is grown and play a greater or lesser role in gardening operations (clearing, digging, fencing, weeding, and so on). Universally, however, it is the wife's identity which is most closely bound up with her pig. As producers of pigs in a domestic context, womens' work is objectified in the pig-as-product, while the husbands' contribution is objectified more in the wife's capability to produce; she (as pig effective producer) objectifies his adequate performance as garden-provider, defender, and so on. Thus, the biological reproduction of pigs is symbolically *eclipsed* by the pig-nurture provided by their human producers, primarily that of the wife, in her unmediated pig-producing relationship with her husband, as shown in Fig. 1.11. 'Eclipsing' is here indicated by the inclusion of BOAR®SOW within the WIFE term of WIFE®HUSBAND.

This initial 'eclipsing' operation, so to speak, gives us our pig; but it is not yet an exchange pig, i.e. a pig in its role as a mediating object in mediated exchange relations, rather than a pig in its role as object-

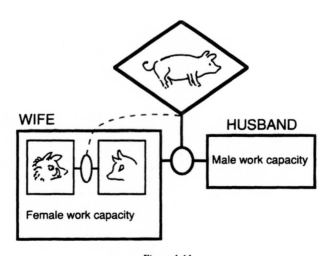

Figure 1.11

ification of unmediated exchanges between boars and sows, husbands and wives.

All exchanges in the system M are between gendered terms, but that is not to say that all exchanges must be between gendered terms of opposite gender, that is, male–female. The instances of unmediated exchange we have considered so far have, indeed, been of this type, but single-sex exchanges are equally possible, male-male and female-female. There are thus a total of six possible types of gendered exchanges, as shown in Fig. 1.12 (six forms of exchange). Reference to our original depiction of an exchange event indicates that the exchange partners who exchange our pig are identifiable as males, and that the whole transaction is a single-sex, male–male, mediated exchange, in which the pig is the mediating gift object. As a matter of ethnographic fact, it is sometimes the case that exchange partners in New Guinea Highlands pig exchanges can belong, genitally speaking, to opposite sexes (cf. Feil 1984 on Tombema Enga *tee*), or be both female, but in terms of Strathern's theorization of these situations, genital sex is overridden by symbolic gender, so that ostensibly female exchangers are transactionally male. (Meanwhile, it must be borne in mind that a single-sex exchange may appear, from another point of view, as a cross-sex one, for reasons which will be explained in due course.)

Two of the six possible combinations of gendered terms and modes of exchange are, so to speak, canonical, though all may occur. These are unmediated cross-sex exchanges, and mediated single-sex exchanges between males. These are the alpha and omega of the system, with the other four possibilities occupying intermediate positions between these canonically opposed types.

	Male–Male	Male–Female	Female–Female
Mediated	Single sex Male–Male Mediated	Cross-sex Mediated	Single sex Female–Female Mediated
Unmediated	Single sex Female–Female Unmediated	Cross-sex Unmediated	Single sex Female–Female Unmediated

Figure 1.12

Cross-sex unmediated exchange relations are those to which the origin of objectifications (such as pigs and children) can usually be assigned. Cross-sex unmediated exchanges are reproductive. Something is drawn out of the parties to such exchanges (their gendered capacity) which is finitely 'used up' in the process of reproduction. The capacity which is lost in the exchange is substituted for by the object which is produced by the exchange: the piglet, grown pig, or child. Cross-sex unmediated exchanges, in other words, (re)produce objects, primarily people, but also foodstuffs and artefacts jointly produced such as the well-known banana-leaf skirts which Trobriand women exchange in female-to-female, single-sex, mediated exchanges (Weiner 1976).

Conversely, mediated single-sex exchanges (re)produce relationships by detaching objects, understood as being parts of persons, from their original owners, and attaching them to other persons. Thus relationships produce the objects which produce relationships, as in Fig. 1.13. Cross-sex unmediated relations turn relations into objectifications, and single-sex mediated relations turn objectifications back into relations.

Why is it that the exchange relations which produce relations should have to be single-sex ones rather than cross-sex ones? This is not to be attributed to ethnographic happenstance or male domination of the prestige economy, but to profounder causes having to do with the logical articulation of the system M, and in particular the mechanics of eclipsing, which I mentioned a moment ago.

The pig, prior to its entry into the ceremonial exchange cycle,

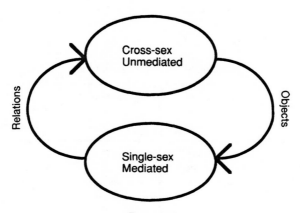

Figure 1.13

objectifies the exchange of cross-sex gendered capacity between husband and wife, biological pig-reproduction being eclipsed within the 'wife' term of this exchange (Fig. 1.11). Now, however, the pig has to objectify not the relations which produced it, but the relations that it produces by being exchanged. The relations that it produces cannot be cross-sex ones, because, in so far as it can serve as the sign-vehicle for any cross-sex exchanges, these can be none other than the cross-sex exchanges which produced it in the first place. Consequently the relationship-producing exchange has to be logically distinguished from the object-producing exchange, and this is achieved by switching from the cross-sex exchange mode to the same-sex exchange mode, in this instance, male–male.

By switching to this mode, it is possible to eclipse the cross-sex reproductive exchanges between humans which produced the pig, and double-eclipse the cross-sex exchanges between the boar and the sow which also produced it, so as to make the exchange pig itself productive, not of pigs or people or other objectifications, but of relations. This twofold eclipsing is shown in Fig. 1.14.

A relation which is brought into being via a single-sex mediated exchange is said to have been replicated. This word is used because it serves to remind us that there is no numerical limit to the number of times the same gift object might be used to produce, that is replicate, relationships (as in Fig. 1.15) via iterated same-sex mediated exchanges. There is an important difference, therefore, between

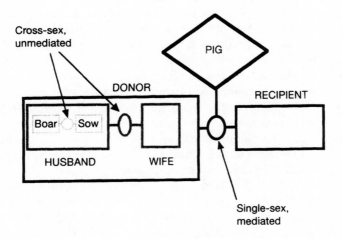

Figure 1.14

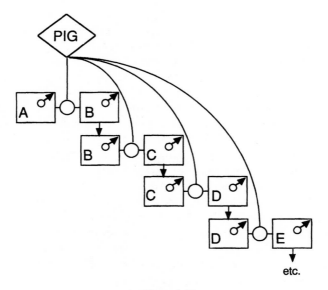

Figure 1.15

replication and substitution. The replication of relations is by mediated exchanges, which have an in-built expansionary potential, whereas, in unmediated exchanges, instead of replication we find substitution, that is, the replacement of the finite reproductive capacities gendered individuals bring to cross-sex unmediated exchanges by the joint product of the exchange of those capacities.

In order to carry this further, I would now like to direct attention towards the male exchangers in the transactions shown in Fig. 1.15, in order to explore the notion of personhood proposed in the system M. Fig. 1.15 is in one respect an illegitimate representation of replicative exchange transactions, in that it breaks a stipulation made earlier, namely, that all the relations between terms objectified by a singular sign-vehicle (the pig) are themselves related, whereas the transactors (as terms) in the sequence of exchanges diagrammed in Fig. 1.15 are shown independently, and their relations are independently symbolized by the unique exchange pig.

In New Guinea Highlands pig exchanges, it is understood that pigs as gift objects are objectifications of the donor's capacity, not to produce pigs himself, but to elicit pigs from others, namely, partners further back along the exchange path. Once pigs enter the path, their origins in domestic labour are eclipsed, and they are imagined to be objects produced by (mediated) relations between transactors, to have been produced by the male capacity to have exchange relations and to engage in exchange. Consequently, a more accurate representation of an exchange transaction represents a male transactor as in Fig. 1.16.

This figure shows the pig as objectifying the relationship produced by the transaction between D (as donor) and E (as recipient).The point this Figure makes is that D, the donor, encompasses, in his person, all the antecedent donor-recipient relations which the pig, in its career as a gift object, has objectified. It is because D is connected to C, and C to B, and B to A, that D has a pig to give to E. The previous exchange transactions, A/B, B/C, C/D, are constitutive of D's person, and it is these constituents of his person (his connectedness to the paths of exchange) which he transfers to E when he hands over his pig, thereby replicating the existing relations A/B, B/C, C/D, with an additional one, D/E.

In the system M, persons are constituted out of relations, and Fig. 1.16 is designed to show exactly what this means, at least in the ceremonial exchange context. In Fig. 1.16 there is no visible person, I should emphasize, only a visible pig which stands for its donor as a term in a relation of exchange, a pig which, in Strathern's terminology, 'reifies' the relations encompassed in this term. But if we direct attention away from the pig and towards the term D, we notice a salient fact, namely, that the attempt to depict visually the structure of the person results in the type of mathematical figure known as a fractal, that is, one which displays self-similarity at different degrees of magnification and minimization. This follows from the rule of eclipsing, which decrees that relations between relations are hierarchized.

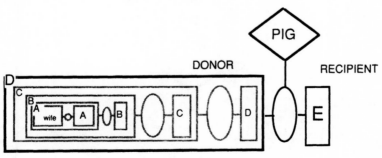

Figure 1.16

The fractal properties of personhood do not get explicitly mentioned in GG, no doubt because fractals were little publicized at the time of its composition (1984–5, revised in 1987). However, fractals were undoubtedly implicit in the argument of GG and emerge very explicitly in Strathern's later writing on Melanesia (notably in *Partial Connections*, 1991). Leaving ceremonial exchange aside, let me dwell for a moment on the notion of fractal personhood in a little more detail. The elementary model of personhood taking person's bodies, for now, to be the objectification, is as shown in Fig. 1.16: that is, persons are the objectification of the gendered exchange relations which produced them, which we may take to be cross-sex. However, the terms of the exchanges which produced S, our person, were themselves persons produced by gendered exchanges, and so on, so that the terms of the exchange shown in Fig. 1.6 must be conceptualized as fractals, as in Fig. 1.17.

This much is mere genealogy; but the eclipsed relations which are hierarchically encompassed within personhood are not effaced, and sometimes it is necessary to evoke them, particularly in ritual contexts. Objectifications can sometimes be seen as totalized constructions, persons being the sum total of their relational constituents. How can total relational identities be detotalized so that objectification can be given to the separate constituents of personhood? Here we encounter a particular symbolic mechanism which the system M gives us privileged access to, which I might call the fractalization of objectifications. That is to say, access to encompassed relations within personhood is achieved via the detotalization of the objectification of personhood, specifically, in this instance, the human body. Thus, in M, the human body is a (non-mathematical) 'fractal' whose part/whole, containing/contained constituents objectify the encompassing/encompassed constituents of relational personhood at the level of terms. The isomorphy between the fractal properties

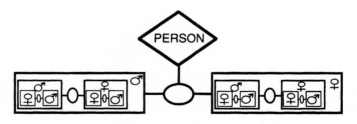

Figure 1.17

of relations within terms, and the fractalization of objectifications is depicted in Fig. 1.18 (the subdivision of our lozenges into sub-lozenges of identical form but different scale expresses this graphically).

Human beings may not only be detotalized, they may also be considered as detotalizations of more encompassing (or collective) terms. Figs. 1.17 and 1.18 are theoretical models, but in order to put some flesh on these theoretical bones let me briefly discuss an ethno-graphic instance, not one dealt with by Strathern herself (in GG) but very apposite to her approach. Jadran Mimica (1988) has made a fascinating study of the number and counting system of the Iqwaye, one of the Anga group of tribes which includes the Baruya and the Sambia, whom I shall come to in a moment. Iqwaye count in twenties, on their fingers and toes, and in powers of 20 (that is, 20 squared, 20 cubed, and so on, in which fashion they can count effect-ively up to about the 1,000 mark). Iqwaye counting is all about total-izing and detotalizing; the base, 20, is equivalent to 'one' , because one man has 20 digits, 20 men (the number 400) are also one, in that 20 men are the 20 digits of one man, and so forth. What is of concern to us, however, is that the Iqwaye very explicitly see the whole cosmos and all its inhabitants in fractal terms, as body-parts of the creator Omalyce, just as numbers are all body-parts of one man, or of a number of men who are equivalent to one man. Omalyce is imagined in the posture depicted in Fig. 1.19[1] (after Mimica), his toes and fingers locked together, his penis, which is also his umbilical cord, in his mouth, through which he nourishes himself by ceaselessly

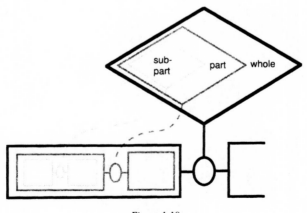

Figure 1.18

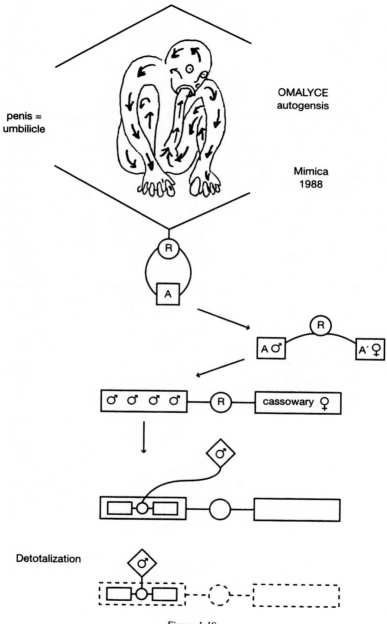

penis = umbilicle

OMALYCE
autogensis

Mimica
1988

Detotalization

Figure 1.19

recirculating his vital substance. This closed position is the zero in the Iqwaye system, but in the light of the stipulations of the system M, closed circulation cannot be sustained, and consequently at a certain point Omalyce must be divided up to form a series of gendered dyadic exchanges. This unfolding is exactly what Iqwaye cosmogonic myth describes; Omalyce releases his penis/umbilicus, in order to breathe, and in this moment sky and earth are created as separate entities, Omalyce's eyes become the sun and moon, and the myriad beings who inhabit the earth and sky are formed from fragments of his body. In other words, creation equals detotalization. Having created the earth, Omalyce takes mud from which he creates the five original men (ancestors). These men, ostensibly of mud, are of course made of Omalyce's body, since the earth is his body too. The fact that these men are detotalizations of Omalyce is further signalled by the fact that Omalyce names these men after his five fingers, the fingers of the hand being the symbolic exponents of

[1] Note by the editor: This figure is Gell's summary of elements in Iqwaye counting and culture (Mimica 1988). Each 'level' (as indicated by the →) is another way of writing the other levels; each is contained in the other. The very top of the figure shows Omalyce in a closed position. Omalyce is the combination of elements that make up every Iqwaye which Gell depicts in the relation with 'A'; this, however, only occurs according to the cosmogonic myth, referred to by Gell, when Omalyce releases his penis/umbilicus, in order to breathe. The next level depicts 'A' as formed of male and female elements, all derived from Omalyce. One version is described in the cosmogonic myth, depicted in the next level. Here it is perhaps useful to quote the relevant portion of Mimica's text:

> Omalyce, the autogeneal being, creates other men. Typically, he made five of them from the lumps of ground. They were his sons. He imbued them with life by an ingenious technique, and finally he inseminated them through their mouths, which is what made them truly men and his sons. All of them drank their genitor's semen, but the last man, Ulaqwa (i.e. named after the small finger), for whom omalyce did not make genitals, ingested it all and became pregnant. While in labour his pains were unbearable for he had no suitable bodily passage for delivery. In this predicament he underwent a series of animal metamorphosis – first into an eel, then a red python and finally a cassowary. As he did so his brother (other men) shot him with arrows, and then, while in the cassowary form, they split open his womb. A red man who appeared as a marsupial emerged from the cassowary's womb. He too was shot and subsequently their bodies were dispatched and some of it eaten. *The cassowary (i.e. Ulaqwa) became the first woman* and her leg bones were used ever after for nose-piercing (Mimica 1988: 80, emphasis added).

What Gell has portrayed are the five men, one of whom was transformed into a woman/cassowary; this accounts for the set of four men on the left of the 'R' and the woman/cassowary on the right.

The next level depicts a 'real' man which is formed of any of the other relations. In other words, any term (rectangle) or objectification (lozenge) is itself being subject to detotalization . This is what Gell indicates at the bottom of the figure.

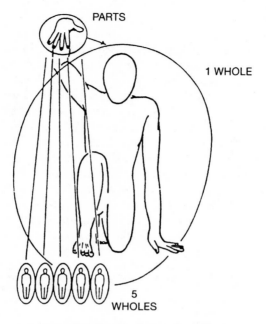

PARTS

1 WHOLE

5
WHOLES

1 whole : 5 parts : : 1 whole : : 5 wholes
i.e. Omalyce : finger : : Omalyce : : 5 mud-men

Figure 1.20

detotalization, as Mimica's own diagram of the situation shows (Fig. 1.20). Omalyce also creates women in his own image (initially as a penisless, pregnant, man) in that he is, if not an explicit woman himself, then an eclipsed one, in that he is said to be male in front and female at the back, or alternatively, male in himself, but casting a female shadow.

All Iqwaye are detotalized body-parts, or fractals, of Omalyce. The practical consequences of personhood as detotalization for the Iqwaye is marvellously brought out by Mimica in his account of the kinship terminology and exchange practices of the Iqwaye, who, like their creator being, are constrained to give birth (indirectly) to themselves. Iqwaye kinship terminology is unusual in that the term for 'father' is reciprocal: that is, a father refers to his son as 'father', using the same term as to his own father, the FF of his son, who are totally socially identified – FF and SS having the same name and addressing one another as elder and younger brother. The prescribed marriage is with the FMBSD or FMBSSD, who is terminologically 'FM'. Thus ego marries the woman who gave birth to his father, and hence it is only logical that his father should call ego (his son) 'father'. As Mimica puts it:

> the *ate* [FM] marriage ... accomplishes at the level of social practice the originary cosmological significance of procreation, namely that the birth of a man is his self-birth. By begetting another male being, the Iqwaye man gives birth to the man who can give birth to himself, or in procreating the son the man has procreated his own father ... my own son can marry my (classificatory) mother, and as such he can give birth to myself (1988: 88).

Next, let me discuss two more examples in which the fractalization of the objectification is combined with gift exchange. One consequence of the system M is that ritual transactions which had not previously been viewed as 'exchanges' come to be so, in that all transactions in the system are exchange transactions. This applies particularly to the transactions which occur, or, more accurately, are seen as occuring, during initiation. Fig.1.22 depicts the transaction which is held by Strathern (basing herself closely on Gillison 1980; 1987) to be thematic in Gimi male initiation, which, like many initiations in the New Guinea Highlands, is centred on the revelation of a

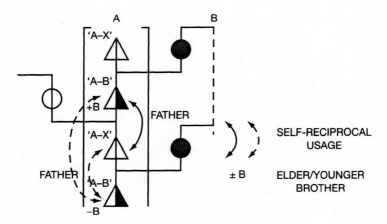

Figure 1.21   from Mimica 1988

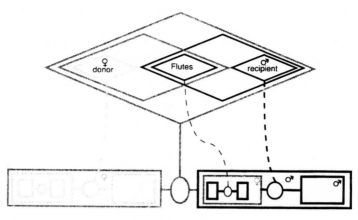

Figure 1.22

pair of sacred flutes to male neophytes in the secret male enclosure. As the flutes are demonstrated to the boys their mythology is imparted, according to which (as is commonly believed in such instances) the flutes were originally female possessions, which were 'stolen' by the men. Initiatory ritual re-evokes this primordial transaction, theft, as an exchange which endows men with the capacity to act as men, that is, engage in unmediated reproductive exchange in relation to women, or in other words to cause them to reproduce. This, after all, is what male initiation has always been understood to be about, namely cranking up the masculinity of male adolescents so as to prepare them for marriage and paternity. On the basis of Gillison's excellent data, Strathern can make sense of the flutes, not just as musical instruments, but as body-parts. The flutes are tubes, the human body consists of tubes and is a tube. The flutes are total persons (autoreproductive androgynes) and, detotalized, gendered body-parts of persons who reproduce only by eliciting the reproductive capacities of the opposite sex. Paradoxically – or perhaps not so paradoxically – the parts of the human body which are most explicitly gendered, namely the genitals, are topologically speaking also the most congruent; the internal female genitalia (the birth canal) is a tube which, turned inside out, is another tube, the penis. Consequently, the Gimi myth which says that the origin of menstruation is the blood flow following the theft of the flutes from women, indicates that the flutes are, in fact, the birth canal, which, in male guise, becomes the penis. In addition, the neophytes are told that the facial hair which they will begin to grow (once initiated) is their sister's pubic hair; the original flutes were stoppered with female pubic hair and the first (male) beards and moustaches originated from this source. The double-sidedness of the flutes as symbolic of gendered parts of both male and female bodies is reiterated in other episodes of Gimi male initiation, as the neophytes have revealed to them the fact that the forest domain, canonically the domain of men, is pervaded with feminine attributes.

Figure 1.22 depicts Gimi flutes as objectifications of gendered exchanges. As Gillison remarks, in themselves, the flutes stand for the indivisible power of reproduction (that is, personhood as such), or, to avoid use of the un-Strathernian word 'power', the capacity for reproduction (the outer, most encompassing lozenge-frame). However, as the flutes in Gimi ritual are transactable mediating objects (gift objects in a mythical instance of mediated negative reciprocity, or theft) they may be detotalized as specific gendered body-parts of males and females respectively. Like pig donors in ceremonial exchange, the women retain, at the level of terms, what they specifically give up at the level of objectifications. The flutes as female body-parts are retained as components of female identities, while being appropriated as objectifications by men, who thus appropriate the means of signifying reproductive capacity, just as a pig recipient has appropriated the means of signifying all the relations which have been replicated by the pig during its career as a gift object. Appropriation of the means of objectifying the capacity to reproduce gives men the ability to elicit or activate the reproductive capacities of women, otherwise contained exclusively within their bodies. A man who (following a series of exchange transactions) has a herd of disposable pigs, can activate the field of exchange relations around him; in the same way, the Gimi men, possessed not of pigs, but of the objectified form of both male and female reproductive capacity, can activate the field of reproductive relations, eliciting the reproductive capacity of women. In this way, it is possible to see Gimi initiations, and Hagen pig exchanges, social events which do not explicitly resemble one another in any way, as transformed versions one of another; which is surely a theoretical result of some interest.

The idea that ostensibly male body-parts, the phallus or the beard, are, in eclipsed form, female body-parts (birth canal and female pubic hair) raises the question of the gender of persons. As I would imagine most people are aware, Strathern has made a particular contribution to anthropology in destabilizing the notion of personal gender as a fixed attribute dictated by nature, and only reinforced (if that) by ritual actions, such as those engaged in by participants in initiatory ritual.

The example which best enables us to come to grips with this problem in terms of the system M is provided by Sambia ritual homosexuality, as described by Herdt (1981; 1982; 1984). Herdt takes an essentialist view of Sambia gender, arguing that homosexual fellatio, experienced first as an insertee, later as an insertor, confirms males in their masculinity, by confining males at a crucial stage in their socialization to an all-male sphere, so that when they have to interact with women (when they get married) they will have transcended the identifications with women which they may have acquired as small, dependent, infants. In Herdt's argument one perceives an attempt, no doubt well-intentioned, to undermine the association which exists in the western mind between any kind of male homosexual activity and effeminacy, a despised characteristic. However, Strathern is surely correct to object that Sambia homosexuality cannot be understood in the light of a problem-definition which stems from the cultural implications of homosexuality in a western frame of reference, and that androgynous attributes in Melanesia are not necessarily evaluated there as they are here.

The starting point for her analysis is Herdt's excellent essay on 'Semen transactions in Sambia culture' (1984), in which semen is treated as a transactable object. The Sambia theory of ritual male homosexuality is as follows. Semen exists in intrinsically limited quantities, and, when not being transacted is contained within a special organ of the male body, the *tingu* or semen organ. Boys are born with a tingu, girls are not. But the *tingu* of small boys is inactive, and can only be activated if, so to speak, it has been primed by the ingestion of semen by male fellatio. Once possessed of an activated semen organ, a male can, alternatively, activate the semen organs of other males, or cause foetuses to grow in the bodies of women, foetuses which once born must be nourished by female milk, which is itself transformed semen, which women can acquire both through sexual intercourse and also through acting as insertees in acts of fellatio performed by their husbands. Three crucial details have to be added to this account. First of all, the semen donated by senior men to neophytes at initiation is explicitly conceptualized as analogous to milk, so that male fellatio is a version of breast-feeding, as may be readily imagined. Secondly the ritual role of primary donor of semen to a neophyte is first of all given to the older male who is the prospective husband of the semen-recipient's sister. Thus a man first of all inseminates his junior male affine via fellatio, then this man's sister, via sexual intercourse and/or fellatio. And finally, consistently with this schema, the recipient of semen is, in the context of the ritual, the 'wife' of his semen donor, female to his male.

The complex of exchange relationships mediated by semen and its analogue, milk, is displayed in Fig. 1.23. Whereas Herdt is inclined to see ritual fellatio as sexual transactions among grades of males, Strathern sees all transactions in semen (and milk as an analogue to semen) as cross-sex mediated transactions in semen, which, as a body component of both males and females, objectifies these relationships and transactions in much the same way that flutes or pigs did in the examples already traversed. Semen is the transactable component of Sambia personhood, standing for the relations internal to Sambia persons as complexes of relations.

What the system M enables us to do is unravel the semiotics of mixed metaphors, because it will be immediately apparent that the same objectification, semen, serves to objectify a series of transactions in which the participants, considered as terms of exchange relations, are simultaneously, or successively, male and female.

We can represent this graphically as follows: in Fig. 1.24. the schema of body-part exchange given for the Gimi sacred flute

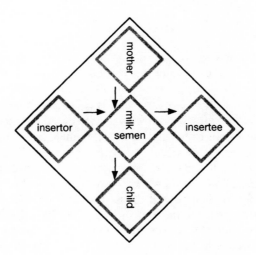

Figure 1.23

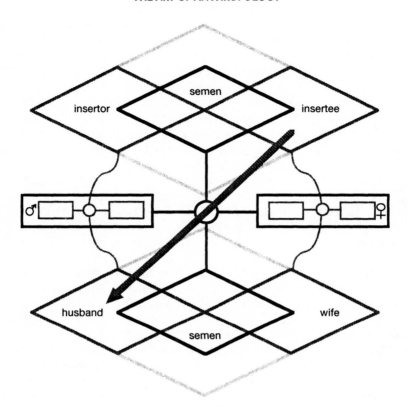

Figure 1.24

exchange is opened up so that the parties to it are represented twice over; the insertee (over the horizontal axis) reappears as 'the husband' beneath it, which he will in due course become (arrow on Fig. 1.24). He will in due course, that is to say, become an insertor, equivalent to the man who is his own insertor. As an insertee, how-ever, he is equivalent to his own insertee, namely his own wife, since in ritual terms he is the 'wife' of his ritual inseminator. Thus, in the light of the semen transactions in which he is involved, a neophyte prefigures himself as a male, while acting the part of his own wife in relation to this prefigured self. This doubling of roles is however achieved, not by pantomime, but through the objectifying power of semen as a sign-vehicle. In order to represent this, Fig. 1.23 abstracts semen as an objectification of two sets of relations, the ones medi-ated by semen as semen, and the other the relations mediated by semen-as-milk. Mothers, in relation to their children, are as insertors in acts of fellatio are, to their insertees. The sign-vehicle, semen/milk, carries with it the possibility for men to play the role allotted to women; thus the older men, in the light of this analogy, are collectively the 'mothers' of the neophytes, but equally in a more eclipsed fashion, women as mothers are playing a role in relation to their nursing infants which is analogically male. This is shown in Fig. 1.25, which is our original Gimi graph unfolded in a different fashion, not this time by unfolding the objectification, but by unfolding the terms and relations in relation to a unitary (fractalized) objectification. How these complementary roles are played out over the life cycle is further diagrammed in Fig. 1.26; as mother is to child, so insertor is to insertee, and husband is to wife; successively, a male is milk-insertee, semen-insertee, semen-insertor, and (indirectly) milk-insertor (via his wife).

In the light of the system M, therefore, the gender of persons is a

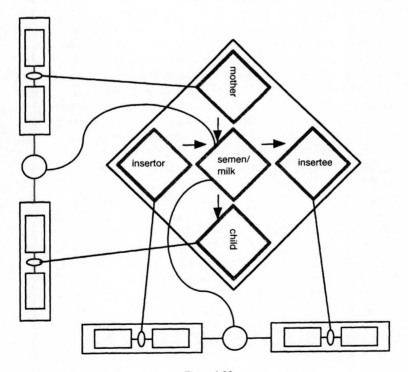

Figure 1.25

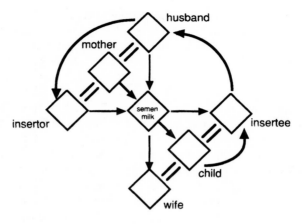

Figure 1.26

function of the particular relationships into which they enter, not something immutable, which is socially constructed one way or the other. Of course, Sambia men, even when they are behaving as mothers, are male, and Sambia women are female, even when they are analogically male as nursing mothers. But this does not arise from some essential property each gender possesses (their genitalia for instance) but from the mechanism of eclipsing, and the hierarchical ordering which prevails among symbolic forms. Thus semen, which in the preceding discussions has been treated as detotalizable as semen/milk, is at the most encompassing level a male body-part, transferable only to females in cross-sex transactions. In just the same way, Omalyce, who can be detotalized as male and female, is in his encompassing, auto-genetic form, male, and only subordinately female. Thus, in the Sambia system, the implicitly female/maternal role of senior men as inseminators is eclipsed by their role as husbands of the neophytes, who are their 'wives'. But just as Freudians speak of the 'return' of repressed material as the key to the interpretation of dreams and neurotic symptoms, so the principle of eclipsing relies on the idea that the content of whatever reading is eclipsed is present in the content of whatever is foregrounded. A view of the sun in eclipse is still a view of the sun, not the moon, though it is the moon one sees. Thus a principle of hierarchical eclipsing ensures that milk is transformed semen rather than the other way about. A woman nursing a child is not spontaneously seen as a senior man inseminating a neophyte. However, a senior man inseminating a neophyte can be seen as a mother nursing her child, because the former image encompasses the latter, but not vice versa.

The Sambia material raises more directly than the Gimi flute exchange the questions of reproduction, marriage and affinity. In rounding-off this conspectus of Strathernian themes, I would like to consider one more example in detail, bearing directly on these matters. The ethnographic example to be considered is the famous case of the Trobriands, but, before I embark on the formidable complexities of Trobriand marriage and exchange, I would like to consider the underlying theoretical problems using a simplified example.

How do marriage, affinal relations and parent-child relations figure in the system M? The first thing to note about marriage/affinity is that any marriage is both collective and individual. That is to say, Melanesian marriage, like other Melanesian transactions, fails to fit the 'western' stipulation that relations are *either* between individuals (interpersonal/private) *or* between collectivities (corporate/public). Individual and society are not opposed there, as they are here, so the question cannot arise as to whether a marriage is a 'private' contract between individuals ('sanctioned' by society) or an 'alliance' between groups. Marriage is always both of these simultaneously. The relationship between marriage (the union between specific spouses) and alliance (affinal alliance linking collectivities such as clans) can be understood in terms of fractal magnification/minimization. As spouses exchange 'parts of themselves' and deliver up 'parts of themselves' in producing children for one another, so intermarrying clans exchange parts of themselves in analogous fashion, and reciprocally reproduce one another, but on a larger scale. But although one can imagine, in general terms, a grand analogy between spouse-to-spouse relations and affinal-group to affinal-group relations, the analogy is not exact; indeed, it is reversed, in that affinally allied clans stand opposed to one another as same-sex units carrying on mediated exchange, whereas spouses stand opposed to one another as cross-sex partners in unmediated exchange. So if we can 'see' the affinal alliance, we cannot see the spouse-to-spouse relation on which, nonetheless, the alliance pivots, and conversely, if we can 'see' the spouse-to-spouse relation, we cannot see (that is, we eclipse) the affinal alliance which gives that spouse-to-spouse relation its systematic significance. The mutually irreconcilable appearances of spouse-to-spouse and affinal-group relations recall those of the well-known 'impossible figures' of Penrose (Fig. 1.27). However,

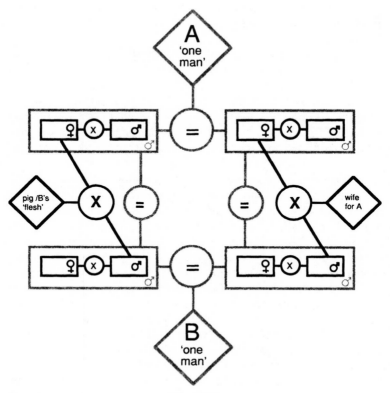

Figure 1.27

the symbolic practices of marriage and affinity depend precisely on continually switching back and forth between cross/sex unmediated and same/sex mediated 'readings' of gendered exchanges, so as to produce the former out of the latter, and vice versa.

The underlying issue here is the conflict between alliance theory (deriving from Lévi-Strauss) and feminist critiques of male-centered anthropological theory. I promised, at the outset, that I would not discuss this subject, but at this particular point it is necessary to raise just one feminist point. Feminist writers have long insisted that Lévi-Strauss's idea that 'groups' (of men) 'exchange women' in marriage makes women unduly analogous to commodities (such as pigs, feathers and shells) which men also exchange, often within the same transactional 'package', as when a bride passes from group A to group B, and pigs, say, pass from group B to group A, as 'bride-price'.

What has happened to the personhood of the young woman here, is she a mere 'valuable' rather than a human being with agency and sensibilities, motives, reasons of her own? Strathern's response to this is twofold; first of all (as already noted) she denies that 'commodity thinking' is appropriate to the elucidation of the symbolism of Melanesian transactions such as these (the ones involving pigs and feathers as much as the ones involving 'women'), and secondly, she denies that 'men exchange women' in any simple sense, because gender itself is not a fixed, given, attribute of the agents involved, either of the givers of brides, of the recipients of brides, or of the brides which pass between them.

One way in which a commodity transaction, or market transaction, can be distinguished from a gift transaction, is that whereas a market transaction makes no reference to the prior history of interactions between parties to an exchange, a gift transaction always does so, and is the means of prolonging, and modifying, these relationships persisting over time. 'Proper gifts' (like Christmas presents but excluding bribes or other covert commodity transactions) only signalize relationships *that already exist*. I have to be already related to my Aunt Mary before I can expect an Aunt-type Christmas present from her. One implication of Strathern's denial of the applicability of the commodity model to Melanesian exchanges (including marriages) is that any given exchange is part of an unfolding history of interactions between individuals and collectivities, rather than a one-off 'swap'. But setting up a marriage is creating relationship(s) where ostensibly no such relationship existed before.

Engaging in gift exchanges as a form of 'action' to realize intentions and to change the world therefore involves a time paradox, in that if I want to change the attitude or behaviour of a potential exchange partner *in the future*, I have to *alter the past* of our relationships, so that he will be obliged to follow suit. One can see crass attempts to do just this in the world of contemporary personalized junk-mail advertising. When I receive an apparently handwritten letter from a perfect stranger addressing me by my Christian name, the implication is being created that at some time I have met this person, the circulation manager of a magazine, say, and indeed have admitted him to my intimate circle. On the basis of this spurious past fellowship, I will be morally obliged to subscribe to the wretched periodical and receive my 'Free Gift'. In Melanesia, we have to proceed on the assumption, foreign to ourselves, that creating a certain past history of exchanges with a view to a future series of exchanges is the bedrock on which intersubjective understanding and mutuality rest; 'altering the past' by objectifying it in symbolic transactions does not, for Melanesians, constitute historical bad faith, because it is only in the light of a 'realist' notion of 'past time' as fully constituted but out of spatio-temporal reach, that this 'bad faith' arises.

With this paradigm in mind, let us consider an idealized Lévi-Strauss marriage-exchange scenario, in which two descent groups (clans) A and B confront one another: A having bachelors in need of wives, and having pigs; B having nubile daughters, and needing pigs. For A just to swap their pigs for B's daughters is not an option, even if this, physically, is what seems (to us) to happen; because it is not possible for these physical events (i.e. appearances) to be read in this (commodity) way. Willy-nilly, the physical transaction will be articulated to the underlying code such that a history of exchanges will be put in place, a past, present and future consisting of overlapping, mutually implicatory transactions in gendered attributes of persons and collectivities.

Initially, let us imagine A and B just confronting one another as collectivities. For Strathern, what is a collectivity such as an agnatic clan? Kinship units such as clans appear before the world as 'like persons' in having a corporate individuality; the clan is 'one man', 'one bone', 'one penis' and so on. Difference between man and man is suppressed (eclipsed) as also are the crucial differences between (*a*) male agnates (brothers) and female agnates (sisters) and (*b*) between the male attributes of *all* agnates (call it 'bone') and the female attributes of *all* agnates, (call it 'flesh') that is, elements of fractal personhood all agnates have derived from matrikin, affines, and so on.

A confrontation between clans is a confrontation between all-male single-sex entities. There is no basis for exchange here, no more than I can exchange the contents of my pockets for the contents of those of my reflected image in a looking-glass. Clans which are identically constituted cannot exchange either; the symmetry is too perfect. It is at this point that the ambiguous switching between 'marriage' (spouse – spouse unmediated exchange) and 'alliance' (group – group mediated exchange) becomes pivotal, because it is by transforming the opposition between same-sex (all male) exchange partners into one between cross-sex partners in unmediated exchange that the imbalance, or asymmetry, essential to the 'ongoing history' of exchanges is introduced.

If we cease to look just at the all-male exterior of the clan, and uncover instead its inner composition, it loses its erstwhile stability as a gendered form – 'one man'. Female agnates, and female elements of male agnates, come into view. It is these female agnates, 'sisters of B', that A want to turn into wives-of-A. The strategy of A must be to make it apparent, first of all, that B is not symmetrical to A, but of complementary gender: that is, B is collectively female to A's collective masculinity, and secondly, that A is 'owed' female elements of B in the light of an exchange linking them both.

B can be opened up and transformed in this manner via a presentation of pigs in the form of bride-price (so called). Let us recall what we earlier noticed with regard to pigs, namely, that they originate as objectifications of gendered cross-sex ummediated exchange internal to the domestic unit. But they can be detached and sent out into the world as mediating elements in same-sex mediated exchanges. In this form they can be used – in ceremonial exchange – to 'replicate' same-sex units in symmetrical relations, as in Fig. 1.15. But now we want them to perform a different task: not to encode the expansion of relations through which one clan measures itself as equal to an 'opposition' clan in the mirror of exchange, but to encode the *difference* between a potentially wife-receiving clan and a potentially wife-giving one. To do this we de-eclipse the cross-sex relationship (husband–wife) encoded by pigs, so that the pig now stands for the dual, male-plus-female composition of the clan which produced it. That is to say, through promoting a different aesthetic of pigs, we can use them to take apart the solidly all-male appearance that clans as ceremonial exchange units normally take on. In the sight of the recipient clan, an all-male unit has dissolved into a cross-sex unit, and moreover one that detaches, and transfers to a reciprocal clan, a part of itself. This dissolution of opposed same-sex clans into their cross-sex components is shown in Fig. 1.27. Since the cross-sex donors of bride-price are ostensibly male, the parts of themselves which they detach and hand over are construed as female; moreover, as we have noted, pigs as exchange objects are thought of as female in that they are produced by female nurture within a framework of male protection and facilitation. We can imagine, at this point, that we have suddenly superimposed a husband–wife 'frame' over what was previously a confrontation between two all-male 'men' (i.e. clans). Clan A as 'wife' produces a pig which is ceded to the 'husband' clan (B), as a wife cedes the pigs she nurtures to her husband as the objectification of his cross-sex persona.

The symbolic mobilization of cross-sex relations in what had been a confrontation between all-male units has a dramatic effect, in that it imposes on the recipients (clan B) of these detachable female elements of a primordially male clan (clan A) a logically inescapable change in perspective regarding themselves, that is, they have to see themselves in cross-sex terms as well. They are no longer all-male, but composite. Thus the strategy of A, in order to wrest apart the all-male counterpart clan B, is to represent itself as cross-sex, in a complementary relationship to B, who also must become cross-sex. But the switch to this mode has other implications as well. As described earlier, 'objects' (pigs, and also people) originate in unmediated cross-sex relations. Cross-sex relations thus raise the question of 'origins' – in this connection the 'origins' of the all-male clan. Presenting an all-male clan with detachable elements of femaleness establishes a *historical debt* in which the all-male clan has not only to acknowledge its cross-sex constituents, but also its cross-sex *origins*; the all-male clan originated in cross-sex transactions (transactions which provided them with their 'flesh') for which the donors of pigs appropriate responsibility. Whether or not the actual 'mothers' brothers' of B are to be found in A, the presentation of pigs makes it so – through the capacity of the gift to establish its congruent past.

In accepting A's pigs, B accept a historical paradigm in which their daughters are ceded, not as commodities traded for pigs, but as 'lost' (female) parts of A, returned to their origins. The pigs serve not as trade-goods, but as symbolic operators, imposing a 'reading' on A–B relations in which B recognize that their sisters are (always were) wives-of-A. B become collectively a 'wife' clan to A. Somebody's sister is always (from another point of view) somebody else's wife, and the only question is – whose? B have to be made to see that the answer to *that* question is: 'A's'.

Clearly, it would be inappropriate to suppose that if, as the preceding analysis shows, 'marriage exchange' between all-male units such as clans involves the positioning of exchanging clans within a mesh of cross-sex exchanges such that each all-male unit (successively) becomes (collectively) 'female' with respect to the other, it makes no sense to speak of 'men' exchanging 'women'. As Strathern remarks, what men exchange is not their women, but their points of view; that is, a man is induced to see his sister (female agnate) from somebody else's point of view, as a wife. That makes *him* a sort of wife, too, which emerges often enough in ritual contexts in which mothers' brothers play 'mother' roles *vis-à-vis* junior affines. The instability, or contextuality, of gender undermines the idea that alliance theory provides an exclusively 'male' view of marriage and reproduction. This is a very significant theoretical development with respect to the feminist criticisms of anthropological ideas about marriage and exchange mentioned earlier.

However, I would not like to give the impression that the preceding discussion fairly represents the actual mechanics of marriage, 'bride-price' and affinity in any concrete ethnographic case (Hagen, for instance). I have simplified matters radically for the purpose of explanation. The actual example I intend to discuss – also, of course, in a simplified manner – raises a further issue so far not touched on at all, namely maternity and paternity. The Trobriands have always been topical from this point of view, ever since Malinowski publicized the Trobrianders' so-called 'ignorance of physiological paternity'. But before I give any details, I would like to make a more general point. In Melanesian ethnography there is much discussion of 'extracting' things (or persons) from other persons, and/or from collectivities. The preceding discussion was all about how the As go about extracting their wives-to-be from the Bs. But the initiatory institutions we dealt with earlier are also about extracting too; the Sambia male child has to be 'extracted' from the collectivity of 'mothers' (who wail and offer token resistance), while in the Gimi instance the men were seen to 'extract' the flutes from women, signalling their control over reproductivity; the flutes enable them to 'extract' children from women.

This concern with extracting and bringing outside, according to Strathern's perspective, is a function of the way in which relationships are 'contained' within other relationships, fractal fashion, and the way in which objectifications (appearances) can be made to signify the prizing away of a 'cover' (say the solidarity of the all-male clan) to get at different, subjacent, relations. The process of birth is quintessentially such a process of extraction. On the one hand, men extract pigs from their exchange partners, and on the other hand they extract children from their wives. This can mean treating the exchange partner as a 'wife'; conversely it can mean treating the wife as an exchange partner.

We, in the west, operate with a (folk) biological understanding of reproduction which treats conception and parturition as 'natural' events, over which 'society' excercises control by imposing rules about marriage, parental rights and responsibilities, and so on, but for which social persons, as such, are not responsible – 'nature takes its course'. In Melanesia the nature vs. culture opposition is not found in this form; women become pregnant and give birth because they are related, in exchange, to other persons in specific ways, not because certain 'biological' things happen to them, or within them. An important aspect of Strathern's theory concerns the attempt to think around our tendency to treat human reproduction as more 'natural' than other events involving social individuals, such as exchanging prestations, or conducting initiation ceremonies.

It is not so hard to think in a non-western way about reproduction, though, if one tries to. Just imagine one is a Martian newly arrived on earth, visiting the Maternity Unit of a high-tech hospital, especially a private one, in which financial as well as medical transactions can be observed to take place. There would be every likelihood that in (his?-her?-its?) report, the Martian would answer the question 'who is responsible for the birth of the child?' by identifying the consultant (gynaecologist), rather than the mother, still less the father, as the one who 'gave birth' to the child. After all, in the Maternity Unit, the consultant is clearly the boss, exercising control over the nurses, the mother, the father, and indeed the infant, with calm authority. Moreover, he and his staff are 'working' and being paid, whereas the mother and father are not 'working'. We do not think we are the offspring of consultants, but according to our Martian we are. The role of the mother is to tender her baby to the consultant, in response to his commands, and the role of the father is to pay the bill at the front desk. (The bill is going to be very big, which explains his anxiety.) To our attempts to ascribe prime-mover status to the 'biological' father, and to explain the 'natural' tie between mother and child, our Martian would reply with the Martian equivalent of a sceptical shrug of the shoulders: 'That's your story and you are welcome to it, but it wasn't what I could see . . .'.

I have introduced the idea of consultants 'giving birth' to babies with the Trobriands in mind, because, in effect, that is what happens there, only the Trobriand 'consultant' is the woman's husband, and the equivalent of the western 'husband' is the woman's (matrilineage) brother. The Maternity Unit is the Trobriand conjugal household. Strathern's ingenious (and arduous) analysis enables us to see this clearly, so I will proceed to summarize her main points.

The enduring, self-reproducing, building-blocks of Trobriand society are matrilineal sub-clans called '*dala*'. *Dala* consist of uterine kin, brothers and sisters. From outside, *dala* are just as much 'one person' as the agnatic clans considered just now, but they have a reproductive problem which is conceptually more intractable.

Agnatic clans convert themselves into cross-sex internal exchange units by detaching and reattaching 'partible' female elements; internally to the clan, this allows for the cross-sex, unmediated, exchanges between husbands and wives through which these units reproduce themselves over time. But this is not possible with matrilineally based units. If one 'opens up' one of these *dala*, they are found to consist, not of cross-sex husband–wife relations of an intrinsically reproductive kind; but of cross-sex brother–sister relations which specifically exclude unmediated reproductive cross-sex exchange. In fact, in the Trobriands, there are particularly stringent sanctions against any kind of intimate, domestic, relationship between male and female siblings. They are forced to lead very separate lives. The *dala* must reproduce, yet, because the *dala* is founded on non-reproductive cross-sex sibling relations, its female members are not 'partible' elements as in the agnatic case. If the *dala* women were made partible (or the *dala* men for that matter) the *dala* would cease to exist. 'Partibility' has to be introduced *internally* to the *dala* woman herself.

The solution is for the brother to enlist the services of the consultant, for a fee, such that the consultant will cause his sister to grow and give birth to a child, for the benefit of the *dala* unit. He does the 'separating' of mother and child. By means of his payments to the consultant, the brother makes his sister give birth, without breaking the incest taboo – though perhaps I should stop talking about consultants and Maternity Units at this point in order not to provide a misleading and derogatory image of life in the Trobriands.

How does reproduction in the Trobriands actually take place? We can begin with the sister, and mother-to-be. A woman of the *dala*, married or not, is always potentially reproductive in that she is always a 'container' of *dala* essence. Trobriand conception beliefs involve the activation of a spirit child contained within the woman through a dream, rather than sexual intercourse with the husband. But what is the implication of the idea of 'containment' here? What makes a container a container is a relation some thing or a person has with itself/herself. Thus a blanket is not a 'container' when it is spread on the ground, but if I tie the corners of a blanket together, hey presto! it has become a useful container. Similarly, a woman-as-container is a woman tied together, related to herself. Such a relation is an internal same-sex. A woman-related-to-herself, expanded, is the *dala* as a same-sex corporate unit; this image encompasses the cross-sex brother–sister relation, and also the relation of the woman and her potential child in a unity. The woman as container is therefore not in a position to reproduce in the sense of having a child extracted from her. For this to happen, a different imagery will have to be imposed; the mechanics of Trobriand reproduction consist of the imposition of this alternative imagery.

The woman is sent to the Maternity Unit, in other words, she is married and resides with her husband, who is of a different *dala* (Fig. 1.28). There she becomes engaged in a cross-sex working/feeding relation with her husband. But the most important transactions are between the woman's husband and her brother, who makes gardens, the produce of which (yams) are sent by him to his brother-in-law, constituting the family food supply. These yams come to objectify the relationship between *dala* I (wife givers, yam donors) and *dala* II (wife-receiver, yam-receivers). But what the brother provides is not so much the yams themselves (which are mere objectifications) as an example of the transformative power of 'work' in the context of cross-sex relations; work leads to substitutions, that is, to transformations. The brother, sweating to produce yams in his garden 'gives' an example to be followed both by his brother-in-law and his sister. The brother-in-law, recipient of the yams, is moved by

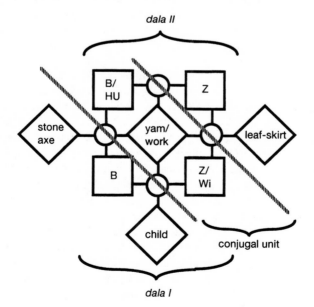

Figure 1.28

them to perform his own work (substitute his own work for them). A cross-sex cover is placed over the single-sex *dala* I/*dala* II relation. The brother-in-law has 'work' to do in 'preparing the way' for his wife's child. Acts of sexual intercourse do this, and they separate it from its mother in that they give the foetus the individual features which will distinguish that child, and later that adult, from other members of the natal *dala*. This sculptor-like activity articulates a difference between mother and child which allows the latter to exist as an independent objectification of the relation, not between father and child, but between mother and child, and mother's brother and sister's child. But this is not all the brother's gardening accomplishes. From Tambiah (whose studies of the role of analogy in magical praxis Strathern does not refer to, though I think she might have (e.g. Tambiah 1968)) we have a clear idea that magic works by giving inspiring examples of how things ought to take place. The brother, in his yam garden, gives an inspiring, but essentially masculine, example of the creation of an extractible product by growing it in a 'prepared bed'. The brother-in-law is preparing the bed (the mother) but the mother is the bed which grows the child. Her procreativity is the female analogue to male garden productivity. His actions pantomime what his sister is going to do. In showing his sister what to do, he magically makes her do it, just as he makes his garden 'do its thing' by reciting inspiring spells over it, laced with metaphors of growth.

This sets up an unmediated exchange relation between brother and sister, not an exchange of things or services (work for a child) but an intangible *exchange of analogies*; analogies, moreover, which decompose the original unity of the *dala* into cross-sex relations between wife-giving and wife-receiving *dala* (I vs. II) between brother and sister, and between sister/mother and child. Simultaneously, however, mediated exchanges are also conducted between *dala*, which are all one-way (from wife-givers to wife-receivers) until after the death of one or other spouse. At this point, the work performed by women in the context of the conjugal household is recouped by the natal *dala* in the form of banana-leaf skirts, presented to the women of *dala* I by the women of *dala* II. Similarly, male valuables (stone axes) recompense the work done by male affines (Fig. 1.28).

At that point I fear I should stop. Perhaps I can end by offering a few remarks on a question which was put to me by Peter Loizos when he heard me say that I intended to produce a user's guide to

GG rather than a critique of it. The question was, given that GG is an illuminating work for those who are already involved in Melanesian anthropology, and know its literature, does this work have anything to say to non-Melanesianists? In the preceding presentation I have emphasized the presence of certain Melanesian constraints in the formulation of the system M, notably that all transactions are gifts, and that all gift transactions are gendered. These modelling constraints are not ones which would have much verisimilitude anywhere except in Melanesia, so the system M, unmodified, is distinctively Melanesian and not African or Indian or whatever. However, there are reasons for wondering whether the system M is really Melanesian either.

I do not believe that the absence of commodity transactions in Melanesia is ethnographically demonstrable, and I have criticized GG on these grounds, as have others. This is not criticism of the system M as a model system, however, only a limitation on its scope. As Strathern makes perfectly clear, the distinction between gifts and commodities is a theoretical distinction which relies on elaborating the contrast between Melanesia and here, and, in effect, imagining the Melanesian 'gift' economy as a default mode of the (imagined) western commodity economy which we can all learn about in the pages of economics textbooks. The system M is a thought experiment which ineluctibly bears the impress of the western system against which it is constructed – one more instance of the return of the repressed. GG is thus not a codification of 'the truth' about Melanesia, but an abstract system which can be aligned with ethnography so as to generate insights into parts of this data, but not, of course, all of it. As such, I think it is exemplary, in that it most effectively destabilized a large number of dogmatic assumptions in sociological analysis which certainly needed destabilizing (society vs. individual, male vs. female, things vs. persons, nature vs. culture, and so on).

To the question posed by Loizos I would therefore answer that the system M is probably quite illuminating in relation to non-Melanesian material so long as it is taken as a fund of imaginings as to what the world might appear as, seen from a counter-intuitive point of view. One can of course also imagine a number of counterparts to the system M, which start from the same idealistic premises, but which replace the specifically Melanesian constraints of the system M with others adapted to different regional cultures; this, I think, has occured as a parallel development in Indian anthropology

via Marriot-esque ethnosociology. But to my mind the real importance of GG is that it instantiates the point that anthropological
research depends on the sustained and concentrated application of
the imagination to sociological problems. To Strathern's imaginings
I have appended some images, which I hope have been helpful.

REFERENCES

Feil, D. (1984) *Ways of Exchange: The Enga Tee of Papua New Guinea* (St
Lucia: University of Queensland Press).
Gillison, G. (1980) 'Images of nature in Gimi thought', in C. MacCormack
and M. Strathern (eds) *Nature, Culture and Gender* (Cambridge: Cam-
bridge University Press).
Gillison, G. (1987) 'Incest and the atom of kinship: the role of the mother's
brother in a New Guinea Highlands society', *Ethnos*, 15:166–202.
Herdt, G. (1981) *Guardians of the Flutes: Idioms of Masculinity* (New York:
McGraw-Hill).
Herdt. G. (1982) 'Fetish and fantasy in Sambia initiation', in G. Herdt (ed.)
Rituals of Manhood: Male Initiation in Papua New Guinea (Berkeley, CA:
University of California Press).
Herdt, G (1984) 'Semen transactions in Sambia culture', in G. Herdt (ed.)
Ritualised Homosexuality in Melanesia (Berkeley, CA: University of Cali-
fornia Press).
Huen, C.W. (1993) 'Nature and culture debate: the natural, social, cultural
and meaningful in the social anthropological discourse on kinship',
unpublished M.Phil. thesis, Clare Hall, University of Cambridge.
Jolly, M. (1992) 'Partible persons and multiple authors' [Book Review
Forum on *The Gender of the Gift*], *Pacific Studies*, 15:137–48.
Josephides, L. (1991) 'Metaphors, metathemes, and the construction of
sociality: a critique of the new Melanesian ethnography', *Man*, 26: 145–
61.
Mimica, J. (1988) *Intimations of Infinity: The Cultural Meaning of the
Iqwaye Counting System and Number, (Oxford: Berg)*.
Strathern, M. (1991) *Partial Connections*, ASAO Spec. Pub. 3 (Savage, MD:
Rowan & Littlefield).
Tambiah, S. (1968) 'The magical power of words', *Man*, 3. 175–208.
Weiner, A. (1976) *Women of Value, Men of Renown: New Perspectives in
Trobriand Exchange* (Austin, TX: University of Texas Press).

CHAPTER 2

INTER-TRIBAL COMMODITY BARTER AND REPRODUCTIVE GIFT EXCHANGE IN OLD MELANESIA

INTRODUCTION

By and large, 'Maussian' gift institutions have had a favourable press in anthropology, and 'commodities' an unfavourable one (for an extreme case cf. Baudrillard 1975). 'Gift–reciprocity–Good/ market–exchange–Bad' is a simple, easy-to-memorize formula. But perhaps the tide is about to turn. Parry (1986; 1989) has exposed the 'moral ambiguity' of the gift in an Indian context. In what follows I propose a critique of 'gift exchange' theory in a more familiar context. Melanesia is deservedly famous for the prevalence of 'ceremonial exchange' institutions there, so much so that it is easy to forget that barter or trade was highly developed in 'old Melanesia' (i.e. Melanesia as it was in pre-colonial times). This fact is often forgotten, witness the paucity of the treatment given to commodity barter in both of the general monographs on Melanesian exchange and economy which have appeared in recent years (Rubel and Rosman 1979; Gregory, 1982). I intend to demonstrate that this myopic stance concerning the presence of an indigenous commodity barter economy in old Melanesia has resulted in serious deficiencies in the theoretical treatment of 'exchange' in non-commercial contexts as well.

In this essay I propose the evidently rather daring hypothesis that Melanesian ceremonial exchange institutions, particularly the category of prestations which I call 'reproductive gifts' are symbolically derived from a 'template' which is provided by commodity barter. I believe that it is wrong to polarize 'gift' economy as if it were antithetical to commodity exchange, when in fact the relation is one of mutual implication, both materially and symbolically or rhetorically.

Thus, I am led to contest the idea that ceremonial exchange is a 'primordial' transactional form from which all other transactional forms may be conceived as deriving – 'after the Fall' as it were. On the contrary, I will suggest that ceremonial exchange is a hybrid product arising out of the ambiguous confrontation of two other transactional modes which may indeed be considered 'primordial', namely 'sharing' ('generalized reciprocity' in the terminology of Sahlins 1965) and 'swapping' ('commodity exchange' as defined by Gregory 1982). The potency of gift exchanges as constitutive features of social reproduction in Melanesian societies arises, not from the fact that 'the gift'expresses some Platonic Essence of sociable conduct, but precisely from the ambiguity of the gift between 'sharing' and 'swapping' – participating in features of both of these, without amounting to either. Neither flesh nor fowl nor good red herring, the gift is admirably calculated to divert attention and conceal motives while certain crucial rearrangements of social relationships occur.

'Reproductive gift exchange' in Melanesia arises through the recasting of social relationships which could be conducted without material transfers of objects-as-gifts, into a relationship-idiom in which these transfers figure centrally. I hold that these transfers of gift objects mimic the processes of commodity exchange which take place on the edges of 'societies' (units for the purposes of social reproduction), that is, inter-tribal barter and the like. This recontextualization of the 'form' commodity exchange from the periphery to the centre of the social field affects it profoundly, so that the commodity exchange 'form' is not easily recognizable in 'the gift' and may be strenuously denied. But commodity exchange is, nonetheless, the prototype for the regime of 'reproductive gift exchanges' in Melanesian society, and, in its 'internalized' form, it provides a cover for the reformulation of crucial social relationships so as to permit a radical severance between reproduction as natural process and reproductive as a social process.

In order to introduce my argument, there are certain points which need to be established.

(1) I have to show that commodity exchange was an important feature of traditional Melanesian society; that is, 'gift exchange' was not the *only* transactional mode available.

(2) I have to show that 'sharing' is different from gift exchange (and obviously from commodity exchange) and that 'sharing' was an important transactional mode in its own right.

Having made the case for (1) and (2), I will then go on to discuss the emergence of gift exchange. For present purposes, 'gift exchange' is to be understood as 'reproductive' gift exchange, that is, prestations explicitly linked to phases in the relations between affinally linked groups (marriage payments, child payments, death payments, and the like). I propose that 'reproductive gift exchange' corresponds to a reconstruction of the relationships involved in marriage and affinity on a 'template' provided by the commodity-exchange relationship, with the result that these relationships are removed from the sphere of economic relationships dominated by the ethos of 'sharing'. I interpret this shift as motivated by certain tensions inherent in Melanesian societies where commodity-exchange forms are contingently underdeveloped. I hazard the empirical generalization that societies, such as Umeda, which have no access to commodity-exchange networks, lack a regime of reproductive gift exchange as a direct consequence of this fact.

The 'tensions' which mark non-commodity-exchanging societies in Melanesia (and which motivate the emergence of the regime of reproductive gift exchange in societies elsewhere) have to do with gender politics. In non-commodity-exchanging societies men are placed in disadvantageous and conflictual relationships through their relationships with women, which are obviated, to some extent, once the transactional mode of 'reproductive gift exchange' is established. Having dealt with the impact of the regime of reproductive gift exchange in those societies in which commodity exchange is only a 'peripheral' element in economic organization, I will conclude this essay by considering the situation in coastal/riverain societies in which commodity exchange is a 'dominant' factor in economic organization. Some of these societies are dependent on barter for their basic subsistence, and here we note a further shift in the patterning of gender relations resulting from the emergence of women as independent commodity-exchange transactors in their own right.

COMMODITY EXCHANGE IN OLD MELANESIA

Let me begin by clarifying what I mean by 'commodity exchange' and by 'reproductive gift exchange' where these two terms are used contrastively. 'Commodities' are items which are alienated in exchange during at least one 'phase' of their existence (cf. Gell 1986). Following Gregory, I define commodity exchange as the exchange of alienable objects between transactors in a state of mutual independence, and the exchange as one which establishes a qualitative relationship between exchange objects. When 'a given quantity' of X moves against 'an equivalent quantity' of Y, a commodity swap has occurred, and the transactors involved in the swap are 'quits' with respect to that transaction, whatever state their relationship towards one another may assume with respect to other transactions and other social contexts.

Gregory goes on to contrast commodity exchange with gift exchange, which he defines as the exchange of inalienable objects between transactors in a condition of reciprocal dependence, which establishes a qualitative relationship between the transactors rather than a quantitative relationship between the objects transacted. Here I differ from Gregory, because I believe that gift exchange is much more like commodity exchange than he is prepared to recognize.

My objections to Gregory's neat definition of gift exchange by simple inversion of the definitional properties of commodity exchange can be briefly outlined as follows.

(1) Objects *are* alienated in gift exchanges. In making a prestation, the donor loses access to the exchange object, which passes to another, and with it the power to donate that object to a different recipient, whereas the recipient gains both of these. In making a prestation, an object of value is 'sacrificed', and the prestige, power, and so on, conferred by the act of giving are proportional to the consensual evaluation of the onerousness of the sacrifice involved. What is not 'alienated' in gift-giving is not the gift object itself, but that which *cannot* be alienated, namely, the social identity of the donor, which still attaches to the object after it has been given away. But there would be no increment of glory to the 'name' which clings to the object after it has been given away, unless the giving-away of the object were a genuine sacrifice or 'loss' to the giver, expressible as a series of opportunity costs incurred in not holding on to the object (for consumption or for disposition in some alternative, and possibly more advantageous, way).

(2) Gift-exchange partners who are in a debtor–creditor relationship, or who are 'mutually indebted' with respect to a multitude of incomplete transactions, are, as Gregory suggests, in a relation of dependency which extends over time. However, this feature cannot discriminate between commodity exchanges and gift exchanges for the following reasons. (i) This situation is just as prevalent in the sphere of relationships based on commodity exchanges, where debt, credit and 'trust' between mutually dependent parties to a trading

relationship may be all-important, and (ii) even if it is true, *de facto*, that gift exchangers are indeed 'mutually dependent' this is not the objective which is actively sought, which is precisely the opposite, namely, to be able to 'call it quits' after a long series of socially salient, high-prestige, transactions. If the objective actually were, as Gregory implies, to maximize outgoings so as to maximize 'indebtedness', the strategy of the 'big man' would be to seek out the 'rubbish man' and ply him with immense prestations, confident of never seeing them return. But nothing of the kind occurs; gifts are given to financial equals, individuals who can be trusted to return them, possibly with increment. The aim is to demonstrate autonomy, the ability to not get into debt or to waste substance on 'bad risks' in the gift/debt economy, while still maintaining a high volume of transactions. 'Dependency' of any kind is contrary both to the spirit and the practice of the economy of reproductive gifts, which is the means available to transactors to demonstrate 'equivalence' with exchange partners through a matching series of reciprocal prestations. And this 'matching' of powers in the sequence of gift exchanges is 'quantitative'. Gifts are accounted for and precisely enumerated, just as they would be if they were commodities moving against commodities.

What distinguishes 'gifts' and 'commodities' is the *social context* of a particular transaction, not the character of relationship between people and things (alienable/inalienable) or between people and people (independent/dependent). For our purposes, 'gifts' are transactions in objects which occur in the contextual setting of social reproduction through marriage, affinity and alliance. 'Commodity' transactions are transactions in objects in a setting definable as 'trade', 'barter' and the like. The objective is to understand the linkage between transactions in these two contextual settings.

Let me return to the first of the two points mentioned above. I promised to show, first of all, that commodity exchange was an important feature of traditional Melanesian society and that 'gift exchange' was not the *only* transactional mode to be encountered there, despite the absence (in general) of money, markets and the state. I could save space by simply asserting this, in the confidence that nobody at all familiar with the literature would be rash enough to gainsay such an elementary observation. However, it is necessary to emphasize the point, because, although well-supported in both the older and more modern ethnographies, it has been lost sight of in some of the more recent theoretical literature, notably the important synthesizing contributions of Rubel and Rosman (1979) and Gregory (1982). In a recent article on Maring trade Healey writes:

> [Gregory] gives insufficient attention to the importance of trade as a stimulus for production, and as a means for acquiring goods for circulation in prestations. The effect is to deconstitute the economy and results in a failure to examine the interconnections between forms and objectives of production, distribution and consumption. The indigenous economy is then effectively reduced to production for subsistence and gift exchange, and the circulation of valuables in prestations alone.
>
> (Healey 1986:129).

These strictures are applied to Gregory, but they are of wider application. In fact, hinterland inhabited areas of old Melanesia were usually, though not universally, criss-crossed by inter-tribal trade routes in pre-contact times, and for the New Guinea Highlands a comprehensive survey of inter-tribal trade has been published by Hughes (1977, cf. Brookfield and Hart 1971) detailing both the routes used and the objects which moved along them. Objects characteristically moved between five and fifty miles, though occasionally much further. In this traffic 'markets' were exceptional (Epstein 1968; Salisbury 1970; Gewertz 1978; 1983). In the hinterland, trade was conducted through individualized trade partnerships between men who met periodically, in person, to exchange trade items. At these meetings information would be relayed about 'demand' for items up and down the exchange road, since traders were involved in trade relationships with a variety of partners located in different places.

Inland, traders were sometimes, but not necessarily, specialized producers of one or more trade commodity, otherwise acting as middlemen between producers and end-users. Here – but not on the coast – there are no recorded instances of communities which could be said to be trade-dependent for basic subsistence (vegetable food). Hinterland trade was 'peripheral' barter between men belonging to distinct social groups, not mutually implicated (by marriage) in 'reproducing' each other. Hughes states that trade in pre-contact days was recalled with a good deal of nostalgia by old men who had been involved in it, as an exciting, prestigious and profitable male pursuit.

But there is no suggestion that the objects distributed through trade channels among hinterland societies were of overwhelming utilitarian significance; the hinterlands could have 'got by' without inter-tribal trade, and the fact that they did not do so must be attributed to factors other than stringent material requirements.

In coastal/riverain Melanesia the situation is different, since here we find a number of communities which are dependent on trade for their continued existence. Trade-dependent communities maintain 'ecological' adaptations which necessitate ongoing trade in vegetable staples as well as 'valuables' (Hogbin 1951 (Busama); Schwartz 1963 (Manus); Harding 1970 (Siassi); Malinowski 1915 (Mailu) cf. Irwin 1983). More recent studies by Gewertz 1983 (Chambri); Lipset 1985; and Barlow 1985 (Murik lakes) have greatly increased our knowledge of such communities and further investigations are in progress (Macintyre, on Tubetube, 1983). Such trade-dependent communities are located sporadically all around the coast of New Guinea (except the south-west coast of Papua) and off the main islands of the Bismark archipelago. Trade-dependent, or partly trade-dependent communities are also to be found along the lower and middle Sepik, whose cultures are in many ways 'coastal' in character, despite being situated inland.

What can one say about the general characteristics of inter-tribal barter trade in old Melanesia? I cannot attempt to provide a summary of the main items involved in the coastal or hinterland trades (for details, see references cited above), but there is one point which emerges from archaeological work in the area which deserves notice. It seems clear that the emergence, particularly along the coast, of trade 'centres' where specialized production for trade is undertaken, and which exercise local monopolies in certain trades, supported by restrictive practices governing the export of technology and 'trade secrets', has been a progressive development in the course of Melanesian pre-history (Irwin 1983). In earlier epochs it would appear, for instance, that pottery production took place at a larger number of sites along the coast (and in consequence, pottery was traded over shorter distances) than was found to be the case at contact. The pottery production centres in operation at the time of contact were, moreover, often dependent on other communities for their raw material (clay) from whom it was obtained by barter, yet the clay-providing communities made no pots themselves. The underlying 'specialization' of the pot-making communities was not in pot manufacture by itself, so much as in the physical and social technologies of trade and distribution. Outside these specialized trade centres, pot-making had become a 'lost art'.

These interesting observations point towards a more general conclusion. 'Barter trade' as an economic phenomenon is often interpreted as a reflection of ecological discontinuities (the inherently uneven distribution of particular resources needed for the production of commodities in general demand throughout a trade region). But, even admitting that the resource-base of particular communities in old Melanesia was of uneven composition, there seems to be a 'drive' towards local specialization in production for barter trade which emanates not from ecological discontinuities *per se*, but from the mechanism (trade) which seeks to redress these discontinuities.

But such a drive towards trade specialization can only be explained on the basis of a cultural mechanism which predisposes communities to participate eagerly in commodity exchange even when local production could provide substitutes for commodities obtainable through trade. It seems clear that commodities obtained by trade are often at a premium simply because they are obtained through these channels: that is, commodity exchange, as a transactional form, confers value on products which they would not otherwise possess. One can see this occurring in connection with the widespread trade in salt in the Highlands. The basic know-how for producing 'salt', by burning leaves, and so on, or wood steeped in natural brine, is known to most Highlands groups, but only a few of them (for example the Baruya) have become specialized salt-producers, and these tribes produce quantities for trade. Once a 'brand' of salt is established, local substitutes are no longer acceptable, despite the existence of the technical means to produce them. The exotic import is at a premium because it is bound up with a transactional mode (commodity exchange) which is positively valued and which confers value on commodities.

But if, as I have suggested, commodity exchange is a favoured transactional mode, gratifying to participants independently of the use-value of the items passing to and fro, does this mean that commodity exchange, in its Melanesian form is really 'Maussian' gift exchange – that is, a 'non-commercial' 'prestige' transaction dominated by political, rather than 'economizing' or utility-maximizing motives?

One can certainly discount the existence throughout most of the region of a 'market' economy in pre-modern times; trade was carried on, and value-ratios between commodities were set, in the absence of the 'market' situation of generalized competition between sellers to find buyers, and among buyers to find sellers. Rates of exchange between trade partners were not arrived at by haggling, but by convention, and were altered only in response to change in overall circumstances (political circumstances as much as economic ones) and had little sensitivity to short-term fluctuation in supply and demand. Ratios were 'lagged' to a very marked degree, or completely immobilized (for an excellent discussion, cf. Modjeska, 1985).

The question we have therefore to face is whether 'avidity for trade' (Sahlins 1972) and relative indifference to 'costs' in energy/labour/time terms gives us grounds for asserting that 'trade' in old Melanesia was motivated by 'social' considerations, so that barter was indeed gift reciprocity oriented towards 'Maussian' objectives. The general argument of this essay depends on giving partial – but only partial – assent to this proposition. The basic format of a 'partnership' sustained by the passage of valuables between partners is indeed common to both gift exchange (reproductive and ceremonial) and barter exchange. But commodity exchange is, nevertheless, distinct, and perceived to be distinct, from the kinds of exchanges which enter into the process of social reproduction.

There can be no suggestion, for instance, that 'big-men' are 'big' traders. An Iatmul big-man, for instance, has two possible sources of shell rings; he can obtain them by participating in internal exchange, or he can trade for them, by offering stone axes (obtained via Chambri from the Sepik hills) to Sawos trade partners. The literature contains nothing to suggest that the 'trade' strategy has a significance, in the careers of known Iatmul big-men, which is comparable to the significance of 'internal' exchange. Yet the Iatmul continued to trade with the Sawos and fought wars with one another over access to Sawos villages. Trade relationships are valuable and politically important, but are not directly articulated to the internal exchange processes which determine internal political standing. The emphasis in the literature is on trade as a source of excitement and social enjoyment, rather than as a basis for power. (For comparison, in the context of Indian 'tribal' society, cf. Gell 1982; 1986.)

Nonetheless, it would be mistaken to suppose that because commodity exchange is gratifying to participants, it is 'ceremonial' or 'ritual', not oriented towards obtaining commodities. It would be no less true to say of a Baniya at an Indian bazaar, a commodity exchanger to his very bones, that he found in the activity of trading a deep source of pleasure and excitement. Indeed, there is a sense in which trading, as an activity, must, almost by definition, be a source of subjective gratification, since to trade is to accept a more-valued commodity in exchange for a less-valued one. That is happiness.

THE INDIGENOUS SERVICE ECONOMY

It may be said, therefore, that in hinterland areas of old Melanesia low-volume inter-group barter trade was pervasive as a valued masculine activity, and that in coastal and some riverain areas 'trade-dependent' societies existed, and trading activity was quite intense. My argument is that this pervasive network of commodity exchange inflected internal processes of social reproduction in most old Melanesian societies in a specific direction. In order to demonstrate this point, it is necessary that I should sketch in the pattern of social reproduction in old Melanesia in the absence of this influencing factor, so as to show the 'baseline' state of affairs, before the commodity-exchange template takes hold. It is possible to do this, because there are a few Melanesian societies in which, for historically contingent reasons, inter-group commodity exchange is not practised; and I am prepared to generalize empirically by saying that in these societies 'reproductive' exchange is not practised either.

One such non-commodity-exchanging society is Umeda, where I did my own fieldwork (Gell 1975). In Umeda, there are no imported shells, valuables, axes, and so on, and virtually no domesticated pigs – and there are no marriage payments, child payments, death payments, and the like; that is, no 'ceremonial' or 'Maussian' exchanges of any importance. I believe that these facts are linked together.

At this point I intend to make certain suggestions about Umeda society which are, from a Melanesian standpoint, rather heterodox, and at variance (interpretatively speaking) with the account of Umeda which I published in 1975. I am now persuaded, shocking as this may seem, that 'exchange' – any kind of exchange – plays no significant part in Umeda social reproduction. It is difficult to make this assertion for two reasons. Firstly, there is the weight of opinion from Mauss, Lévi-Strauss, and so on, which holds that social communication, the exchange of women, gifts, commodities, messages, and so on, are essential to the constitution of any social order whatsoever, and Umeda cannot possibly be an exception to this universal rule. Secondly there is the 'received version' of the trend in Melanesian social evolution, which is expounded in both of the recent general monographs on the subject, by Rubel and Rosman (1979) and Gregory (1982) and which is referred to in more general terms by other writers, such as Godelier (1986). This received version holds that even where exchange of valuables, such as pigs and shells, is poorly developed, 'exchange' is still fundamental because social reproduction is based on the exchange of women between exogamous clans or lineages, that is, on affinal reproductive 'gifts'.

The foundation of the social order is the exchange of women, described by Gregory (echoing Williams) as 'the supreme gift'. Gregory, and Rosman and Rubel, both suggest that the most 'elementary' forms of social organization in Melanesia are manifested by societies which practise direct woman-exchange, that is, 'sister-exchange'. Marriage payments and the like come in subsequently as a means of obviating direct woman-exchange, replacing a ceded sister not with a sister, but with an array of valuables, so as to expand the scope and complexity of social organization beyond an exogamous moiety structure. These authors propose what one could call a 'from the bottom up' interpretation of reproductive gift exchanges; these exchanges 'were once' (at the bottom of the scale) woman-for-woman exchanges, and have been transformed and expanded into exchanges of women against valuables, and latterly, in response to intensification of production, into exchanges of valuables against valuables, as in ceremonial exchange systems of the Moka/Tee type.

My interpretation can be contrasted to this one as a 'from the top down' interpretation: reproductive gift exchange results from the extension of 'external' commodity-exchange type relations into the domain of affinal relations between groups interested in each other's reproduction. In order to substantiate the 'from the top down' interpretation, I have to show that 'reproduction' can be carried on *without* exchange, and that is what I will now attempt to show.

It is conceivable, to me at least, that all socially necessary activity can be carried out by individuals as a result of moral obligation, not because these individuals stand in relations of reciprocal 'exchange' with other individuals. Thus, to cite the most fundamental instance, the sexual division of labour is not sustained by reciprocity between the sexes (a pact to make mutual sacrifices for the benefit of the other) but is sustained by role expectations applying to men and women respectively, as duly socialized persons. Women behave as women, and perform the duties appertaining to the roles of daughters, wives, sisters, mothers, and so on, not because the services they perform are reciprocated, but because they are obliged to do so, and are morally responsible for their behaviour. Services are performed according to role-definitions, and, although there is 'harmony' (more or less) in the patterning of interlocking role-relationships, so that they form a coherent system for practical purposes, this systematicity is not sustained by an ethos of the mutual exchange of equivalent sacrifices, that is, 'reciprocity'. The prescribed role-definitions oblige each and every person to perform services towards prescribed others in accordance with the division of labour by sex and age, and the recognition of kinship statuses. Moral obligation dictated by role-definitions provides a basis for a political economy and social-reproductive regime, which I will name 'the indigenous service economy'. In such an economy, material transfers between individuals (food changing hands between one person and another, for instance) occur as a function of the existence of a moral obligation, incumbent on the transferring party, to 'provision' the transferred-to party to the transaction in some respect. For instance, the provisioning of children by parents involves material transfers which flow directly from the moral definition of role-relationships between parents and children, and are not 'prestations' which produce, or repay, 'debts'. In the Indigenous Service Economy material transfers are the physical embodiment of 'service' obligations.

The Indigenous Service Economy corresponds, partly, to what Sahlins calls 'generalised reciprocity' in his (all too) well-known paper on the 'sociology of primitive exchange' (1965). But to call 'sharing' (and domestic provisioning) 'reciprocity' is most misleading, because in households reciprocal relations are just what one doesn't find. Asymmetrical role-relationships are the order of the day (Hu/Wi, Pa/Chi, EBr/Ybr, Br/Si, etc.). One cannot discuss, under the rubric of 'reciprocity', transfers of objects and performance of services in a transactional context, which is specifically designed as the one in which role-relationships are asymmetrical and incommensurable, accounts are not kept, and in which recompense for sacrifices made cannot be demanded, and need never be forthcoming.

It is therefore quite wrong to imply, as Sahlins does, that gift exchange (balanced reciprocity) is emergent in the transactional context of intra-household generalized reciprocity. Gift exchange – in which accounts are kept, and recompense must be forthcoming – is defined in *contrast* to what goes on inside households, or, more generally, in the Indigenous Service Economy. 'Generalized' and 'balanced' are not two alternative forms of reciprocity; balanced reciprocity is reciprocity, because 'balance' (comparability of mutual sacrifices) is built into the notion of reciprocity as such: 'generalized' reciprocity is the absence of reciprocity, that is, non-reciprocity.

My general point, in all this, is that the exchange economy (the reproductive gift exchange) is to be understood as the means for the reformulation of the basis of human relationships in terms *other* than those set by the Indigenous Service Economy. 'Exchange' provides an escape route from a social order in which objects are transferred, and services performed, out of moral obligation, substituting for it one in which transfers and services can be conceptualized in terms of the schema of the mutually advantageous exchange of sacrifices.

I introduce Umeda, at this point, in order to exemplify social reproduction in a regime in which the Indigenous Service Economy is dominant. But societies of this kind have been given another, and more perspicuous, name: 'bride-service' societies. It is under this rubric that they have been described by Collier and Rosaldo (1981) in an article which has decisively altered my understanding of Umeda society and affinal relations, as will become very apparent as I proceed.

'Bride-service' societies are simple societies in which the main expression of affinal relations is the imposition of service obligations on married persons *vis-à-vis* their in-laws, rather than the institutionalization of marriage payments or other reproductive exchanges. What most distinguishes bride-service societies, especially from the standpoint of the argument currently being advanced, is the onerous and 'marked' character of the son-in-law *vis-à-vis* the wife's parents. Sons-in-law become, to a greater or lesser degree, appendages of their wife's parents, obliged to serve and provision them while they live, and these obligations descend to the junior generation as obligations to serve and provision the mother's brother. Collier and Rosaldo point out that in bride-service societies, women are not seen as group 'reproducers' but as bait for sons-in-law and the focus of male sexual rivalry. As points-of-attachment for client-like sons-in-law, they have room for manoeuvre, and enjoy a degree of pre-marital sexual freedom as well as having scope for adulterous liaisons subsequently. Their position with respect to male peers is relatively advantageous. On the other hand, the position of young men is relatively disadvantageous, since, though they all desire to get married (eventually), to do so is to come under the sway of their wives' relatives.

Umeda is a bride-service society' on Collier and Rosaldo lines. Unfortunately, I did not understand this fully when I was in the field, or immediately afterwards, because at that time I was still under the sway of the 'exchange/reciprocity' model of Melanesian society, and was determined to see 'sister-exchange' as the primordial transaction in Umeda social reproduction. If (anachronistically) Collier and Rosaldo's essay could have been brought to my attention at the relevant time, I might have been less scornful of the emphatic testimony of my informants, who were mostly young men belonging precisely to the category for whom the down-side of marriage, for males in a bride-service society, loomed most ominously. Vain regret! Misled myself, I have been all too successful in misleading others, notably my colleague Chris Gregory.

UMEDA AFFINITY : BRIDE-SERVICE AND SISTER-EXCHANGE

Umeda is situated in unfavourable terrain in the Border Mountains of the West Sepik Province, Papua New Guinea. Umeda was excluded from significant inter-tribal barter trade by a number of factors. To the north, there is a trade route which runs along the relatively densely occupied Wasengla valley, which articulates with trade routes along the north coast of New Guinea and West Irian. But informants' accounts suggested that relations with Wasengla valley tribes were unremittingly hostile in pre-pacification times, and the Umedas did not dare venture into the no-man's land lying between themselves and the Wasengla valley (the *Aw-sis* the limit of their world) across which Wasengla raiding parties would periodically make forays. I found no artefacts of Wasengla manufacture in Umeda, suggestive of active trade; the Umedas having nothing to offer that was coveted by the Wasenglas except their hunting territory. To the south, Umeda had social relations, but not trade relations, with Punda, and Punda with Yafar, and so on, but these inter-village relations did not involve trade, and were tenuous at best. The Sepik, with its abundance of trade routes, was inaccessible to all of these communities, which were exceptionally small, scattered, and basically nomadic. Umeda was entirely self-sufficient in items which, elsewhere, are typically exported and imported. Umedas manufactured their own salt, lime and paint; created their own dog- and pig-teeth ornaments, decorative net-bags, purses, hair-ribbons; and obtained their plumes, furs, and so on, by hunting. Umedas also made all their own stone tools, sago-pounders (still manufactured and in universal use in 1979–80) and small axes, which were obsolescent by the time I arrived.

Umedas were nomadic for most of the year, working in family groups at isolated sago-stands, hunting, gathering, and engaged in desultory gardening. They were, in fact, hunter-gatherer-like in many respects. They possessed the 'sharing' ethos to a marked degree, and the corresponding lack of interest in amassing personal property. Umeda women had the 'sexy', rather than 'reproductive', image so well-described by Collier and Rosaldo. The basic theme in Umeda society was male sexual rivalry, fired up by the capriciousness and sexual manipulativeness of women.

The essential point about Umeda, in terms of this discussion, is that sons-in-law were obliged to live and work in the bush with their in-laws for extended periods. In the bush, men practised shifting residence between camps located in their own clan-territory, their wife's clan-territory, and the clan-territory of their matrikin. While residing with affines, husbands undertook two main kinds of work, namely, hunting and pounding sago. Umeda is rather unusual in that the heavy work of pounding-up the pith of the sago log, preparatory to washing the starch out of it (which is done by women) is exclusively a male task. This pounding work is done by sons-in-law while residing with affines, and they eat and live as members of their affines' sago-working camp. They also hunt, collect wild food, and assist in gardening. This account of Umeda bride-service obligations is duplicated among the neighbouring Yafar described by Juillerat (1986) except that, among the Yafar, men leave pounding sago to women.

Umeda youths with whom I discussed these matters were most demonstrative about the disadvantages of marriage, of which the outstanding one was the 'shame' (*loweh*: the word for brother-in-law) of having to live intimately with in-laws in a subservient and patronizable condition. Only after many years of marriage and the demise of the wife's parents did these obligations disappear, at which time sons assumed obligations towards their fathers' affines (as sisters' sons) and, through having daughters, men might begin to patronize sons-in-law of their own.

But Umeda youths were most unwilling to step onto this treadmill, and dreamed of escaping to the coast and to a condition of permanent bachelorhood (and access to prostitutes, since, in their eyes, sex on a 'strictly cash' basis was as enticing as it was unobtainable locally). At the same time, however, they did everything within their power to attract the favourable attention of potential wives and fathers-in-law. They hunted assiduously, beautified themselves, and would, in earlier times, have sought occasions to demonstrate their bravery in war.

Bride-service institutions give rise to a basic tension because men as hunters, fighters and lovers are encouraged to become equal and independent, but hunting, fighting and love-making inexorably lead to affinal servitude, a condition of subservience from which only increasing age offers any escape, and that a very uncertain one. One finds a pervasive contradiction between the 'autonomous' values of the 'male republic' (male–male solidarity, hunting, 'sporting' warfare between traditional enemies and so on) and the 'shameful' inequality which comes from marriage, domesticity and affinal servitude.

But if this is a correct interpretation of Umeda marriage, why did I not perceive this originally? Why did I find it so easy to represent Umeda (as on the whole I did) as one dominated by an 'exchange' mentality?

There are two features of Umeda society which seem, at first glance, to support an 'exchange' interpretation of Umeda marriage and affinity. They are (1) the systematic transfer of meat (of wild game, notably wild pigs) from wife-receivers to wife-givers, and (2) the common and recognized practice of 'sister-exchange' in this society.

Let me deal briefly with (1). As in many hunting-gathering societies, Umeda hunters were strictly forbidden to eat any part of game which they had killed themselves. Meat was given, as a matter of stringent obligation, to those individuals to whom the hunter was connected via a female tie, namely, wife's parents, matrikin, sister and sister's husband, and so on. Of these gifts, the largest and most important went to the wife's parents. Once the affinal and maternal portions had been packed and distributed, the remainder of the animal was shared generally in the camp.

Now it could be argued that these portions of killed game sent to affines are 'prestations' which reflect the presence of woman-debt incurred by wife-receivers with respect to wife-givers, and that is indeed how I originally interpreted them. But this is not correct. The affinal portions are not 'presents' which are 'given' – they are 'shares' which are 'sent' (*asmhui-piav*). No debt is repaid, instead, it is an obligatory service which is being carried out, that is, the son-in-law's obligation to hunt for his parents-in-law. The meat is not an exchange object at all, but a by-product of a service obligation dictated by the Indigenous Service Economy. It is in this respect comparable to the pounded sago pith, or gathered wild foods, with which the son-in-law is likewise obliged to furnish his parents-in-law. On the other hand, meat differs from these in being associated with 'prestige' male values, and this is a point I will return to later.

Next let me take up point (2) above, that is, 'sister-exchange'. Quite a high proportion of the marriages I recorded were between sets of siblings and could be counted as 'sister-exchanges'. However, there was absolutely no question that sister-exchange marriages were more legitimate or approved than any other kind of marriage. What 'legitimated' marriage was the recognition of affinal service obligations, not recompense of a woman for a woman. In fact, when I asked about sister-exchange, Umeda informants claimed that it was an innovation of the recent past, having been imposed on them by the first Dutch patrols in the area, as a device to lessen fighting. Umedas went on to say that it was much better, in their eyes, to seduce a woman or obtain one by violence, and that exchanging sisters was an unappealing strategy which would procure only unappealing girls (too young or too old, or with skin rashes) but that they were obliged to follow it because to do otherwise was to run the risk of being imprisoned on charges of fighting or rape by the colonial authorities.

I discounted all this and went on doggedly totting up 'exchange' marriages so that I could represent it as a 'rule' of marriage, despite the fact that I never discovered an Umeda term which specifically distinguished 'exchange' from 'non-exchange' marriages. And of course I could do this since there were many marriages of this kind, and a clear awareness, on the part of informants, that certain movements of girls in marriage had been precipitated by the need to square accounts between sets of siblings united by previous marriages. 'Sister-exchange', as a practice, is not at all mythical; but the question is – does sister-exchange really count as 'exchange' in the commonly understood sense?

In a sense, the whole notion of 'sister-exchange' is nonsensical, because if A and B were really to 'exchange sisters', A's sister would become B's sister, and B's sister A's sister, and neither would be any nearer obtaining a wife for himself. Given that *by definition* A's sister is unmarriageable for A, and B's sister is unmarriageable for B, which we may assume, then in permitting their sisters to marry elsewhere they are 'giving up' nothing for which reciprocation might reasonably be demanded. In fact, when B marries A's sister, she continues to be A's sister, just as she was before, and B's sister, now married to A, is B's sister still; A and B's sisters are A and B's *married* sisters, which is what, in the nature of things, they must become. There is no logical reason for supposing that marriage interferes in any way with descent or siblingship. It can be represented as doing so, but it certainly does not do so by necessity. If A getting married to B's sister is not an infringement of any right or power that B, as her sibling, has over her (which certainly does not include the right to expect wifely services from her) then her marriage to A is in no sense a sacrifice, made by B for the benefit of A. And if this marriage, considered in isolation, is not a sacrifice made by B for the benefit of A, it follows that the reciprocal marriage of B to A's sister is not the means of requiting this never-outstanding sacrifice. Since neither has made any sacrifice, sacrifices cannot be mutually exchanged.

The rationale for sister-exchange is quite different, as the Umedas made clear, had I been prepared to listen. In bride-service societies, males compete for women, and gaining a wife is a mark of social approval with respect to prowess in hunting, fighting, and the art of making one's self sexually attractive. The 'losers' with respect to any marriage, are not the girl's male kin, but the eligible competitor males, who might have got to marry the girl, but in the end did not prevail. Sister-exchange does two things: (1) it establishes parity of social esteem between men in relationships of symmetrical affinity, and (2) it reduces conflict between men who are not affines and who might otherwise come into damagingly competitive struggles over a restricted number of available marriageable women.

Despite the existence of sister-exchange as a means of moderating male conflict over the distribution of brides, social reproduction in societies such as Umeda is not founded on reproductive 'gifts' taking the form of women. In fact social reproduction is carried out via the institution of marriage, and the accompanying obligations of services and provisioning, that is, by the Indigenous Service Economy.

In the absence of 'exchange' as a primordial institution in this 'simple' Melanesian society there seems no reason to posit the 'elaboration' of exchange institutions (sister-exchange→marriage payments→ceremonial exchange) as the trajectory of social evolution in Melanesia, as envisaged by the 'from the bottom up' interpretation mentioned above. In the simplest Melanesian societies, the ones cut off from the commodity-exchange nexus, there is no 'exchange' to be elaborated. There is no 'gift' economy, no gifts either in object form or in the form of persons.

But there is, so to speak, 'space' for exchange, a space which, in Umeda, for contingent ethnohistorical reasons, remains unfilled. This space lies within the confines of the masculine republic, within which men can exchange blows or caresses, insults or compliments, but not *objects* unless they have objects to dispose of, which in Umeda they do not. But, even in Umeda, they almost dispose of giftable objects, in two senses. Firstly, men are, by virtue of their hunting specialization, associated with transfers of high-prestige, high-value, low-volume food (meat), which, as a comestible can be focalized and quantified in a way which bulk staples (cooperatively produced by both sexes) cannot be. These meat transfers are, so to speak, precursors of gifts within the Indigenous Service Economy. Secondly, the seductive notion of 'sister-exchange' as an exchange of women – false though this is – exercises its enchantment not only on misguided anthropologists, but equally on many of the practitioners of this strategy. Sister-exchange is not exchange, but, given the conceptual possibility of construing affinity in general as an exchange process, it can readily be made to appear so. It is a rhetorical trope ripe for strategic misuse. Thus a society like Umeda can be considered 'pre-adapted' for the emergence of a regime of reproductive gifts, while remaining itself within the confines of the Indigenous Service Economy.

The next step in the argument must be to attempt to isolate the mechanisms for the transformation (in structural, rather than historical, terms) of systems of social reproduction conducted on the basis of the Indigenous Service Economy into systems of social reproduction conducted on the basis of reproductive gift exchange. My claim is that commodity exchange plays a crucial role in this transformation.

THE OBVIATION OF BRIDE-SERVICE: MARING TRADE AND MARRIAGE-PAYMENTS

Commodity barter, as Marx pointed out, arises at the boundaries of social systems. These boundaries are a male preserve, physically and symbolically, because men are specialists in hunting and violence. In the hinterland, barter trading is masculine and disarticulated from social reproduction – in particular from the processes of the Indigenous Service Economy, and the inequalities inherent in affinity. At the margins of the world, men encounter other men in war and trade, but not as parties interested in reproducing one another.

In this mutual disinterestedness there is exhilaration, danger (violence is never far from the surface) but also solace. Solidary relationships, no longer fateful, no longer charged with the inescapable burdens of moral conflict, assume a sharply positive diacritical weighing against the background condition of generalized suspicion and hostility. They assume the form, not of role-complementarities or the uneasy rivalry of social peers obliged to support one another yet always pitted against one another, but of 'partnerships' – alliances maintained against all the world, peers and enemies alike. Trade partnerships are in a sense subversive, in the way that Simmel claimed that our love relationships are subversive.

At these social boundaries, it would be vain to look for a 'market' because there is no hegemonic power to exert the peace of the market-place. The 'trade partnership' in which each partner guarantees, as far as possible, the safety of the other in their mutual trading activities is the absolutely necessary condition for the existence or commodity exchange. As such, it stands as a primordial form of social relationship, antithetical in every respect to the moral basis of relationships dictated by the Indigenous Service Economy.

Traders do not meet to exchange compliments, but to exchange commodities; the voluntaristic amoralism of a partnership 'against all the world' can only be sustained through the transactional schema of object exchange, because, lacking 'personal' referents, the relationship can only be established with reference to things, which are all that the parties to it have in common. In exchange, objects are focalized, quantified, valued, and so on; and there is recognition of debt, credit and reciprocity. It is the transaction of these objects, now commodities, which sustains the partnership, and, because the partnership relation is valued as an end in itself, the objects involved carry a symbolic charge stemming from this source; they are over valued because their presence evokes a valued relationship and a privileged kind of social interaction. Where there could be enmity and danger, lo! – there is this shell, the axe . . .

Let this suffice as a sketch of the ideological associations of commodity exchange in the hinterland. I turn now to a more detailed consideration of commodity exchange, marriage and reproductive gifts in a New Guinea Highlands society which is no longer dominated by the Indigenous Service Economy. The example I have chosen is the Maring (Healey, 1978, 1984, 1986). What is the relation between commodity exchange and reproductive gift exchange in a medium-intensity highlands society of this type?

The first point which needs to be made is that among the Maring the physical inputs into reproductive exchanges are originally derived from barter sources. Maring society is not trade-dependent, yet the Maring have contrived to make themselves 'artificially' trade-dependent in that the volume of their reproductive and ceremonial exchanges, both in valuables and pigs, could not be sustained without inter-tribal barter trade. This is indeed the almost invariable state of affairs among comparable societies in Melanesia having significant levels of reproductive exchange. Not physically dependent on enemies and trade partners for subsistence, they are dependent on them for essential contributions to the internal circulation of symbolically essential items; for which they must pay with their exports.

In recent times Maring have participated in two major trading complexes: the trade in salt against axes (in which they acted as middle men, producing neither themselves), and the trade in shells and pigs against fur and feathers in which they acted both as middle men and as producers (of fur and feathers). Axes were a component of marriage payments, as were shells. Nowadays, money functions as a 'valuable' in exchanges of this kind, replacing shells. This is not to be interpreted as 'commercialization' of exchange, just because a modern medium of exchange, which has been partially inflation-proofed, is preferred to shells, which have been in excess supply. The availability of money enables Maring to conduct transactions in 'sound money' which is what shells used to be, but are no longer. Money is what has saved the 'traditional' exchange system from total eclipse, here and elsewhere in the Highlands, and is by no means the factor tending to subvert it.

Healey has provided a detailed account of Maring trade (1978; 1984). The theoretical issue raised by his work is that, whereas it is clear that Maring traders regarded their trade partners as 'exchange partners' in the usual Melanesian fashion, nevertheless these men are indisputably engaged in commodity barter, and their relationship is terminologically distinguished by the Maring themselves from the relationship existing between parties to 'internal' exchanges.

Partners are constrained to trade with one another and to keep the relation alive with a flow of valuables; laggard performance may invite retribution in the form of sorcery. The objective of trade is the transaction of valuable objects, but the accumulation of wealth is not the aim in view; once acquired, trade items must be passed on or fed into internal exchanges. Maring trade, according to Healey, has a strongly 'sociable' character. 'In practice [trade] is a mode of expressing social relationships via a balanced exchange of valuables' (1986: 141). But, if barter is an 'expression of social relationships', does it not collapse into Maussian exchange, the Maring rhetorical distinction between gift- and trade-transactions notwithstanding?

Current orthodoxy might favour this very conclusion, but consider:

(1) Social reproduction without gift or commodity exchange is possible, as the Umeda example shows.
(2) Maring gift exchange is physically dependent on inputs which are commodities (i.e. alienated).

In other words, the question is not whether Maring commodity exchange equates with gift exchange, but the other way about: that is, whether gift exchange equates with commodity exchange. It seems more logical to suppose that commodity exchange is 'primordial' in that (1) commodity exchange is logically separable from the processes of social reproduction *per se*, and (2) social reproduction can occur without exchange, either of commodities or gifts. Hence 'reproductive gift exchange' is logically a dependent variable of social reproduction and commodity exchange, which are independent variables (not dependent on each other or on reproductive gift exchange). Whereas reproductive gift exchange is dependent on both.

Let me pass on to an examination of the constituents of the Maring regime of reproductive gift exchanges. Here, I think, one is better able to grasp the essentially artificial character of gift exchange – mimicry of commodity exchange in an internal, reproductive, context – and the way in which the Indigenous Service Economy continues to exist in a disguised and modified form under a veneer of reciprocal exchange of sacrifices in 'gift' form.

Marriage payments are made to the bride's father and brothers after a number of years of marriage and usually the birth of one or more children. Payments are made in two media (pork and shells/valuables) and is divided into two components comprising both media of exchange. The first component is assembled by the groom himself and is transferred to the bride's father and brothers. This component is never reciprocated in kind. The second, and much larger component (two or three times larger) is contributed by members of the groom's clan and political support-group, is passed by him to the bride's father and brothers, who distribute it to their clan and supporters. This component has to be reciprocated subsequently by the recipients. The assembling, redistribution, and eventual reciprocation of the second component of the marriage payment articulates both intra- and extra-clan male–male relationships in an idiom of the reciprocal exchange of valuables. But it also serves as a 'cover' for the actually unreciprocated component paid by the groom himself to his wife's agnates.

In this way Maring achieve two contradictory objectives simultaneously. The second component and its reciprocation serve to locate marriage in a transactional setting dominated by equivalent and reciprocal male–male exchange relationships, as if, so to speak, marriage were little more than a pretext for the serious business of life, which concerns men exclusively and which places them, as exchangers, in the centre stage in the process of social reproduction. At the same time, this screen of 'diversionary' transactions serves to cover the really crucial, but relatively covert, unreciprocated payment of the 'real' bride-price. But what does this payment represent?

It seems to me that what this payment does is to permit the groom to get on equal terms with his affines, that is, to obviate the direct expression of obligation through the performance of bride-service by means of a payment in lieu. It is the means of converting a potential 'patron' into a 'partner'. Reproductive exchanges do not abolish social distance, they create it; and in so doing they liberate Maring husbands from the intimacies which so terrify an Umeda youth contemplating his matrimonial future.

Through the reformulation of affinity in the idiom of exchange, the peripheral is made central, and relations between men, mediated by valuables (which they control) replace relations between men mediated by women (whom they do not control). The peripheral barter-exchange schema provides an idiom for an all-male social universe, weakening the position of women accordingly. Moreover, as this transactionalization and masculinization of the processes of social reproduction takes place, the Indigenous Service Economy becomes an almost all-female affair, in which male participation becomes more and more marginal.

One can see this most clearly if one takes a closer look at the 'pork' constituent of the groom's component of the marriage payment (the meat of three or four pigs from the groom's herd slaughtered for the occasion). An Umeda son-in-law sends quantities of meat to his father-in-law; a Maring son-in-law gives quantities of pork to his father-in-law as part of his marriage payment. On the surface, this looks like precisely the same institution. But it is not so by any means. The source of an Umeda son-in-law's contributions in the form of meat is himself (i.e. a pig hunted and killed by him personally and actually identified with him), whereas the source of a Maring son-in-law's pork gifts is his wife, since she is the 'mother' who has raised the pigs from the produce of her own gardens during the lifetime of the marriage. In this way Maring women contribute heavily to their own marriage payments.

But these are, nonetheless, said to be made to 'compensate' her agnates for the 'loss' of their sister/daughter. An instant's reflection is all that is required to ascertain that no such 'loss' has actually been sustained by them; and that it is, in fact, only when she becomes a married woman, contributing to her own marriage payments, that male agnates are able to derive benefit from her productive activities. But this fact is obscured by the idiom of object exchange between male transactors. The Maring wife ends up not only performing wifely services for her husband, but also performing the services an Umeda son-in-law performs for his father-in-law.

The conclusion, which seems to me inescapable, that the regime of reproductive gifts in societies such as the Maring rests on a special kind of bad faith, is further supported if one considers another important element in the conventional (local) justification of marriage payments. These payments are considered to be compensation for the (fictitious) 'loss' of a sister/daughter as a productive/reproductive group member, and secondly to be compensation for the loss of 'substance', that is, agnatic essence derived from ingesting the produce of agnatic land. Marriage payments 'replace' lost physical substance imbued with agnatic essence. Pork gifts symbolize this return of lost substance. But, as we have seen, the source of the pork gifts is the woman herself, who is obliged to replace herself in porcine form. As she is a 'mother' of pigs, her progeny are reclaimed by her agnates, just as, later on, her female offspring will be reclaimed by them according to the local preference for delayed bilateral cross-cousin marriage (known as 'the return of the planting material').

The superficial appearance of marriage payments suggests that affinally linked groups are independent 'units' which engage in exchange. The flow of gifts and personnel following from the mutual exchange of sacrifices, the 'loss' of a woman over here, the corresponding 'loss' of pigs, shells and so on, over there. But the underlying situation is quite different. Women are not 'lost' to their natal group in marriage; they remain 'female agnates' charged with a three-fold reproductive task; to reproduce their own group as 'mothers' of pigs and as mothers of 'returnable' daughters, and to reproduce their husband's group in the ordinary way. Affinal prestations are not therefore a 'buying-out' of agnation (compensation, say, for a rupture in the relation between an agnatically linked brother and sister). They are actually the expression of an agnatic monopoly on agnates of both sexes; the onerousness of exchange obligations vis-à-vis affines and matrikin increases as a positive rather than a negative function of the perdurable nature of the tie between cross-sex siblings. The 'exchange' idiom creates the appearance of a rupture between affinally linked groups which does not actually exist, at least for married women.

In short, Maring reproductive gifts achieve two things: they establish a male domain, internal to the society, in which relationships of 'equivalence' between 'partners' can be represented as crucial to social reproduction through attaching 'reproductive' meanings to transactions in valuables and pork. Meanwhile, these transactions provide an ideological cover for the fact that 'women' are not being 'transferred' between groups at all, but are simply being charged with reproducing, according to service obligations incumbent on them as married women, both their natal and affinal group.

WOMEN AND COMMODITY EXCHANGE

Oversimplifying somewhat, one might say that in the Melanesian hinterland, reproductive exchange arises out of a strategic reformulation of the Indigenous Service Economy, such that women remain within its orbit (as producers and reproducers) while men escape from it, as transactors (i.e. as commodity exchangers and through the mimicry of commodity exchange in reproductive gifts). But the situation changes radically once one brings into consideration those coastal and riverain Melanesian societies among whom commodity exchange has penetrated deeply into society, so that it is no longer a matter of the 'periphery' of society, but, so to speak, its inner core. At this point the association between masculinity and commodity exchange breaks down, because the commodity-exchanging activities of women become as fundamental to social reproduction as their productive and reproductive activities; indeed, they are one and the same.

It has often been noted that in coastal Melanesia, and along the Sepik, women enjoy a greater degree of social prestige than is commonly the case, in hinterland societies such as the Maring. Few would dispute that there is a causal link between this somewhat elevated status and the role of women in commodity barter, and in the manufacture of barterable commodities. The classic instance of this from the older literature is Mead's (1963 [1935]) account of female 'dominance' among the Tchambuli (Chambri), and although Mead's account has been qualified and historically contextualized by Gewertz (1981) basic elements of the picture remain intact. Chambri women enjoyed social advantages because they were the manufacturers of mosquito-bags in great demand along the Sepik before the introduction of mosquito netting, and they also maintained a fish-for-sago trade which was essential to the provisioning of Chambri society.

In societies such as Chambri (Gewertz 1983) and Murik, which I will describe in more detail shortly (Lipset 1985; Barlow 1985), both sexes are involved in commodity exchange, and subsistence depends on the import of food (sago starch). Under these circumstances two things can be observed to happen. The status of women is altered, and inequality reappears in affinal relations. Whereas, in the highlands, wife-givers rank equal to wife-receivers (or even below them, where the marriage payments are 'officially' valued more highly than the woman herself, because they represent the value to the group of the 'opening of an exchange road') – in the coastal/river setting wife-givers always rank above wife-receivers.

The Murik lakes provide us with an example in terms of which we can explore the relationship between social reproduction and commodity exchange in a trade-dependent society (Barlow 1985; Lipset 1985). The Murik are an (agriculturally speaking) 'landless' people living at the mouth of the Sepik river, whose continued existence depends on trading links with neighbouring inland sago-suppliers, and who trade up and down the coast. They are specialists in sailing-canoe transport, trading as middle men, and as producers/ manufacturers of various high-value foods, valuables, and 'immaterial' valuables such as songs, cults, designs, and so on. Myths of the foundation of Murik society do not recount a cosmogony, but a series of migrations from an ancestral site in Chambri lake to their current location, involving numerous sojourns at various places along the coast and up the river, where they now maintain trading links. These trade partnerships are personal and hereditary, descending cognatically within families.

The Murik are involved in three distinct nexuses of trade. For

basic starch, the Murik women barter fish for sago with trade partners in neighbouring sago-producing 'bush' villages. This trade is
exclusively female, and sago-suppliers are called 'mothers'. Exchange
rates are fixed, but are strikingly unfavourable to the Murik, who
appear to get only one-eighth the quantity of sago per fish as the
Chambri women, engaged in exactly the same trade with their
neighbours in the Sepik hills, did for theirs. This reflects the fact that
in their heyday the Chambri were under the military protection of
the Iatmul, whom they supplied with mosquito-bags, axes, and so
on, and who were prepared to back up 'stand-over' tactics in the fish-
for-sago barter market (Gewertz 1983; Modjeska 1985). No such
outside protection is afforded to the Murik whose indigence in sago
obliges them to accept very stingy treatment from their 'mothers'.
But the fact that this difficult-to-obtain starch is traded for, and
dispensed, by women, contributes materially to the 'moral superiority' of women in Murik society (Meeker, Barlow and Lipset 1986).

The second trade nexus in which the Murik are concerned is
coastal canoe trade in low-volume, high-value items, pigs, decor-
ations, shellfish, pots, and, above all, high-quality decorated baskets,
in whose manufacture the Murik women are specialized. Women
travel in canoes with their menfolk on expeditions along the coast,
and maintain their own personal trading partnerships, which they
have inherited. On these expeditions, it was the tradition that women
would conduct affairs with lovers in their partner's village, in which
they were supposed to take the initiative (rather reinforcing the point
made above regarding the 'subversive' element in both trading
partnerships and love relationships).

The social position of a man in Murik society was dependent on
the contributions made by women to trading ventures, both as transactors and as manufacturers of 'copyright' baskets. A Murik man
married to a notorious termagent, who frequently harangued him in
public, declared to Barlow that he remained married to her because
his reputation in trade depended on it:

> [my trading partners] can all come at once and try to overwhelm
> me. But I always win. Everything goes to them. Not one debt stays
> with me. I always pay back every one. This is the way of my wife,
> which is why I hold on to her. Her way is to make baskets very
> quickly. Like a machine she makes baskets.
>
> (1985: 108)

The third nexus of trade is long-distance inter-island trade in large sailing canoes, handled by all-male crews. But even here women are crucially involved. Inter-island trade partnerships are inherited, and women inherit such partnerships as well as men. Women depute their husbands, brothers, and so on, to trade for them with their overseas partners. Moreover, much of the merchandise is of female manufacture and, so to speak, emblematic of the powerful women who have created and patented much sought-after basket designs.

But perhaps more important to inter-island trade is the role of women as 'negatively' responsible for the success of the expedition through restraint in sexual and other behaviour while the canoe is at sea. Chastity and elaborate taboos are imposed on women during this period; a woman's skirts must not blow in the wind or the canoe will be swept away, she must not remove the plug from a water jar lest the canoe start to leak, and so on. These precautions do not just reflect the Malinowskian dictum that hazardous and uncertain enterprises are hedged about with magic and taboos. They correspond, rather, to the reassertion of an element of gender-exclusiveness in this kind of commodity exchange, as opposed to the lack of any such exclusiveness in the coastal trade. The open sea plays the same role in this as the 'frontier area' between tribes plays in the hinterland trade: that is, it is given over to the masculinity, and female influences must be shunned there (though attacks by flying witches are an ever-present possibility). Long-distance seaborne trade is the last bastion of the masculine republic, and the sea itself comes to be a sort of nature reserve for men, when all else has been lost through the active presence, or even predominance, of women in commodity exchange. No wonder overseas trade is elaborated even when, as in the Kula, there is no commercial rationale for it, so that it becomes a purely 'ceremonial' traffic. The Kula is mimicry of commodity exchange, just as I have suggested that marriage payments are; which is not to say that it actually is commodity exchange. Its purpose is to sustain, and expand, a transactional relationship between men, originally associated with external commodity exchange, in circumstances in which commodity exchange as such is no longer a male monopoly.

Among societies such as the Murik (and Chambri, Iatmul, etc.) we find paradoxically both a heavy emphasis on onerous and unreciprocated reproductive gifts (passing from wife-receivers to wife-givers) and a re-emergence of bride-service, that is, specific work obligations incumbent on sons-in-law to contribute to projects

undertaken by their wife's kin. However, these bride-service obligations do not stem from a recrudescence of the Indigenous Service
Economy, but from the final triumph of exchange, as a principle of
social relationship. Sepik marriage payments are conceptually, and
really, 'payments' for the effective alienation of women from their
natal groups; payments for women who are, however, regarded as
being 'without price' by their status-conscious agents. Return gifts
are never sufficient to cover the debt incurred by the wife-receiving
group, who remain permanent (indebted) inferiors. Sepik bride-
service is not a matter of moral obligation, but a matter of working-
off an unrepayable debt. At this point, one can certainly agree that
social reproduction is carried on according to a regime of reproductive gifts and the universal transactionalization of relationships.
But it must be stressed that this development does not take place
against the development of pervasive commodity exchange, but precisely because of it, because it is only in this context that women
become so pre-eminently valuable.

In this essay I have tried to show that 'barter' was much more than
a sideshow in old Melanesia, since it provided both the physical
resources and the ideological template for the elaboration of the
kinds of Maussian 'reproductive gift' institutions for which the
region has become so well known. I hope that I do not need to
reiterate that reproductive gifts, though derived from a commodity
exchange 'template', never amount to commodity exchanges in
themselves. There is a density of metaphor in Melanesian life-cycle
prestations which is *sui generis*, not to be reduced to 'mere' commercial transactions. Brides are not really 'bartered'. But I hope that
I have also argued convincingly that there is a basic conceptual mistake underlying our willingness to collocate words like 'mere' with
words like 'barter'. Commodity barter transactions do not take place
in a social vacuum, nor do they occur without provoking powerful
symbolic associations, not least under the conditions prevailing
in old Melanesian societies. These conditions necessitate the development of so-called 'trade partnerships' – an innocuous-sounding
label for what is, in effect, a momentous symbolic precedent.
Under the 'sign' of barter, social relationships come into existence
which are no longer pre-empted by the morality of reproduction and
its service obligations. At the social margins, a constructed world
comes into being, mediated by flows of objects along transactional
pathways, which increasingly infiltrate the reproductive sphere from
which it was originally excluded, but not without itself undergoing a

sea-change. I have traced certain of these transformations in the course of this essay, but there is clearly much more that might be done in this direction, which might lead to a general revision of current ideas about the evolution of 'exchange' in Melanesian society.

REFERENCES

Barlow, K. (1985) 'The role of women in intertribal trade among the Murik', *Research in Economic Anthropology*, 7: 95–122.

Baudrillard, J. (1975) *The Mirror of Production* (St. Louis: Telos).

Brookfield, A. and D. Hart (1971) *Melanesia: A Geographical Interpretation* (London: Methuen).

Collier, J. and M. Rosaldo (1981) 'The politics and gender in simple societies', in S. Ortner and H. Whitehead (eds) *Sexual Meanings* (Cambridge: Cambridge University Press).

Epstein, T. (1968) *Capitalism, Primitive and Modern* (Canberra: ANU Press).

Gell, A. (1975) *Metamorphosis of the Cassowaries* (London: Athlone).

Gell, A. (1982) 'The market wheel: symbolic aspects of an Indian tribal market', *Man*, (n.s.) 17: 470–91.

Gell, A. (1986) 'Newcomers to the world of goods: consumption amongst the Muria Gonds', in A. Appadurai (ed.) *The Social Life of Things* (Cambridge: Cambridge University Press).

Gewertz, D. (1978) 'Tit for tat: barter markets on the middle Sepik', *Anthropological Quarterly*, 51: 37–46.

Gewertz, D. (1981) 'An historical reconstruction of female dominance among the Chambri of Papua New Guinea', *American Ethnologist*, 8: 94–106.

Gewertz, D. (1983) *Sepik River Societies* (New Haven: Yale University Press).

Gregory, C. (1982) *Gifts and Commodities* (London: Academic).

Godelier, M. (1977) '"Salt money" and the circulation of commodities among the Baruya', in *Perspectives in Marxist Anthropology* (Cambridge: Cambridge University Press).

Godelier, M. (1986) *The Making of Great Men* (Cambridge: Cambridge University Press).

Harding, T. (1967) *Voyagers of the Vitiaz Strait*, American Ethnological Society monograph no. 44 (Seattle: University of Washington Press).

Healey, C. (1978) 'The adaptive significance of ceremonial exchange and trade in the New Guinea Highlands', *Mankind*, 11: 198–207.

Healey, C. (1984) 'Trade and sociability: balanced reciprocity as generosity in the New Guinea Highlands', *American Ethnologist*, 11: 42–60.

Healey, C. (1986) 'New Guinea inland trade: transformation and resilience in the context of capitalist penetration', *Mankind*, 15: 2. Special issue on recent studies in the political economy of PNG societies, ed. D. Gardner and N. Modjeska, 127–44.

Hogbin, H. (1951) *Transformation Scene* (London: Routledge & Kegan Paul).

Hughes, I. (1977) *New Guinea Stone Age Trade (Terra Australia 3)* (Canberra: ANU Press).

Juillerat, B. (1986) *Les Enfants du Sang* (Paris: Maison des sciences de l'homme).

Lipset, D. (1985) 'Seafaring Sepiks: ecology, warfare and prestige in Murik trade', *Research in Economic Anthropology*, 7: 67–94.

Irwin, G. (1983) 'Chieftainship, Kula and trade in Massim prehistory', in J. Leach and E. Leach (eds) *The Kula* (Cambridge: Cambridge University Press).

Macintyre, M. (1983) 'Kune on Tubetube and in the Bwanabwana region of the Southern Massim', in J. Leach and E. Leach (eds) *The Kula* (Cambridge: Cambridge University Press).

Malinowski, B. (1915) 'The natives of Mailu', *Transactions of the Royal Society of South Australia*, 39: 494–706.

Mead, M. (1963) [1935] *Sex and Temperament* (New York: Morrow).

Meeker, M., K. Barlow and D. Lipset. (1986) 'Culture, exchange and gender: lessons from the Murik', *Cultural Anthropology*, 1: 6–73.

Modjeska, N. (1985) 'Exchange value and Melanesian trade reconsidered', *Mankind*, 15: 2. Special issue on recent studies in the political economy of PNG societies, (ed.) D. Gardner and N. Modjeska, 145–63.

Parry, J. (1986) 'The gift, the Indian gift, and the "Indian Gift",' *Man*, (n.s.) 21: 453–73.

Parry, J. (1989) 'On the moral perils of exchange', in J. Parry and M. Bloch (eds) *Money and the Morality of Exchange* (Cambridge: Cambridge University Press).

Rubel, P. and A. Rosman. (1979) *Your own Pigs you may not Eat* (Chicago: Chicago University Press).

Sahlins, M. (1965) 'On the sociology of primitive exchange' in M. Banton (ed.) *The Relevance of Models for Social Anthropology*, ASA 1 (London: Tavistock).

Sahlins, M. (1972) 'Exchange value and the diplomacy of primitive trade', in *Stone Age Economics* (Chicago: Aldine).

Salisbury, R. (1970) *Vunamami* (Berkely, CA: University of California Press).

Schwartz, T. (1963) 'Systems of areal integration in the Admiralty Islands of Northern Melanesia', *Anthropological Forum*, 1: 56–97.

CHAPTER 3

THE MARKET WHEEL

SYMBOLIC ASPECTS OF AN INDIAN TRIBAL MARKET

Dhorai is the name of a market village located deep in the hinterland of North Bastar district, Madhya Pradesh (central India).[1] On non-market days Dhorai is a sleepy, tree-shaded hamlet straddling an unsealed road which winds its way through the forest. Occasionally its rural peace is shattered by the roar of a passing truck laden with massive logs of teak (timber production being the major industry in the region) or loud blasts from the horn of the local bus; but these interruptions are not frequent. Social life in Dhorai revolves around two primitive teashops with a clientèle of low-ranking employees of the State Forest service, whose misfortune it has been to be stationed in such a distant and insignificant spot. Dhorai boasts a tumbledown school, which doubles as a post office, an imposing Forest Rest House (usually empty), a few substantial homesteads belonging to Hindus, a penumbra of rather less substantial huts inhabited by tribal Muria Gonds,[2] and not much else.

Dhorai on non-market days – every day except Friday, that is – hardly exists at all; but Dhorai on a market day might be a totally different place. Parked trucks jam the road, in charge of their drivers, burly Sikhs from the north, or dark, polysyllabic Telegus from Hyderabad. The lowly Forest Guards bustle about in smart, newly pressed uniforms, while the more important officials of the Forest service, down for the day, oversee operations from the verandah of the Forest Rest House. They disburse payments to the tribal labourers, and check through the mounds of documentation which are the bane of a forest officer's life. In their quasi-military khaki they look like the officers of an occupying colonial power, whose successors they have indeed become.

While the officials hold court in the Rest House, files of tribals continue to pour in from all directions, laden with the produce of the forest, of their fields and of their own manufacture. They are joined by Hindu vegetable-sellers, and by specialized craftsmen, potters, weavers and blacksmiths. The general impression is one of richness and confusion, compounded by the fact that a religious ceremony, as well as a market, is in process. In front of the temple of the state goddess, which faces onto the market-place, the untouchable oboeist and drummer are performing, and a long-haired ascetic insults his back with chains. The whole world, it seems, is at the market, men and their Divinities alike.

The market-place is a roughly quadrangular patch of ground, about 100 yards square, at the centre of which there grows a magnificent banyan tree. The thatched market stalls are arranged in a concentric pattern, and are divided by narrow streets or defiles, along which customers manoeuvre themselves as best they can in the crush, trying to avoid treading on the goods of less established traders, who make use of every nook and cranny between the permanent stalls to display their wares.

Beggary and poverty are not to be seen at the Dhorai market: the young are all dressed smartly, and their elders contrive to convey, at the very least, an impression of respectable solidity. The dressiness, the showiness of the market scene – the oiled hair, the ornaments, the brilliant-hued saris, the immaculate shirts and turbans – is not, indeed, an aspect of the market to be ignored: for it reveals, as clearly as anything, the fact that the market is a ceremonial as well as a commercial occasion. Participants adopt modes of heightened and stereotyped role-playing, appropriate for a ceremonial occasion, and the obligatory 'dressing up' is an aspect of this. Indeed, on closer examination, it is possible to perceive in the design of the market occasion an enactment of the social order in the widest sense, as it impinges on the people in the locality. For distinctiveness is at a premium, and the market provides an occasion *par excellence* for the differentiation of groups and for the articulation of inter-group relations, in ways not possible in the context of the daily routine of village life, where these diverse groups come into contact only spasmodically. The market gives tangible expression to principles of social structure which transcend the village context. It locates the villagers in a holistic system of sociological categories, and binds them to this system by means of market relations. The intention of this article is thus to explore the Dhorai market from the point of view of its symbolic importance as an indigenous model of social relations.

THE STUDY OF MARKETS

'Markets which meet periodically in India have been neglected by geographers', writes Harriss (1976; cf. Bromley 1974), and despite some additions (Wanmali 1976; 1977; Agrawal 1978) this remains true. The anthropological literature on rural markets in India is no less sparse, though the monographs by S. Sinha *et al.* (1961) and D. Sinha (1968) are interesting exceptions. This neglect is curious, especially in the light of the copiousness of 'market' studies carried out in India's congener-societies in the developing world, a genre inspired by the example of *Trade and Market in the Early Empires* (Polanyi *et al.* 1957) and culminating in such major syntheses as Bohannan and Dalton's *Markets in Africa* (1962) and Skinner's 'Marketing and social structure in rural China' (1964–5). In many non-industrialized societies markets are arguably central in the understanding of the social system as a whole. But this view would be completely heterodox in the Indian context, and for perfectly good reasons, no doubt, stemming from the self-sufficient nature of the traditional village economy and the prevalence of the *jajmani* system (Mandelbaum 1970). Nonetheless, periodic marketing systems are a common feature of rural India and are worthy of more attention from sociological observers than they have received. The question is, what *kind* of attention should they attract? Hitherto, they have been mainly the concern of economic geographers, interested in locational questions, periodicities, catchment areas and administrative problems (Wanmali 1976) and with problems of the general efficiency of rural marketing arrangements as means of distributing food cheaply and fairly (Harriss 1976). My concerns are quite different, which does not of course imply that I mean to deprecate the geographers' approach to applied social research. What follows can best be described as a 'thick description' of a rural market, undertaken in order to demonstrate the structural parallels which exist between the microcosmic system of the local market and the macrocosmic system of North Bastar society. The method is the one adopted in Geertz's famous account of the Balinese cockfight (1975; cf. Geertz *et al.* 1979).

Following Geertz, I take the market at Dhorai as an enacted 'text', whose meaning can be construed by providing the appropriate specification of context. My argument is that, for the participants, the market gives concrete representation of the ground-plan of their society, its hierarchical organization and the scheme of values which sustains it. The market is a secular event, but it is also part of the ritual of social relations. Critics of this 'interpretative' approach may consider that it leaves untouched crucial questions having to do with 'why' things are as they are in Dhorai market and in Bastar society generally, and I am willing to concede this. However, it is heuristically practical to maintain a methodological separation between problems of cultural interpretation on the one hand and problems of causal/historical explanation on the other. It is all the more likely that I might arouse unfulfilled expectations with respect to the latter class of problems, in that my topic is the market, and 'market' studies have most frequently been undertaken with causal/historical analytical goals in mind; were I describing a festival or a *rite de passage* my interpretative intention would be more understandable, though still, no doubt, objectionable to certain points of view. The present choice of problem definition is not dictated as a consequence of a theoretical prejudice against causal analysis,[3] but arises from data at my disposal which seem sufficiently suggestive to warrant analysis within a narrowly structural framework. My theme happens to be the market, but this article is not intended as a contribution to the theory of markets, nor more generally to exchange relations. I am more preoccupied with the elucidation of a secular ceremonial, following the proposal made by Leach in a famous passage in which he advises anthropologists to make themselves aware of the 'ritual' component in normal everyday actions (Leach 1954: 13). Dhorai market has a significant ceremonial component in that it provides a *mapping*, in space, time and in the form of market interactions, for the gamut of social relations found in the wider society in the region of North Bastar where Dhorai market is located. This 'mapping' is quite overt in the spatial layout of the market, and here I am extending the range of spatial representations of social relations already exemplified in such familiar instances as the layout of the village of Omarakana in the Trobriands (Lévi-Strauss 1964) or the arrangement of the negotiating table at the 1971 Paris peace talks over Vietnam (Douglas 1973).

This approach is familiar enough and only the context, perhaps, is novel. But in the Indian ethnographic milieu it would be strikingly aberrant were I not centrally concerned with the symbolic representation of hierarchy in social relations, since the inegalitarian premiss is so rooted in India, even in 'tribal' Bastar. Here I am perhaps entering an uncharted area, in that previous discussions of hierarchy in India have not taken into account the hierarchical aspect of market relations. I would acknowledge the impetus provided by the work of Carol Smith (1975; 1976) towards the germination of the ideas presented here. Smith has summarized her arguments in the following terms:

> Regional central-place organisation in Guatemala acts as a 'negative' or deviation-amplifying feedback loop between the irregular organisation of many local central-place systems, the ethnic divisions of the region, uneven rural development and underdevelopment and political inequality in the region
>
> (1976: 293)

While it should be apparent that Smith is dealing with questions of the most ambitious causal/explanatory kind, whereas I am not, the causal processes of hierarchy-accentuation *via* marketing organization adverted to by Smith can be accompanied by processes of symbolic reinforcement of hierarchical relations of the kind I do discuss. This seems to be particularly a feature of those parts of India most distant from major centres of power, where state administration and Brahminical ritual dominance are weakly developed. Work on tribal Bihar (Sinha *et al.* 1961; Sinha 1968) supports this view: markets are most sociologically salient in areas which are 'backwaters' according to the historic-geographic regional typology of Schwartzberg (1967). I must defer, to a later occasion, the provision of the kind of regional geographical economic analysis provided by Smith, which leaves as an open question the applicability of her Guatemalan model to the very different circumstances, and very different cultural premisses, of North Bastar. But there seems to be scope for suggesting some degree of convergence between the microcosmic perspective adopted here (the world as seen from Dhorai) and the macrocosmic perspective so elegantly presented in Smith's work.

SOCIAL CATEGORIES

If we are to see the Dhorai market as, in some sense, a 'map' of social relations, it is necessary to enumerate the major categories of people to be found in the market area. I propose to list these groups, simply for the sake of quick exposition, but must forestall a reasonable objection to this admittedly rather old-fashioned procedure. It may be felt that to list separate 'groups' in this way is to obscure the very point that I am seeking to demonstrate, namely, that the market reflects patterns of inter-group relations in the wider social field, since by simply enumerating groups as separate entities I leave unclarified the nature of the inter-group relationships supposedly reflected in the market arena; I would, by implication, be imputing to the market itself causal priority in the structuring of inter-group relations inasmuch as it is in the market alone that such inter-relationships can be concretely shown to exist. It would be more appropriate, such a critic might insist, to depict the different groups as organically related *outside* the market context – in a manner well known from the vast bulk of studies of multi-caste village societies in India – before turning to the market-place where such a given dis-position of relationships between socially and ritually ranked and economically differentiated groups could be seen as 'reflected' rather than as in any sense primarily constituted or established. This objec-tion is perfectly in order, and it is not indeed my intention to argue that the market has causal priority in bringing about the pattern of existing inter-group relations. However, the objection loses a great deal of its force as a result of certain considerations peculiar to low-density, dispersed-settlement societies, such as characterize the Dhorai hinterland. It is simply a fact that there is very little sustained daily interaction between the major groups here discussed, a situ-ation quite unlike that normally encountered in densely packed, nucleated, multi-caste villages where a complex web of inter-caste relations is daily mobilized and continuously elaborated. If com-munal relations in the Indian village are usually, in Srinivas's famous phrase, 'back to back', it would be truer to say of the villages in the Dhorai area that they are out of sight, out of mind. But this is not to say that these inter-group relations are not clearly articulated, though they are expressed, outside the market context, by the absence, rather than the presence, of association. For this reason it is not misleading to give an initial account of 'groups' in the Dhorai area in the form of a listing of discrete social categories, rather than in the form of an account of dynamic interactions between them.

Gonds. The majority of people in the area served by the Dhorai market are *Adivasis* or Tribals. Around Dhorai the tribal population consists of Muria Gonds (the largest single group in North Bastar) and, to the west, in the mountainous and unadministered Abujhmar region, the Hill Muria, another Gond group speaking a slightly dif-ferent dialect. Gonds live in mainly single-caste communities, to which may be attached enclaves or colonies of 'caste' Hindus of various kinds. Purely Hindu settlements cluster around the lines of communications – roads, rivers and market centres – while the hinterland is predominantly tribal (Elwin 1947; Grigson 1938; Agarwal 1968).

The dispersed pattern of settlement seen in Gond villages – houses being scattered widely through the village territory – contrasts strongly with the much more nucleated pattern seen in Hindu settlements. The Muria Gond are settled agriculturalists, growing paddy on fields surrounded by water-retaining dykes but not otherwise irrigated. The main annual paddy crop is followed, weather permitting, by a cash crop (oil-seeds, pulses). Muria also derive cash from labouring for the Forest Department – work concentrated in the slack agricultural season – and from collecting such forest products as tamarind, teak-seeds and silk cocoons.

Around Dhorai, if not always elsewhere, Muria tribal society is essentially intact, its institutions including the famous youth-dormitory (*ghotul*) still fully viable, and it would have appeared to have reached a stable *modus vivendi* with the Hindu presence, and with the government and its agencies. The older system of forest swiddening is closely controlled, where it is not banned altogether, but in exchange the Tribals receive protection for their land rights from the government, plus a permanent availability of a modest cash income from labouring for the Departments of Forests and Public Works, as well as from the sale of forest products, for which there is always a ready market.

Maraars. The most numerous non-tribal group in the Dhorai region are the Maraars. They claim to have migrated from the Kanker – Chhattisgarh district where they were market-gardeners and purveyors of flowers (*maraar* is said to be a corruption of *mali*, Hindi for 'gardener'). Maraars are skilled agriculturalists and vegetable-growers. Their settlements abound in the proximity of rivers, on whose banks they practise irrigated horticulture at a level of intensiveness far in advance of the Gonds.

Since the type of low-lying river-land used by the Maraars for irrigated cultivation and the use they make of it hardly overlap with the more extensive pattern of agriculture seen among tribal Muria, it would not be too far-fetched to see Maraar–Muria relations in terms of occupancy of separate and non-competing ecological niches. This is not altogether true, since Maraars also have paddy land of the ordinary kind, and cultivate more land on sharecropping arrangements from Muria landlords from whom they are prevented by law from buying land outright. It would be true to say, though, that the two groups do not see themselves as economically competing, and they are related by ritual ties which stress the primacy of the Tribals' ownership of the earth.

The Maraars are specialist agriculturalists with a strongly market orientation. They claim high ritual rank (as providers of flowers) 'like Brahmins' they say – and as there are no Brahmins for miles about to say them nay, they go uncontradicted. They are distinguished from the tribal population not only in their observance of Hindu dietary taboos and such, but also linguistically, in that they rarely speak any Gondi (the Dravidian tribal language). They speak instead an Indo-European regional *lingua franca*, Halbi, and Chhattisgarhi Hindi.

Other Hindu groups. The most numerous non-tribal group in the mountainous area to the west of Dhorai are the Halba, descendants of the Maharashtrian soldiery of the kingdoms of Bastar and Chanda. They have lived among the tribal population for so long that they are classified as Tribals in the census. They are not numerous in the Dhorai area. A more significant group, though not a numerous one, are the Rawits or herdsmen. Most Muria villages contain a family or two of Rawits, migrants from the north who claim kinship to the important northern caste group of herdsmen known as Ahirs. Rawits, though maintaining their Hindu identity (not eating beef, wearing the sacred thread like the Maraars) are in effect a service caste to the Muria Gonds, whose cattle they look after and whose clients they are. They mostly cultivate land of their own as well, but are rarely well provided for in this respect. They milk the cows and sell milk in the market. Finally, mention should be made of the Kallar or distillers. This small Hindu caste was enabled to enrich itself during the period, up to the mid-1960s, when it held a legal monopoly of the trade in distilled liquor. Distillers rank high in the caste hierarchy, and own considerable amounts of land, from which they now derive their livelihood, as the sale of liquor has been officially banned.

Outcasts. Untouchability in its more extreme forms is not encountered in the region, but certain beef-eating, non-tribal caste groups have low social status. Of these the largest is the Ganda or weaver caste. Gandas are mostly poor, landless or nearly landless labourers. They are also musicians, and to a certain extent practitioners of their caste occupation of weaving. Gandas sell their cloths, which are expensive but exceptionally hard-wearing if somewhat old fashioned, in the market. Blacksmiths (Kachchi) are another low-ranking occupational caste. They are a subcaste of Gonds, rather than Hindus, and produce mainly agricultural implements in the villages, from iron smelted from local ores. Bronze-workers (Ghassia) form a separate group. Ghassia are Hindus, and specialize mainly in the production of temple images, ritual drinking-vessels, trumpets, bells and so on. Ghassias are also occupationally specialized as assistants to jewellers-cum-moneylenders, for whom they perform debt-collecting and strong-arm-man functions. Kumhars (potters) are low-ranking and generally very poor; they carry on their occupational specializations and sell their wares at the market.

Outsiders. The previously mentioned groups are all traditional occupants of the area, whose arrival in the region predates the turn of the century at the latest. But there are many much more recent and less assimilated caste Hindus in the area, particularly among the market traders. The caste status of these outsiders is for the most part irrelevant, especially if they are transient government employees. Their status depends on their importance in terms of the local government and Forest Department bureaucracy. But sometimes an outsider's caste status is significant (for example, a forest officer who is a knowledgeable Brahmin will be consulted on matters appertaining to astrology). This is particularly so in connection with a key individual in the Dhorai market, the main jeweller, whose stall is the very hub around which the market revolves. This man comes, like most jewellers in the area, from Rajasthan. He carries with him a distinct air of northern, aristocratic culture, and he claims himself to be a Rajput. Most market traders of manufactured goods are Hindi-speakers from metropolitan areas, culturally quite distinct from the local Hindu groups. I return to the significance of this point later on.

Having discussed the major groups of people assembled at the market, I will now provide a brief sketch of the pattern of market relations they enter into. There are five main kinds of goods transacted:

(1) Imported manufactured items originating outside Bastar (which has no manufacturing industry), including jewellery (silver and gold), machine cloth, beads, trinkets, and more mundane items such as lamps, brass pots, knives, plates.

(2) Non-locally produced food, notably salt, rice, pulses, turmeric, dried chillies, refined sugar, flour (and other consumables such as *bidi* cigarettes, perfumed hair oil, 'Himalayan Snow' face-cream, talc).

(3) Locally produced food, fresh vegetables such as tomatoes, *muli*, onions, and luxury foods such as *gur* (locally made sugar) and parched rice, to which should be added locally cured tobacco.

(4) Local manufactured (craft) items such as bamboo baskets and grain-bins, sleeping mats of woven rushes, the complete range of earthenware pots, locally made ironware, axes, knives, arrowheads, and local khadi cloth.

(5) Forest products and cash crops collected in bulk at the market and despatched to metropolitan centres, mainly tamarind, oil-seeds, silk cocoons, leaves for use as wrapping, and teak-seeds.

Corresponding to these major categories of goods are market roles which can be listed as follows:

(1) Stallholders. These are without exception Hindus, not from the immediate locality, trading goods in categories 1 and 2. They can be subdivided into (*a*) jeweller/moneylender; (*b*) trinket sellers; (*c*) machine-cloth sellers; (*d*) hardware/drygoods (manufactured items and imported foods); (*e*) tea shops (local Hindus).

(2) Open-market-produce traders. These consist of local Hindus (Maraars) and tribal Muria Gonds. They are divided into (a) parched rice/*gur* sellers (Chhota Dongar Maraars); (b) fresh-vegetable sellers (other Maraars); (c) tobacco sellers (Maraar men and one tribal); (d) tribal vegetable-sellers; (e) milk sellers (Rawits).

(3) Open-market non-produce traders. These include (*a*) traders in baskets/mats/bamboo-work (Tribals from the Abujhmar); (*b*) potters; (*c*) blacksmiths; (*d*) weavers.

(4) Middlemen. Hindus who buy up tribal forest products and cash crops, paying with salt or money.

To this list we can add the three major categories of customers, who tend to be in the market for rather different things: (*a*) non-local Hindus (e.g. forest officers, officials); (*b*) local Hindus; (*c*) Tribals; and the non-customer roles policeman (Kotwal), beggar (Hindu Sadhu) and spectator.

The following matrix diagram (Fig. 3.1) summarizes the pattern of transactions between the major categories of participants in the market. The structure of market relations shown in Fig. 3.1 reposes ultimately on the purchasing power of the tribals, who are the main customers for all categories of goods. The tribals' cash is derived from the exploitation of their relatively rich resource base. Wealth derived from the sale of cash crops, forest products and from wages also circulates inside the village, where there is a thriving cash economy. The intra-village economy is rather different in character from the market-place economy, since it is largely bound up with the buying and selling of livestock, both as draught-animals and for slaughter at ceremonies and feasts. The sale of livestock plays no part in the market at all. The intra-village economy is the arena for competition between tribal men of power and influence (*sian*) who finance feasts and marriages, which involve copious expenditures and long-term debtor–creditor relations. As I describe below, institutionalized credit is absent from the general run of market-place relations, and is confined to the intra-village context. There are, in effect, two distinct frameworks for economic relationship: the village, and the market, with somewhat different economic ground rules in each case. The 'village' economy is embedded, 'personalistic', geared to the struggle for *internal* prestige between individuals who are equals in terms of the value system of the wider society, while the 'market' economy is hierarchical, anonymous, and geared to the values implicit in the state, the widest framework of social relations.

TIME AND SPACE

The Dhorai market is primarily an institution of 'vertical integration' (in the sense of Mintz 1959). It integrates three levels of North Bastar society: (i) the village, (ii) the market area and (iii) the district as a whole, including its articulation to metropolitan centres. Market relations, seen from this point of view, are relations of encompassing and encompassed, macrocosm and microcosm. The ranking of market places by size and distance from a centre, first established as a theoretical scheme by Losch (1954) and Christaller (1966) and since that time extensively studied by geographers (Berry 1965; Smith 1976), is significant not merely to students of locational problems *per se*, but also to any kind of sociological analysis of communities that takes regional factors into account. The view of the world that members of a particular community maintain is determined by the

	TRIBAL	LOCAL HINDU	NON-LOCAL HINDU
Jeweller	Jewels Money Credit / Credit Money	Jewels Money Credit / Credit Money	
Finery	Trinkets / Money	Trinkets / Money	
Tobacco Parched Rice Gur	Tobacco Parched rice Gur / Rice Money	Tobacco Parched rice Gur / Money	Parched rice / Money
Fresh vegetables	Vegetables / Money	Vegetables / Money	Vegetables / Money
Dry goods	Staple foods & objects of use / Money	Staple foods & objects of use / Money	Staple foods & minor luxuries / Money
Cloth	Cloth / Credit Money	Cloth / Credit Money	
Tribal vegetables	Garden vegetables / Money	Wild forest vegetables / Money	
Potter Smith Bamboo	Craft items / Money	Craft items / Money	
Middleman	Salt and Money / Forest products Cash crops	Cash crops / Money	
	TRIBAL	LOCAL HINDU	NON-LOCAL HINDU

Figure 3.1 Transactions between categories of participants at market.

nature of the access that they have to it, and this in turn is crucially modified by the hierarchialization intrinsic to any regional system of communication, transport, exchange and distribution. It is outside the scope of this article to discuss market hierarchy theory in detail (cf. Smith 1976; Skinner 1964–5) Here it is sufficient to identify three levels only: namely, '*tehsil*' markets (the highest level of weekly markets), 'intermediate' markets which provide a full range of goods and marketing services in areas away from district towns, not served by permanent bazaar areas, and finally, 'minor' markets which provide less than the full range of market facilities.

In the hierarchical order of the market system of Bastar as a whole, the Dhorai market occupies an intermediate place; it is superordinate in relation to the village economy, definitive in relation to the Dhorai-market-area economy, and subordinate in relation to the *tehsil* economy. People in the Dhorai market area are of course aware of the existence of other market centres, of various hierarchical orders, beyond the Dhorai market itself, and from time to time – especially when the market in question is combined with ceremonies connected with the goddess cult – they participate in these markets. In other words, it is through the regional articulation of the market system that people in the Dhorai market area conceptualize the structure of what can be called, in general terms, the state.

The market system of coordinates structure time (cf. Bohannan 1967). The week, of seven days, is the cycle between successive markets in any one market area, and the days of the week are distinguished, and hierarchialized, according to the markets which occur on given days at given places. The fundamental rhythm of the market-day cycle is established at Jagdalpur, the state and previously royal capital, over 150 km away. The Jagdalpur market is held on Sundays, which becomes, so to speak, the highest-ranking day. However, Bastar district (whose total area is greater than that of Kerala) is much too large to function as a single market system, so each *tehsil* has its own Sunday market, in imitation of the one at Jagdalpur, at the *tehsil* headquarters. Dhorai is in Narayanpur *tehsil*, so Sunday is Narayanpur market day, a day consecrated to the centre and the state. Time and space coincide in expressing political hierarchy. Ranked beneath the Sunday markets, are the second-order market centres such as Dhorai. The market traders of a *tehsil* concentrate in the *tehsil* headquarters on Sunday, and visit other, smaller market centres on other days. Monday, Tuesday and Wednesday are not market days (Tuesday is ruled out as the Hindu unlucky day,[4] and

Monday and Wednesday are devoted to rest and replenishing stocks) leaving Thursday, Friday and Saturday as second-order market days. Second-order markets are arranged along routes of communication fanning out from the *tehsil* headquarters, as shown in the hypothetical model in Fig. 3.2.

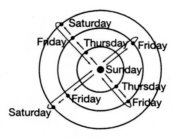

Figure 3.2   Model of time coordinates.

Pharasgaon and Chhota Dongar markets are thus third-order markets (Fig. 3.3). The spatio-temporal hierarchy of market centres articulates between village-level society and the state: the *tehsil*-wide market system of Narayanpur recapitulates the organization of the state (centering on Jagdalpur and divided into subordinate *tehsils*) while the pattern obtaining within the *tehsil* as a whole is itself recapitulated, on a microcosmic scale, by the order of events within a single second-order or third-order market area; thus, returning to Fig. 3.2 we can see that *tehsil*-wide market organization consists of an alternation of market concentration and dispersion (systole/ diastole) which is mirrored within the single market area – the Dhorai market area let us say – by the concentration of people in the market (on market day) and their dispersion back to the villages on non-market days. In other words, Dhorai (and the other second-order centres) are to Narayanpur, as the component villages of the Dhorai market area are to Dhorai; and as Dhorai is to Narayanpur, so Narayanpur is to Jagdalpur.

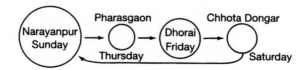

Size of circles expresses the relative importance of each market

Figure 3.3   Spatio-temporal hierarchy of four market centres.

Markets are symbols of the social order because they are its product. Along with battles, ceremonies and political assemblies, they fall into the class of necessarily rather than contingently public occasions. They demand the renunciation of individual autonomy for the sake of ends (the exchange of goods and information) which can only be achieved collectively. Because of their logistic coordinating functions, markets exert a profound influence over concepts of time and space in peasant societies and peasant states. The rhythm of market systole and diastole, emanating from Jagdalpur, is indeed nothing less than the pulse of the state itself.

THE MARKET-PLACE: EQUALITY AND INEQUALITY

I turn now to the implications of Fig. 3.4 which shows the layout of the Dhorai market-place. The Dhorai market-place is nothing less than a compendium of social relations in the Dhorai market area. These can be classified as relations between coordinate groups of approximately equal social rank, and relations between groups of different rank. These relations are expressed in two ways: (1) in the traditional layout which regulates where each group sits and transacts its business in the market-place, and (2) by means of an implied hierarchy of *goods*, which ranks any kind of goods in the market as higher/lower/equivalent in relation to others, and accords them a more central or more peripheral place as the case may be.

In abstract terms the market can be imagined as a wheel; at the hub of the wheel is the central banyan tree, where sits the 'Rajput' jeweller, and on the outermost rim of the wheel are the basket-makers, potters and smiths. On the basis of this analogy, we can define two axes of market relations (1) the 'radial' axis along which participants are assymetrically related as more/less central and along which different kinds of goods are arranged as more/less prestigious; and (2) the 'circumferential' axis along which participants are linked by relations that are symmetric, equal and competitive, and along which goods of equivalent symbolic value are ranged. Let us examine these propositions in more detail.

The market map is divisible into five concentric zones. The central zone is occupied by the jeweller, the richest, most sophisticated and best-educated trader in the market. The stock he carries, only a portion of the stock-in-trade of his family, jewellers with a permanent shop in Jagdalpur, must be worth something in the region of 20,000 rupees,[5] and he has large sums of cash as well. He mainly sells

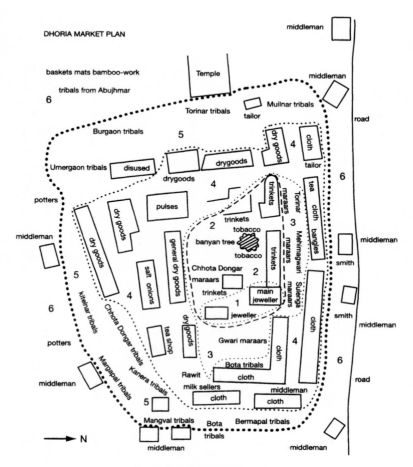

Figure 3.4 Dhorai market plan.

relatively inexpensive trinkets in silver (such as hairclips at 25 rupees each) but every so often he sells a more valuable object, such as the heavy silver neck ornaments favoured by tribal women (700–1,000 rupees), and more rarely a gold necklace, prices for which range up to 5,000 rupees depending on the number of gold beads used. Just for comparison, land is sold between tribals (non-tribals not being permitted to acquire land from tribals) at little more than 500 rupees a hectare, and a team of ploughing cattle is worth about 350 rupees. These gold necklaces can be worn by either sex but are most often worn by wealthy and influential tribal men.

The main jeweller's stock-in-trade are the symbols of rank and prestige in tribal society: and he himself is the most prestigious market trader on both cultural and economic grounds. Surrounded by his Ghassia henchmen, he dominates the centre of the market, overseeing what may be, at times, quite enormous transactions by local standards. But at the same time he is a familiar and perfectly accessible, indeed genial, man: when more important transactions do not claim his attention he will occupy himself in extolling the virtues of his cheaper hairclips for the benefit of vacillating tribal girls with every appearance of complacency. And this is an important point, for in the market the jeweller is the symbolic exponent of ideas of pre-eminent value – power, superiority – but, like all symbols, he remains within the ordinary, everyday world, while the values he *represents* lie outside it and transcend the villagers' ordinary experience.

Facing the main jeweller's stall there is a second, smaller, jeweller, also from Rajasthan. This second jeweller depends more on the sale of cheaper items, and is intermediate in position between Zone 1 and Zone 2.

Zone 2 is interesting because it is so seemingly heterogeneous. On the basis of the hypothesis of symbolic equivalence between items transacted in a given zone of market space, our problem is to determine the implications of the following structure:

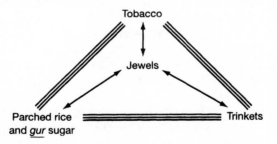

We may note, first of all, that all these goods are luxuries, but that only jewellery is a luxury which is also a permanent store of value. Trinkets are low-grade, perishable jewels: but what makes parched rice/*gur* and tobacco different from the general run of 'consumables' sold in Zone 3? The key seems to be the fact that they are processed or refined. Parched rice and *gur* are the local high-status luxury foods, and are produced by the local 'aristocratic' group – the Chhota Dongar Maraars, the wealthiest, most ancient, and the largest landowners among local Hindus. Women from this group are the main local traders and they dominate the trade in luxury food. Their traditional role in the market as 'adders of value' is interestingly brought out in the convention by which they exchange parched rice with tribals for its equivalent *volume* in dehusked paddy. Thus tribals, who are prevented by a taboo from selling paddy for money, will barter one pound, say, of paddy for the parched rice equivalent of perhaps half that amount, since in the processing of parched rice the grains swell up considerably. The tribal has not offended the rice by 'selling' it: he (or more likely she) has 'valorized' it in the interchange with a high-status group. Similar considerations apply to *gur* and tobacco, both of which have been elaborately processed. Zone 2, then, is shared by luxuries: down-graded jewellery and up-graded consumables. Sociologically speaking, it is the zone of the locally dominant Hindus.

Zone 3 is also a 'Maraar' zone of vegetable sellers, mostly from Maraar communities which are offshoots from the ancient Chhota Dongar settlement, or more recent immigrants from elsewhere in Bastar. Maraars cultivate vegetables in irrigated gardens, specializing in items which cannot be produced, or not in quantity or not of such good quality, in the tribals' own gardens. These vegetables (such as onions, chillies, tomatoes, *muli*, squashes, aubergines), are semi-luxury items, appreciated by tribals as additions to their basic diet of rice, pulses and millet. It is noteworthy that the Maraar traders in Zones 2 and 3 (mostly women, except for tobacco sellers who are all male) while they do not avail themselves of stalls, do always carry to market a stool to sit on, so as not to sit on the ground in the fashion of the tribals. On the other hand no tribal would presume to make use of a stool, so the Maraars are not only figuratively but actually 'higher' than the tribals.

Zone 4 consists of the stalls of Hindu traders in non-luxury items. One half of this zone is comprised of the street of cloth sellers who deal in cheap machine-made saris, blankets and such, the other half by the stalls of the dry-goods merchants. Cloth is not a luxury item, and the sale of cloth is not a prestige occupation as is the sale of jewellery or luxury foods. Cloth sellers behave in an unrestrained, vociferous, bumptious manner, quite different from the civilized standards of other Hindu traders. The dry-goods stalls also mainly sell non-luxury items, such as small utilitarian objects or staple foods. They do carry some luxury items such as *bidi* cigarettes or biscuits, but these are not such as to appeal much to the tribals, and are mainly sold to local Hindus, for whom they are not perhaps luxuries anyway. One form of local produce is sold in the fourth zone, namely milk. Milk is not a luxury food, and is indeed generally disliked as a food by the tribals, so that the Rawit traders' output is purchased exclusively by Hindus. The intermediate status of the Rawits – lower than Maraars but higher than tribals – is clearly expressed in the confinement of Rawits to Zone 4.

The fifth zone consists of tribal sellers of vegetables. Here we find the mass of tribal women selling small quantities of vegetables in season, seated on the ground in lengthy rows, each according to their villages of origin. Tribal men also sit in these areas, sometimes selling, sometimes merely sitting. Men are more mobile though and spend much of the time in more exclusive huddles off in the bushes at some distance, conducting meetings relating to inter-village affairs and drinking.

The sixth zone, finally, includes the low-ranking sellers of non-prestige craft items: smiths, basket-makers from the Abujhmar and potters. Also located in this zone are the middlemen who buy up forest produce as it is brought into the market by tribals. These middlemen (*seth*) are not really 'in' the market at all (they are there to buy rather than sell) and I discuss them separately.

The zonal arrangement of market space provides – with certain exceptions – a clear articulation of hierarchical relations, and serves very much as a ground plan of inter-group relations, both within the single market area and beyond it.[6] There is nothing immediately problematic about the hierarchy of people expressed therein ('Rajput' in the middle, the Maraars, local caste Hindus, then tribal, then Abujhmaria low-ranking Gonds and polluting castes); what is perhaps more subtle is the way in which this hierarchy of people is correlated with a hierarchy of goods. Here the opposition seems to be between jewellery and luxuries versus consumer goods and craft items of a utilitarian nature.

The two axes mentioned earlier – the radial and the circumferential – may also be said to define two axes of economic choice for participants (buyers) in the market. Choices within a zone (circumferential choices) are selections made, on the basis of value for money, between objects whose symbolic value is equal, while choices between zones (radial choices) are of a more fundamental kind, between different types of value. The zones are hierarchically ranked in that implicitly a buyer of an item in a higher order zone (1 or 2, say) must already have a sufficiency of the gamut of utilitarian goods sold in lower order zones (2, 4, 5), or in other words higher-order zones *encompass* lower-order zones, just as according to Dumont (1970), Brahminical religious values encompass secular-political and economic values in the caste system generally. The full rigours of caste ideology are attenuated in Bastar society, where, in contrast to the typical Indian pattern, it is *only the state* which is hierarchically organized. Villages are virtually single-caste and politically egalitarian. Lacking grass-roots expression, the concept of hierarchy becomes attached to the market, and is communicated via the symbolic oppositions between goods of various orders. Higher-order goods communicate messages which mediate between individuals – themselves confined to the village/subsistence sphere – and the higher reaches of society. Here we encounter a profound paradox in tribal consciousness. The paraphernalia of 'tribal' body ornamentation, the heavy silver bangles, the golden earrings and necklaces, the mirrors, the bells, the pompoms, the whole panoply of exotic finery, is wholly manufactured by Hindus, largely outside Bastar, to supply the tribal market – since Hindus themselves have mostly abandoned these particular ornaments. These symbols which so strongly bespeak 'tribal culture' – particularly to the metropolitan Hindu – mean precisely 'Hindu' in the estimations of the tribals who adopt them. They are glittering fragments of the Hindu world, for which the tribals readily surrender their spare cash, as would an orthodox Hindu to secure a Brahmin's blessing.

The radial axis of market space, and the sequence of choices which lie along the radial axis, relates the world of subsistence production, the domestic unit, the fragmented village, to the unifying core of the state and to the symbols of value which emanate from the state. But what of the circumferential axis? In the market people are 'put in their place' in a sense rather stronger than is usually implied by that idiom and this applies equally to circumferential relations. These relations are symmetrical and competitive, as opposed to hierarchical (encompassing/encompassed by), and competition does not lie between unequal groups. In effect, circumferential relations in the outer zones are territorial and segmentary. It is an unspoken, but almost universally observed, rule that sellers and spectators from a given locality will be seated together, and that their customary position will reflect the disposition of their village of origin *vis-à-vis* other villages in the area. Thus tribals from Torinar (Taragaon, due west of Dhorai) sit on the western side, the Mehima-Gwari people (whose village is slightly north) to their left, and the Burgaon people (slightly south) to their right (see Fig. 3.5). Maraars sit more cen-

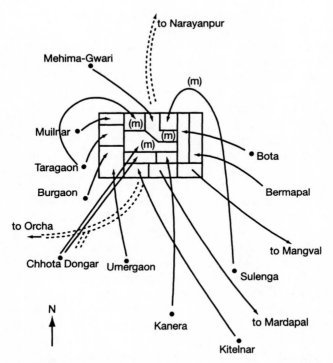

Figure 3.5 Diagram showing the relation between market space and the territorial arrangement of villages.

trally (reflecting their different position in the state hierarchy) but within their zone they, likewise, occupy positions which correspond to the geographical disposition of the settlements they come from.

If one takes a tour round the periphery of the market-place one is, in effect, traversing a small-scale model of a spatial/territorial relation in the Dhorai market area. One can readily see the significance of this for the hypothesis that the market provides a cognitive model of society at large. The next section, which is concerned with symbolic aspects of interaction in the market-place, says a little more about the content of these circumferential relations.

INTERACTION IN THE MARKET

The market is a paradigm of social relations; interaction in the market-place is coloured by factors external to the market-place, so that a tribal interacting with a market trader does not see him simply as the purveyor of some good that he has in mind to buy, but as a representative of a category, relatively ranked in accordance with a sociological scheme of values. It is necessary to distinguish this categorical aspect of market relations (the replacement of the purely economic relation buyer-seller with the sociologically determined relation tribal–Hindu) from the economic personalism often found in peasant markets elsewhere (cf. Davis 1973). Relations of a *personal* nature are precisely what these categorical relations rule out. One looks in vain for any analogue to Haitian *pratik* or similar kinds of clientèle-formation through the institutionalized extension of credit by traders in the Dhorai market. It would be going too far, though, to deny that credit is ever extended, by any class of trader in the market, towards individuals whose places of origin and degree of wealth happen to be known to the trader. The concept of extending credit (*laga arihana*) is familiar enough from the intra-village economy, and tribals are not too shy to ask for credit if they consider they have some chance of obtaining it. But it remains the case that the great majority of transactions in all categories are for cash, with the possible exception of purchases from cloth sellers. More importantly, price levels are set on the assumption of immediate cash payment: traders do not quote asking prices which are implicitly assumed to contain the costs they incur in carrying their customers' long-term debts, carried over from week to week, as the price of clientage. The dearth of higgling-haggling, which so sharply differentiates Dhorai from others described in the ethnography of markets, derives, I think, from the prevailing notion that an asking price is an 'objective' price associated uniquely with the goods transacted, to the exclusion of factors deriving from the nature of the social relationship between buyer and seller. Where credit is extended, this is not indicative of a 'personalistic' element in the economic relation between the parties to the transaction, but reflects a straightforward commercial judgement, on the part of the seller, of the purchaser's ability to clear the debt in the reasonably near future. There is no expectation, on either side, of a continuing or exclusive relationship thereafter.

In spite of the absence of bargaining, either over the price asked for goods, or the quantities offered at a given price, in the general run of market transactions (again with the exception of purchases from cloth sellers) it remains the case that there is an obvious advantage to the trader in increasing sales by offering marginally more attractive terms than competitors. Customers' goodwill is not won through leniency in the bargaining process or offers of attractive credit terms, since these mechanisms remain undeveloped, but is nonetheless sought through a device which is much more in tune with the anonymous and hierarchical ethos characteristic of this particular market. This is the device of *pura kiana* ('completing'), which, characteristically, places the buyer in the position of the recipient of the trader's *largesse*. This is seen particularly in the practice of the Maraar sellers of foodstuffs, who will invariably – but only when the sale has been agreed on – add a 'sweetener', in the form of an extra handful of rice or a couple of additional tomatoes, to the amount paid for. The buyer usually remonstrates at the inadequacy of this extra quantity, and may be successful in extracting a little bit more. This could be mistaken for bargaining over the quantity of goods offered at a fixed price, but it is important to stress that the sale is in no way dependent on the size of the 'extra' amount, having been concluded before anything additional is offered. What is bought and sold is a straightforward commodity, paid for at a given price; what is given as 'extra' is a *gift*, supplicated for as traditional *largesse*, which reinforces hierarchical relations between social categories.

Category relations laid down in the market are the coordinates of social distance: where transactions mutually involve persons who belong to different orders, this distance is not lessened as a consequence – on the contrary it finds tangible expression. When a tribal seeks to buy something from (say) a dry-goods merchant, there is a notable absence of sustained interaction; the tribal indicates his wishes (often by pointing to or holding the object); the merchant, as curtly as possible, states a price. If the tribal considers the amount excessive he puts the item back and takes himself off, and if he is satisfied he pays cash on the nail. None but the minimum of words are exchanged, eye contact is restricted, and no extraneous social signals pass between buyer and seller.

Radial relations are *ipso facto* relations between socially distant persons; the reverse is true of circumferential relations. The circumferential axis of market interaction corresponds to the major channel of inter-village communication and is intensely sociable. In particular it is at the market-place that marriages are arranged and meetings which have to do with intra-village affairs (performances of ritual, apprehension of runaway couples, negotiations about brideprice and the return thereof in the case of divorce and so on) are conducted. Individuals seeking spouses visit the market-place, so that a man who says 'I got my wife at the market' does not mean that she was purchased, but simply that he sought her out there. For tribals, most of whom in any given week have little enough to sell and no inclination (if they have the money) to buy, the most important aspect of the market is its circumferential aspect. This gives rise to a great deal of what can only be called pseudo-marketing, particularly by tribal women whose strongly engrained work ethic prevents them from simply attending for pleasure and social enjoyment. A tribal woman, desirous of visiting the market for purely 'social' reasons, will nevertheless provide herself with a 'stock-in-trade' (and hence an excuse) in the form of, say, a handful of microscopic and mostly rotten tomatoes, and will proceed to 'sell' this unsaleable item for the entire morning. In this way she manages to see her neighbours, friends and relatives, opportunities for social contacts outside the immediate family or hamlet being uncommon at other times because of the dispersed pattern of settlement in tribal villages.

One can therefore generalize by saying that interactions on the radial axis are characterized by distance and anonymity, while interactions on the circumferential axis are personal and specific. Social distance on the circumferential axis corresponds to segmentary and territorial oppositions, while on the radial axis it corresponds to category oppositions between ranked groups. However, there are certain anomalies, which may be discussed at this point.

The middlemen who station themselves around the paths leading into the market-place, but outside the main area, are an exception to the normal rules first in that they are Hindus, but are peripheral, and secondly in that they solicit trade directly, sometimes using what appears to be physical coercion (grasping a tribal woman's basket of tamarind and attempting to prevent her going to another buyer); they often speak Gondi, and have Gonds as assistants. The aggressive, vociferous means they employ is deceptive to the extent that tribals are not genuinely coerced into selling forest products to a buyer not of their choice, and investigations did not turn up any significant differences in the prices being offered by different middlemen. Their profits are proportional to the volume of trade, and each is in competition with his colleagues to maximize volume short of actually offering an increased price over the consensual one, which does not fluctuate over a short-term period. They are consequently obliged to concentrate on building up a clientèle of regular suppliers, by developing social relationships with tribals. Each one has a stall which adjoins one particular path leading to the market, and they concentrate on forming relationships with people from particular villages which lie along that path. They employ as assistants men drawn from the selected village or villages, who in turn influence the choice of middleman for their co-villagers. Their stall becomes a kind of meeting place where tribals like to relax and exchange gossip. They also advance money to individuals known to them, against future contributions of produce (not for interest, which is illegal). In short, they really operate in terms of the 'village' credit/debt economy – the personalized, embedded economy, in contradistinction to the anonymous 'market' economy. Hence their peripheral position, and the lack of social distance between them and their clientèle, confirms, rather than upsets, our general hypothesis.

A second slightly exceptional group are the cloth-sellers. Bargaining is not normally a feature of interactions between socially differentiated participants in the market, but this is not so where the cloth sellers are concerned. Tribals do usually contest the asking price for cloth, and cloth sellers engage in patter routines to try to convince passers-by that their prices really are rock bottom. Cloth sellers extend credit to individuals known to them, but do not depend on a regular clientèle. The explanation for the rather more egalitarian interaction between cloth sellers and tribals may be due to a conceptual identification between them and weavers (Gandas) who have low social status. It would of course be normal to haggle with a Ganda the price of a handloom cloth (Gandas visit the market but do not sit in any special place, wandering around the periphery hawking their wares).

CONCLUDING REMARKS

The present account is intentionally limited in scope; it would be necessary to conduct more extensive researches into markets in Bastar, and in other parts of India, to explore the full ramifications of the relationships between village society, the market, hierarchy and the state. I hope that I have said enough at least to justify the idea that the Dhorai market provides, for those who come within its ambit, a ground-plan of group relations, and in the hierarchy of goods, a scheme of values through which village dwellers encounter, on the level of *praxis*, superior values emanating from the state. All of which is only to say that the market has an ideological significance, very much as a ceremony, the performance of a religious rite, or the installation of an office holder has significance. The problem that I wish to raise, by way of a conclusion, is one common to all such value-laden performances: namely, the issue of truth versus mystification. We have become accustomed not only to tease out the implicit meanings of ceremonies but also to subject them to criticism, finding in them labyrinths of semantic manipulation, the net effect of which is to represent reality under such a guise as favours the interests of certain elements in the social whole, to the detriment of others. If it is true that the market occasion is ideologically significant, as I have claimed, is it also true that it is manipulative in this sense, depicting the forms of social reality so as to favour sectional interests, by mystifying the real basis of social relations?

There is one good reason why one might hesitate to draw this conclusion. The Dhorai market is not overtly a ceremony at all, but a straightforwardly instrumental institution, geared to the economic needs of people in the area. There is no element of make-believe, no communicative intent, behind the purchase of a packet of nails for eight annas, then, or the myriad of other, equally matter-of-fact transactions which collectively make up the market. The market cannot distort reality because it *is* reality. The money medium of the market accurately reflects relative economic strengths and weaknesses (in a way that the credit/debt economy within the village may not). Markets are information exchanges, but they differ from ceremonies in that the information exchanged is verifiable and overwhelmingly true – the market price of tomatoes is only in dispute until a sale is made; once made, the price is indisputable – while symbolic statements made in the course of a ceremony are always, and only, *claims*, for which no validation can ever be finally found.

There is thus no element of mystification in the instrumental aspect of the market as an exchange of (price, demand) information and goods. But at another level I believe that the Dhorai market is profoundly mystifying, yet not in a way which benefits a dominant sectional interest only, but in a way which reinforces the position of the very group who come off worse in the symbolic exchange, namely the tribals. I have indicated the extent to which the market defines tribals as peripheral and low, by contrast to Hindus, who are central and high. Moreover, the pattern of tribal purchases, their focus on obsolete jewels, trinkets, finery and traditional luxury foods (as opposed to the Hindu trend towards symbols of modernity such as biscuits and filter-tipped cigarettes) categorizes them as childish and weak, easily seduced by baubles.[7] In other words, tribal market participation, both in terms of the spatial organization of the market and the image projected by their evaluations of goods, perpetuates and reinforces the stereotype of cultural backwardness and political inferiority. This stereotype, however, has historically had certain advantages, and conceals a rather different reality. The tribal population of Bastar traditionally enjoyed the patronage of the state, without much interference in the course of their daily lives. The Rajah of Bastar was in effect a Divine King, the living embodiment of the state goddess, and the duties of the tribal population in regard to him were of a ritual nature. Subsequently, as a result of various convulsions in the state, which cannot be discussed here, the tribals of this part of Bastar, if not elsewhere, have developed a rather similar relationship with the government and its agencies. Legislation which protects tribal interests is enforced, and the continuation of the internal autonomy of tribal villages is permitted. The tribals' basic motivation is the continuation of a hedonistic lifestyle to which they are deeply attached, but the price paid for it is the continuous exchange of myths – the myth of tribal primitiveness, Hindu patronage – with the Hindu population. Intelligent tribal men have firm views on the threat to themselves posed by any attempt by tribals to infiltrate the Hindu-dominated power structure. It is because the interests of tribals are protected by the aura of myth which surrounds them that the exchange of these myths, which one can see taking place very clearly in the market-place, assumes such importance. But they are only myths: the resource base on which tribal society rests is a rich one by Indian standards, and it has not passed into the hands of outsiders. The effect of the market is to establish a stereotype of tribals, and tribal–Hindu relations, in which tribals retain actual control of their resource base, at the expense of becoming symbolically peripheral to Hindu society, wards of the state. For Hindus it is the establishment of symbolic hegemony, for tribals, real security.

NOTES

The fieldwork reported on here was conducted in 1977–8 and was supported by the Department of Prehistory and Anthropology, School of General Studies, Australian National University, to which I am very grateful. I was accompanied in the field by Simeran Gell who played a large part in collecting the data for this study. This article was first presented at the 1979 meeting of the Australian Anthropological Society at Sydney University.

1 Data relating to Dhorai market as it was in the late 1950s are to be found in Jay 1968.
2 The terms 'tribal' and 'Adivasi' are standardly used to cover Scheduled

Tribes as listed in the Indian Constitution and enumerated in the Census. It is not to be supposed, however, that these terms have definite sociological meaning.

3 I propose to turn to such matters in the future; in collaboration with Dr C. Gregory and with the support of the SSRC and the International Centre for the study of Economic and Related Disciplines (ICERD) the author is engaged on a detailed survey of marketing in North Bastar.

4 Wanmali (1977) states that in Singhbhum, Bihar, Tuesday was, in 1926, the most popular market day. Tuesday has since been displaced by Friday (now the most popular) and by Wednesday, Thursday and Monday as well. The reasons for changes such as these remain a matter for further investigation.

5 The rupee was valued at Rs. 14 to the £ sterling at the time of fieldwork in 1977.

6 If it is true, as I have argued, that the hierarchy of groups in the Dhorai market area is encoded in the hierarchy of goods offered in the marketplace, it naturally becomes a question as to how this hierarchy of goods is sustained in the process of exchange, that is, the way in which prices both reflect the symbolic aura of different kinds of goods, and at the same time operate so as to perpetuate the relative economic positions of the groups who bring each category of goods into the market. The question of price setting is too considerable to be dealt with here, and could only be elucidated in the context of a full-scale regional economic survey, a project the author and his collaborators have on hand at present.

7 My colleague, Dr J. Parry, points out that amassing quantities of jewellery and gold ornaments is an objective shared by virtually all sections of Indian society, for reasons which have little enough to do with 'backwardness' in the sense implied here. While I accept this qualification, I think there is a distinction between the Muria estimation of jewellery as high-status-conferring by virtue of its symbolic associations with the admired metropolitan ideal (mediateu by the high-status trader) *versus* the more sophisticated attitude which sees jewellery as a convenient way of storing capital in a form which is both safe and ostentatious.

REFERENCES

Agarwal, P. (1968) *Human Geography of Bastar District* (Allahabad: Gogra).

Agrawal, B. (1978) 'Economic networks and cultural integration in Madhya Pradesh', *Man in India*. 58:285–297.

Berry, B. (1967) *Geography of Market Centres and Retail Distribution* (Englewood Cliffs: Prentice Hall).

Bohannan, P. and G. Dalton (1962) *Markets in Africa* (Evanston: Northwestern University Press).

Bohannan, P. (1967) 'Concepts of time among the Tiv of Nigeria', in J. Middleton (ed.) *Myth and Cosmos* (Garden City, New York: Natural History Press).

Bromley, R. (1974) *Periodic Markets, Daily Markets and Fairs* (Melbourne: Monash University, Dept. of Geography).

Christaller, W. (1966) *Central Places in South Germany* (Englewood Cliffs, NJ: Prentice Hall).

Davis, W. (1973) *Social Relations in a Philippine Market* (Berkeley, CA: University of California Press).

Douglas, M. (1973) *Rules and Meanings* (Harmondsworth: Penguin).

Dumont, L. (1970) *Homo Hierarchicus* (London: Weidenfeld & Nicolson).

Elwin, V. (1947) *The Muria and their Ghotul* (London: Oxford University Press).

Geertz, C. (1975) *The Interpretation of Culture* (London: Hutchinson).

Geertz, C., H. Geertz and L. Rosen (1979) *Meaning and Order in Moroccan Society* (Cambridge: Cambridge University Press).

Grigson, W. (1938) *The Maria Gonds of Bastar* (Oxford: Oxford University Press).

Harriss, B. (1976) 'Social specificity in rural weekly markets – the case of Tamil Nadu', *Mainz. Geogr. Stud.*, 10.

Jay, E. (1968) *A Tribal Village of Central India* (Calcutta: Anthropological Survey of India).

Leach, E. (1954) *Political Systems of Highland Burma* (London: Athlone Press).

Lévi-Strauss, C. (1963) *Structural Anthropology* (New York: Basic).

Losch, A. (1954) *The Economics of Location* (New Haven, CT: Yale University Press).

Mandelbaum, D. (1970) *Society in India* (Berkeley, CA: University of California Press).

Mintz, S. (1959) 'Internal market systems as mechanisms of social articulation' in V. F. Ray (ed.) *Social Mobility and Communication* (Seattle: American Anthropological Association).

Polanyi, K., C. Arensberg and H. Pearson (ed.) (1957) *Trade and Market in the Early Empires* (Glencoe: Free Press).

Schwartzberg, J. (1967) 'Prolegomena to a study of Asian regions and regionalism', in R. I. Crane (ed.) *Regions and Regionalism in south Asia*, Duke University Program in Comparative Studies in South Asia, Monograph no. 5:89–111.

Sinha, D. (1968) *Cultural Change in an Intertribal Market* (Bombay: Asia Publishing House).

Sinha, S., B. Dasgupta and H. Banerjee (1961) 'Agriculture crafts and weekly markets of South Manbhum', *Bulletin of the Anthropological Survey of India*, 10:1–163.

Skinner, G. W. (1964–5) 'Marketing and social structure in rural China', *Journal of Asian Studies*, 24:3–44, 195–228, 363–400.

Smith, C. (1975) 'Examining stratification systems through peasant marketing arrangements: an application of some models from economic geography', *Man*, (n.s.) 10:95–122.

Smith, C. (1976) *Regional Analysis* Vol. 1 (New York: Academic).

Wanmali, S. (1976) 'Market centres and the distribution of consumer goods in Rural India', *Mainz. Geogr. Stud.*, 10.

Wanmali, S. (1977) 'Periodic markets in south Bihar', *Management Lab. Stud.*, 3:1–16.

CHAPTER 4

STYLE AND MEANING IN UMEDA DANCE

The objective of this chapter is the application of structural analysis to the dance, in particular to a sequence of ritual dances performed in the Waina-Sowanda district of the West Sepik Province, Papua New Guinea.[1] I made a study of this ritual, which is known as *ida*, in Umeda village in 1969–70, and the results of this study were published in a monograph (*Metamorphosis of the Cassowaries*, Gell 1975), which readers of the present essay may consult for more background information than can be provided here, both concerning the ritual itself and the sociological setting. More recently, I revisited the area in the company of a film maker (Mr Chris Owen of the Institute of Papua New Guinea Studies, Boroko, Papua New Guinea), who made a film of the *ida* ritual. This was subsequently put at my disposal, making the analysis reported on here possible (Owen 1977 [1979]).[2]

The *ida* ceremony occupies two nights and two days, and consists of the appearance of a sequence of masked dancers, who dance in the ritual arena before an audience of villagers and visitors from elsewhere. Music is provided by a band of wooden trumpets, and women also dance, though without wearing masks or adopting named ritual roles, like the men. In the above-mentioned book I provide an analysis of *ida*, which takes as its starting point the idea that each of the successive roles danced in the arena is a transformation of preceding ones, and an approximation towards the final apotheosis of man in the guise of a red bowman, the *ipele*. The initial dancers to appear are 'cassowaries' – black-painted men wearing bushy masks of treelike aspect. They stand for nature, the wild, the uncontrolled, the primordial. This role confers the greatest individual prestige, but is at the same time negatively evaluated. In Umeda the cassowaries are accompanied by two junior dancers (*motnatamwa*), whose repressed style of dance and red body paint underline the symbolic significance of the black paint and wild cavortings of the senior cassowaries. As the ritual progresses, the dancers enact roles that depart, ever more radically, from this initial stereotype. The cassowaries are followed by 'sago' dancers, still wearing treelike masks, but lacking the warlike black paint, and then by the 'firewood' dancers with masks constructed on similar lines, but with a tall decorative shaft. Then during the daytime come the 'fish' dancers, emblematic of masculinity, erotically attractive, but also evoking cultural themes, particularly through their masks, which are constructed of the 'cultural' coconut palm (as opposed to the 'natural' sago/arecoid constituents of the cassowary mask) and are painted with clan designs.

During the second day, the fish are joined by more dancers, who diverge even more sharply from the cassowary. The 'termite' dancers lack the enlarged, weighted penis gourd which previous dancers wear (and exploit in their dancing in a manner to be described below), and have only the smaller penis gourds of everyday attire (cf. Gell 1971 for illustrations and discussion). Their masks are highly simplified versions of the cassowary mask. The termites represent domesticity and the care of children (they may be given babies to carry). On this day there are throwbacks to the uncivilized state represented by the cassowary, in the form of ogres of various sorts who make brief appearances to frighten and amuse the spectators. One is a transvestite man parodying the female dance style, another is the hateful creeping *kwod*, whose distinctive dance will be described below.

Finally the ritual culminates in the appearance of the *ipele* bowmen, who differ from all previous dancers in being identified as men, rather than natural species (sago, fish, etc.). They are accompanied by preceptors, because although they are hunters, they are 'new men' who have not yet learned how to shoot their arrows. They perform the final ritual of loosing off the *ipele* arrows, and with this the ritual is concluded.

The dancing at *ida* is very striking and varied. Most notable, perhaps, is the orgiastic style adopted by the cassowary, sago, and to a lesser extent the fish dancers. All these (male) dancers wear a weighted penis gourd, and a belt strung with hard seeds around the abdomen. They dance in a leaping, undulatory fashion, which causes the penis gourd to fly up, striking the abdominal belt with every step, so that it emits a sharp clicking sound. This dance is very overtly sexual, and I have discussed the symbolism involved elsewhere (Gell 1975:

232–4). But this dance is only one of many different styles seen at *ida* and in this account I want to concentrate more on Umeda dances as a *system*, rather than on the symbolic meaning of individual dances. In my previous account, I was only able to indicate very gross contrasts between wild unrestrained dancing, associated with the ritual roles that fall at the cassowary end of the wild–civilized continuum, versus restrained dances appropriate to such figures as the *ipele* bowmen, whose relatively cramped style of dancing expresses the repression of spontaneity that culture imposes (Gell 1975: 289–90). With the aid of filmed material, I think I can now go a bit further than this and construct a model of Umeda dance as a set of variations on a basic armature. This model that I propose is an 'observer's model' utilizing behavioural data, not an indigenous model provided by the Umeda themselves. A model is a codified, simplified description, within which relationships between variables (here, patterns of movement) can be made explicit. It may be helpful to the reader to indicate the application of structural analysis of the kind I have in mind, by means of an example. Fig. 4.1 is a flow chart showing the transformations of mask styles worn by various ritual actors in *ida*. It will be seen that there are obvious generic resemblances between the styles of mask worn by the cassowaries, the sago dancers, the firewood dancers, and finally the termite dancers; and there is also an obvious relation between the fish mask and the *ipele* mask. One can also see that the firewood mask is a kind of bridging example between the cassowary/sago mask and the fish/*ipele* masks. In other words, the masks worn at *ida* form a *set* and each mask can be transformed into the others by means of simple operations (for example, the *ipele* mask is a miniaturized fish mask, the firewood mask is an elongated cassowary mask, and so on). It is through the patterning of these contrasts and continuities that the masks, as a set, encode meanings; that is, as mask A is to mask B, so ritual role A is to ritual role B, and so on. The masks are visible and tangible exponents of implicit dimensions of symbolic significance. Moreover, the mask set is not an isolated domain, but incorporates many references to the world outside the ritual – which is also the world to which the ritual ultimately refers. It will be seen in Fig. 4.1 that there is a parallel between the bushy hairstyle of the senior married man and the bushy top of the cassowary mask, versus the controlled bachelor hairstyle and the neatly constructed *ipele* mask, while the mask set taken as a whole obviously makes references to, and is based on, the everyday traditional hairstyle whereby the hair is

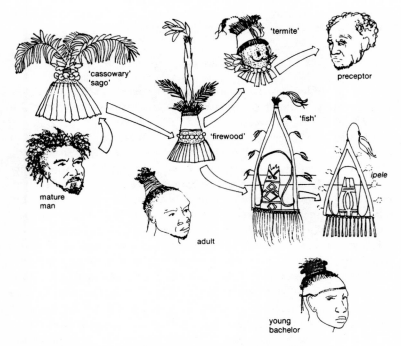

Figure 4.1 Transformation of mask styles in the *ida* ceremony

drawn up into a decorative open cylinder of woven rattan. Thus the mask set (as a group of transformations on an armature, the basic mask) draws upon elements of mundane life in elaborating its specific ritual meanings; in particular it recapitulates the sociological oppositions between various classes of men at differing stages of the life cycle via references to the variety of hairstyles these classes of males adopt. This, in effect, is the strategy of the ritual as a whole, since the purpose that lies behind it is precisely the acting out, through a ritual drama, of the general processes of biosocial regeneration, a task that culminates in the appearance of the *ipele* bowmen, who are new men, produced during the course of the ritual itself. The masks, through a variety of references too complex to be pursued further here, encode this regenerative cycle, but the point that I wish to stress here is the way in which in order to grasp their meaning it is necessary to consider them as a transformation set, rather than simply as a set of individual masks. The objective now in view is to provide an analogous analysis where the dance proper, rather than the accoutrements of the dancers, is concerned. This raises a number of rather special problems.

GRAPHIC ANALYSIS

One of the difficulties that has prevented progress in the field of the anthropology of dance being as rapid as that in, say, the anthropology of visual art, has been the need for a notation of dance movements that combines accuracy with some degree of readability for the non-dance expert. Art objects, such as the masks mentioned in the previous section, can be simply *reproduced*, but this simple graphic reduction is not feasible where dance movements are concerned. Laban notation and Benesh notation both have their advocates, but are equally incomprehensible to the rest of the anthropological profession, who are unlikely to undertake the task of learning complicated systems of hieroglyphics lightly. It seems to me that this problem can only be attacked piecemeal, in terms of particular analyses with specific ends in view. For present purposes I have devised a system, for whose crudity I make no apologies, that reduces Umeda dance movements simply to movements of the leg, seen sideways on. Of course, when dancing, Umedas move the whole body in extremely complex ways, but the leg movements are sufficiently crucial to serve as discriminators between Umeda dance styles for the purposes of the model. Umeda dances can all be construed as different forms of gait, and can be analysed using techniques derived from the kinesiological study of human walking and running (Carlsöö 1972: 94–120; Hoenkamp 1978). Gait can be described, among other ways, by measuring the angles formed by the upper leg (thigh) and the lower leg (from the knee down) to the vertical at successive points during the step cycle. As the limb swings and bends at the knee during walking or running – or dancing, for that matter – these angles vary continuously and can be plotted as functions on a graph.

Working from film, which is the most feasible way of measuring angles, we can produce functions for (*a*) the upper leg and (*b*) the lower leg. We only need to consider one leg, not both, because each leg goes through the same sequence of movements, only in counterphase. But the leg is an indivisible entity, and we need to combine the lower- and upper-leg functions, so that we can see how lower- and upper-leg angles correlate with one another. This is easily done by making use of a two-dimensional graph (which represents a two-dimensional phase space) in which one axis (north–south) corresponds to upper-leg angles, and the other axis (east–west) corresponds to lower-leg angles. Two parabolic waves plotted against one another in this manner yield an ellipse. However, the functions for leg movements are not parabolic, especially not the lower-leg function, which is quite irregular, so the graph for 'normal' western walking looks more like a leg-of-mutton shape.

This kind of graph was developed by Hoenkamp (1978) for use in conjunction with computer registration of data, but its original form is both too sensitive and too abstract for the analytical purposes I have here in mind. I measured angles off the film in five-degree steps, and subsequently rounded off even these figures when plotting them on my diagrams, which are calibrated in terms of ten-degree steps. This dramatic, but necessary, shedding of information at each stage of the model-making process should alert readers to the fact that this apparently 'mathematical' approach to dance analysis is not aimed at numerical accuracy, but simply at uncovering certain gross features of the shapes produced by plotting Umeda dance movements on to graphs. This raises the second problem of such graphs, which is the difficulty of mentally translating them back into concrete movements. I have tried to overcome this problem by constructing a master figure, which consists of an array of cells, inside each of which is depicted a little leg, which corresponds to the combination of upper and lower leg angles (calibrated in ten-degree steps) located at that point on the overall two-dimensional graph (Fig. 4.2). The shape of this figure is that of a right-angle triangle, because many combinations of upper leg/lower leg angles are ruled out by the fact that the knee only bends one way (these are all the ones on the top right-hand side). I should stress that this depiction is valid only for specific purposes: many more possibilities exist but these are the ones relevant to the analysis.

The graphs can therefore be read as follows. On Fig. 4.2 I have outlined two sets of cells. Sequence A→B read in the direction of the arrow shows a leg kicking forwards (kicking a football, say) while sequence C↔D shows a leg performing a series of knee bends – here the arrows go in both directions. One can imagine each cell as a separate frame in a cine-film. It may be helpful to bear in mind, when reading the remainder of the graphs I will present, that the southeast–northwest axis always corresponds to sequences in which the upper and lower parts of the leg are both moving in the same direction with respect to the vertical, while the southwest–northeast

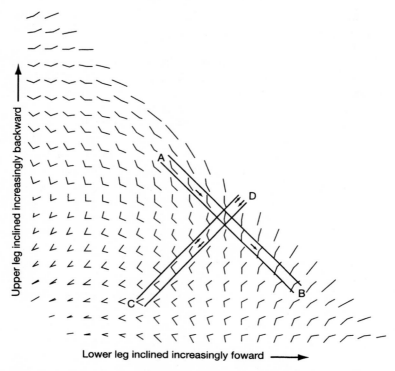

Figure 4.2 Graphic representation of upper and lower leg angles (after Hoenkamp 1978)

axis corresponds to movements in which the upper and lower parts of the leg are moving in opposite directions with respect to the vertical (i.e. the knee joint is being flexed or extended). The north–south axis, meanwhile, corresponds to movements where the angle of the lower leg remains constant while the upper leg moves with respect to the vertical, and the east–west axis corresponds to movements during which the lower leg swings from the knee while the upper leg remains at a constant angle.

In Fig. 4.3a I have projected a normal western walking step cycle on to the master graph, and (dotted) a deviant version of walking. This version would be more characteristic of the Umeda standard walking pattern, which is not quite the same as the western one (for explanation, see below). This latter shape is the basic armature of Umeda dance.

The advantage of this method of representation is that it permits instant visual comparisons between different versions of the step cycle seen as wholes, with the possibility of easy identification of the distinctive features wherein they differ. Moreover, it becomes possible, in this way, to see the different styles of movement adopted by participants in *ida* as a set of transformations of a single form (the cycle of Fig. 4.3a), which is expanded, contracted, stretched this way and that, transposed bodily, and so on, maintaining its essential unity. Edmund Leach once advised his anthropological colleagues to approach the analysis of anthropological data as a problem akin to the topological analysis of figures drawn on rubber sheeting (1961:7). The transformational approach to the analysis of mask styles presented earlier was intended to exemplify Leach's approach in the analysis of visual forms and meanings. We are now in a position to do the same for dance.

DANCE AND NONDANCE

There is not, in Umeda or perhaps anywhere, a clear boundary between dance and nondance; we always find the self-consciously graceful walk that seems continually to refer to the dance without quite becoming it, and the half-hearted dance that lapses back into the security of mere locomotion. Yet it also remains true that there is a gap, a threshold however impalpable, that is crossed when the body begins to dance, rather than simply move. This gap is less a matter of movement *per se* than of meaning, for what distinguishes dance movements from nondance movements is the fact that they have dance meanings attached to them. But here is a paradox, fundamental to the whole question of dance, because what source can these dance meanings possibly have except the patterned contrasts, the intentional clues, embodied in everyday, nondance movement? Dance seems to separate itself from nondance by its atypicality, its non-normal, non-mundane character, but dance acquires its meaning by referring us back always to the world of mundane actions, to what these performers would be doing, were they doing anything but dance. Even the most delicate ballroom dances seem to present us with innumerable scenarios of provocation, pursuit, flight, capture, rape; and what would one make of Umeda dance, the endless cycles of tumescence that fill two days and leave the dancers wearied to exhaustion? Dance escapes from nondance only to return to it in the course of symbolically transforming it, and dance analysis can only succeed by following this double movement, back and forth.

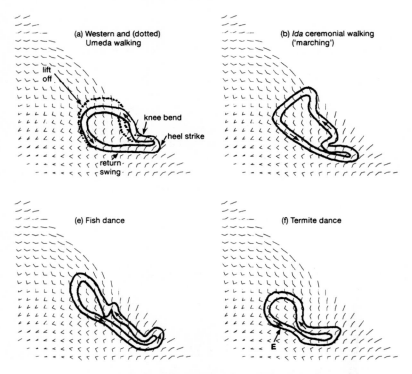

Figure 4.3   Graphic representations of *ida* step cycles

Dance meanings originate through a process whereby elements, or components, of nondance motor patterns are seized upon, stereotyped (usually with some degree of formalization and exaggeration), and are set within a particular context. The logic of dance is, in this respect, highly akin to the logic of play; the message 'this is dance' (like the message 'this is play': cf. Bateson 1972: 151) is a metamessage, one that sets the subsequent communicative transaction in its correct logical context (. . . .I am going to pretend to stab you with this knife, but only in play, really we are the best of friends. . .). The function of style in dance, the immediately recognizable but usually very impalpable mannerism that colours the complete gamut of dance forms in a specific culture, is to mark this logical boundary between dance and nondance, ambiguous though it may become in particular instances. We may profitably begin our analysis of Umeda dance, therefore, by seeking out the motor stereotype that conveys this context shift, that establishes the category of dance as one with

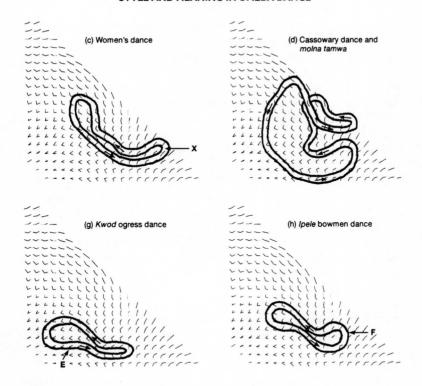

(c) Women's dance

(d) Cassowary dance and *molna tamwa*

(g) *Kwod* ogress dance

(h) *Ipele* bowmen dance

ground rules that are distinctively different from those that govern the interpretation of behaviour in the nondance context.

Yet even here we do not escape from the nondance world, because the most notable mannerism that separates dance from nondance in Umeda proves to be no more than a caricature of a feature basic to Umeda motor style in *all* contexts, not just dance. Let me refer to Fig. 4.3a, where I have indicated a certain deviation from the norm of western walking that seems to me characteristic of Umeda. Umedas, especially when they are walking in a deliberate, careful way, seem to me to manifest a step cycle that differs significantly from the western one at one point in particular, the commencement of the so-called support phase, following the moment when the heel of the leading foot lands on the ground. At heel strike the leg is quite straight in the western walk, and the heel is brought sharply down. Subsequently there is a brief bending of the knee, which serves to bring the whole foot into contact with the earth, and then, almost at once, the leg straightens again so that before it has reached the vertical the knee joint is locked straight and remains so for the latter part of the support phase until the heel lifts off again. In the Umeda walk, on the other hand, the front leg may already be bending at the knee before the heel hits the ground, and the knee bend following heel strike is more pronounced and prolonged, the knee straightening and locking only after the upper leg has passed the vertical.

It is interesting to pause for a moment to consider the source of this apparent anomaly. The whole subject of the cultural ecology of walking is, so far as I know, unsurveyed at present, though copious materials which would shed light on the matter must be available in the film archives of the world. It would appear to me, at any rate, that the way Umedas walk is related to their environment (dense jungle, no roads, many obstructions in the form of exposed roots, thorns, rocks, and so on) and their technology (lack of shoes of any kind). Like all anthropologists, no doubt, who have worked in similar circumstances, I have spent time attending to the wounded feet of my hosts, and have had occasion to marvel at the wonderful callosities that the unshod develop; nevertheless foot injuries are common, painful, and pose a distinct threat to production and social viability. It must be reasonable to suppose that the gait pattern of the unshod reflects constraints not only of locomotor efficiency *per se*, but also constraints imposed by the need to minimize the chances of foot injury – constraints that impinge very much less heavily on ourselves. Examination of a worn pair of shoes is suggestive in this respect: the heaviest wear is always at the heel with another patch of heavy wear under the ball of the big toe, yet the feet of the unshod do not seem to show markedly thicker callosities in these regions, nor in my experience were injuries concentrated there. It might be the case, therefore, that the unshod walk in such a way as to minimize the possibility of damage (which is proportional to the local pressure on the part of the foot in contact with the ground at any one time) by maximizing the area of weight-bearing surface of the sole of the foot at all stages of the step cycle. The exaggerated knee bend during the support phase has this effect (*a*) because the foot lands on the ground relatively flat, with no sharp impact of the heel, (*b*) because when the knee bends, weight is only gradually transferred from back foot to front foot (that is, the time during which both feet are on the ground and sharing the weight of the body is maximized) and (*c*) because the knee bend dampens the angular momentum of the body weight as it changes direction (moving down when the legs are widely separated and up as the support leg swings underneath the body). Although the knee bend increases the amplitude of this up-and-down motion of the body, it smooths out the wave-form so that there are no sharp shocks that would cause increased local pressure to be communicated to the foot–ground contact area. This is the same principle as the suspension of a car.

As I remarked earlier, the knee bend in normal Umeda walking becomes most pronounced when the individual is walking in a deliberate, intent fashion: there seems to be a clear carry-over between this and what I call 'ceremonial walking', which is a borderline form of dancing seen particularly in the case of the musicians – men playing wooden trumpets – who parade round the arena throughout *ida*. Fig. 4.3b (taken from film) shows the step cycle of a man marching vigorously with the band of trumpet players. It is clear that this form of walking emphasizes and exaggerates elements that are already present in normal walking; the ceremonial walk in Umeda, if I may be permitted the expression, is an hypostatization of the normal walk, and as such is already a dance. We have an analogous case in our own culture that may help to clarify the point: military marching. What is most notable, comparing the Umeda 'march' with the western one, is the way in which each selects, for formalization and emphasis, quite different elements in the step cycle, which is only at a very abstract level a true human universal. I feel it quite appropriate to describe the Umeda ceremonial walk as a march, because that, functionally speaking, is what it is; but I am sure that any British soldier whose parade-ground style approximated to the Umeda one would spend most of his military career in the guardroom, peeling potatoes. Marching is a cultural, not a natural category, and as such is constrained by technology and environment. It would not be possible to perform the western military march with bare feet, since it achieves its effect mainly in the simultaneous crashing down of rank upon rank of iron-shod boot heels (heavy boots have a natural tendency to swing out at the beginning of each stride). The Prussian goose-step is the apotheosis of this 'shod' approach to ceremonial walking (indeed the prominence that it gives to the boot as an item of military technology is not misplaced), but it stands at the opposite end of the spectrum from the Umeda ceremonial walk. The features to note in the Umeda ceremonial walk are (*a*) the increased stride length – this is the only feature that is in common with the European military march, (*b*) the exaggerated knee bend and the sharp upward rise during the latter part of the support phase, and (*c*) the tendency to exaggerated follow-through during the swing phase, the knee becoming quite sharply bent during the return travel of the non-support leg. The Umeda ceremonial walk is not just a means of locomotion, but is at the same time an expression, mediated through cultural categories, of the *idea* of walking. We have crossed the threshold of the dance.

The examples of dancing proper, which I will now go on to consider, all share with the ceremonial walk the features of stylization of knee bend, follow-through, and (in some instances) abnormal stride length. These deviations from the norm, which at the same time seem to caricature or exaggerate the norm, reflect the Umedas' own perception of the structure of their motor repertoire, and the meaningful articulation of different modes of motor performance. It is these perceptions that lie at the heart of their dance system.

FEMALE DANCE

Fig. 4.3c (taken from film) shows a woman dancing in an unusually vigorous manner: the graph diverges sharply from normal walking and is clearly a dance step. This gait is characterized by greatly extended stride length, deep and prolonged knee bending during the support phase, but lacks the upward spring characteristic of masculine leaping dances (see below). The dance as a whole might best be described as a stretched walk; particularly the exaggerated forwards extension of the leading leg (marked x on the graph).

What the graph cannot convey, useful as it is for comparative purposes, is the way in which female dancing exploits female dress in a sexually suggestive way. The purpose of the outstretched front foot (the ankle is maximally extended and the toes angled down) is to bring the body weight on to the front foot early on in the stride. As the foot lands it is angled sharply in, so that the dancer seems pigeon-toed. As the leg continues to move back during the support phase, the body rotates so as to align itself with the angle of the supporting foot, with the result that the hips swing sideways, causing the dancer's long grass skirt-tails to fly out in that direction. This pigeon-toed step and swaying skirt are also visible in the gait of women in non-dance contexts. Some degree of hip rotation is present in any normal gait, but the curious angling in of the foot may, I think, be related, once again, to cultural adaptation of the gait pattern to specific circumstances. Umeda women are used to walking through bad terrain with heavy loads, carried in net bags, which they suspend from their foreheads and which rest on their backs. This obliges them to keep the weight on the front foot, which does not strike the ground heel first, but toe first. The reader may care to experiment for him/herself, but my observations lead me to believe that toe-first walking gait requires a pigeon-toed approach, while walking on tiptoes with the feet angled out feels extremely unnatural. If pigeon-toed walking is indeed related to load carrying in net bags, then it would be true to say that the female dance is an exaggerated version of a normal but specifically *female* gait, since men do not carry loads on their backs, nor do they dance in this pigeon-toed way. It is certainly notable that women always dance with net bags hung over their backs, and lean their bodies forwards as if they were carrying loads.

The female dancers at *ida* are not performers in the full sense, but rather active spectators. The ritual is an occasion for self-display by both sexes, and the female dance is intended to be, and indeed is, provocative. The point to note, however, is that female dancing is not a separate sphere of motor behaviour, but the occasion for realizing, to the fullest extent, certain potentialities that are already present in female gait. Skirts sway whenever and wherever women move, only the amount of thigh on view is not usually so extensive. Only during *ida* are the distinctive characteristics of female gait permitted full expression: women become truly themselves only when they are permitted to behave abnormally – but this is true of most ritual behaviour.

MALE DANCE

I do not have any film of the dance of the cassowaries, which occupies the first night of *ida* and which is performed in darkness, so the next graph, Fig. 4.3d, is a reconstruction, making use of the film, which shows roughly similar forms of dancing that take place during the daytime. Four masked dancers appear in Umeda during this night: the two cassowaries, who, I mentioned before, represent the wild, primordial state, and two *molna tamwa* (neophyte fish) played by newly initiated youths wearing the penis gourd (the small one in everyday use, not the weighted one like the cassowaries). The *molna tamwa* are insignificant, ritually, but are interesting because they are so completely contrasted in every respect with the cassowaries (their paint is red, not black, their status junior rather than senior, their masks of coconut fibre, not sago, and so forth). I have discussed the cassowary/*molna tamwa* relation at length elsewhere; they stand for opposite ends of the male life cycle, whose trajectory leads in the direction of asocial autonomy (represented by the cassowary) and a progressive casting off of the social constraints that impinge on youth (supposedly devoted to the ascetic pursuit of hunting) – represented here by the *molna tamwa*, and more fully, later on, by the *ipele* bowmen (for more detail cf. Gell 1975: 243–4).

As one would expect, the dance of the cassowaries and that of the *molna tamwa* are highly contrasted, and in ways that clearly reflect their opposed symbolic roles. The *molna tamwa* dance is, in fact, a highly reduced version of the ceremonial walk: stride length is radically curtailed, and only the springy knee bend marks this out as a dance at all. This suffices, however, to impart that sinuous, up-and-down bobbing that is the hallmark of Umeda male dance and causes the feathers on masks to wave (a feature of ritual display to which Umedas attach great aesthetic significance).

The cassowary dance is a very different affair and represents the most extreme departure from normal gait that the Umeda dance repertoire contains. The objective of the cassowary dance is to impart maximum momentum to the bushy mask (whose arms wave dramatically in the air) and to the dancer's penis gourd, which must strike resoundingly against his abdominal belt all night through. The phallic character of the cassowary is strongly emphasized and indeed his penis is believed to grow to enormous length during the performance. In the graph we can study the leaping movement whereby this effect is achieved. The leg movements approximate to those of a hurdler negotiating a series of closely spaced hurdles (much closer together than they would be at an athletics track of course). A deep knee bend precedes each leap, which is produced by the simultaneous straightening of the upper leg/trunk angle and flexion of the non-support leg, which adds upwards momentum to the leap (Fig. 4.3d). The cassowary graph reflects this in its strong north–south emphasis, which is the hypostatization of the episode of leg straightening (marked S on Fig. 4.3d) visible even in the normal Umeda walk. Here this episode is grossly exaggerated and becomes the basis of the cassowary dance style.

It is interesting to contrast the graphs showing female dancing with the graph for the cassowary dance. Both are very divergent from the norm of standard walking gait, but in contrasted ways. The female dance is a normal walk pulled out lengthways, while the cassowary dance is a normal walk pulled out in the vertical axis, so that it becomes a series of leaps. Different aspects of the common armature of standard gait are used to encode the formal opposition of the sexes in ritual terms. The wildly swinging weighted penis of the dancer only makes this more explicit: but just as women's skirts sway even in normal walking, so the penis gourd of everyday male attire is subject, though to a much lesser degree, to up-and-down motions, especially if the man is running. The seemingly bizarre penis-gourd dance is only a caricature of normality, if a rather remarkable one.

In general, the cassowary dance is designed to convey the idea of uncontrolled, wild, primordial energy: the cassowaries, Lords of Misrule, represent the socially autonomous role of senior men in an acephalous society, a society where to marry, to control female labour and reproductivity, to live sufficient unto oneself, is to achieve all that is open to a man to do. Such men are, like cassowaries, independent of society, while also being those responsible for reproducing it. Around this paradox *ida* has grown. The subsequent dances show the gradual process of incorporating the primordial autonomous man into the restraining fabric of society. With this, there also ensues a gradual transformation of dance style, a curtailing of motor exuberance, whose course we may follow in the ensuing graphs.

Fig. 4.3e shows the more restrained type of fish dancing style, which is most typical, though fish, especially the brightly painted *tetagwana tamwa* played by young men, do occasionally engage in bouts of more vigorous dancing. Fish dancing is always more orderly and controlled than cassowary dancing – the fish maintain single-file formation and go round a regular path, while the cassowaries may gyrate all over the arena in a quite random way.

Structurally, the fish dance is a reduced version of the cassowary dance: the upward spring which gives momentum to the weighted penis gourd is present, but much moderated, and the athletic leaps become smooth and sinuous. There is one nondance parallel to the fish dance that is worth mentioning. During the fish dance the support leg is kept relatively straight, and the dancer gets his spring by extending the ankle joint rather than the knee (this cannot be shown on our graphs). In other words, fish dancers tension the leg much more stiffly than the other dancers, and dance on their toes rather than on the flat of their feet. This is very reminiscent of the typical stride pattern of Umeda bowmen making a rush in battle, which was demonstrated to me while I was in the field (there were no actual battles). Rather than creep up on their enemies, Umeda warriors preferred to look as tall as possible as they ran forwards to fire their arrows at an adversary (they were, moreover, protected by their woven cane body-armour). The springy tiptoe run of the advancing warrior seems to be incorporated into the fish dance style, which is very suitable because the fish dancers represent the male strength of the village, and moreover they carry bows and arrows, which they use to threaten spectators and one another. The fish dance, in Umeda terms, is therefore a warrior style of dancing.

The stiff-legged, vertical emphasis of the fish dance is progressively reduced as the ritual proceeds, though there are fish in the arena until the very conclusion of the ritual, usually between five and ten at any one time. The fish represent the aggressive and phallic aspects of Umeda masculinity, while later figures represent more domesticated and sexually repressed aspects. In dance terms this is reflected in a reduction in spring height, and a more creeping or loping style of movement.

Fig. 4.3f is the graph for a termite dancer. Termites represent domesticity (because of their seemingly inexhaustible reproductivity) and the termite dancers, who appear on the afternoon of the second day of *ida*, are followed around by the children of the village, and are given babies to carry. They herald the successful culmination of the ritual, the taking over, by society, of the processes of natural regeneration. But they are, at the same time, figures of fun, lacking the autonomous, untrammelled freedom of the cassowary, or the erotic and military prestige of the fish. Their dance is a slow, undulating, loping step, designed to show off the glossy cassowary plumes on their headdresses to best advantage. They wear only the ordinary penis gourd, their sexuality having been neutralized by domestic responsibilities.

Looking at the termite graph, we can see the deep knee bend, which is the signature of Umeda dance, but what is lacking, compared to the cassowary, for instance, is the powerful spring at the end of the support phase, or the tense warrior stride of the fish. The whole termite graph is bodily displaced, relative to the fish graph, or indeed the ceremonial walk, towards the southwest corner of our master graph, Fig. 4.2. This is indicative of the fact that during the termite dance the knee remains more sharply bent than heretofore, never becoming straight at all. This gives the impression of invisible fetters restraining the freedom of the dancers, epitomized by the gaggle of yelling children by whom they are followed. Another detail of the termite dance reinforces this impression. This is the feature of 'exaggerated follow-through', marked E in Fig. 4.3f; it takes the form of a little backwards kick at the beginning of each return swing, as if the termite was scraping the dust with his feet, like a restive horse. This exaggerated follow-through is partly necessitated by the sharp bending of the knee at that point in the stride by the other (supporting) leg, but seems to be emphasized for its own sake. It seems to express the idea of excess energy, which the rather cramped termite dance style cannot quite accommodate. As we will see it is even more marked in the *kwod* dance, which I will discuss next.

In general, then, the termite dance, although still reflecting the generic up-and-down bobbing of Umeda male ceremonial display, does so in a muted and restricted form. Structurally this is achieved by a dimensional reduction of the general pattern of male dancing combined with a transposition of the whole cycle into a different and darker key (the key of bent knees, so to speak). But the exaggerated follow-through still refers obliquely to the exuberant style of the cassowary, just as, in a rather similar way, the termite mask reflects the cassowary mask (cf. Fig. 4.1).

Fig. 4.3g shows the dance style of a *kwod* (ogress). It will be seen that this dance resembles the termite dance but is an extreme form of it. The southwest transposition is carried even further, and the exaggerated follow-through is even more marked. This is interesting because the dance analysis here allows me to go a little further in my overall analysis of this figure than I was able to do in my original account, where, by ignoring the dance, I failed to see the very close relation between the *kwod* and the termite, and so failed to pick up some important clues.

Kwod is a kinship term that means 'father's sister/father's sister's husband' – that is, it is an *intersexual* term for people who, in ego's kinship universe, are interstitial between (patri-) kin and (matri-) allies. *Kwod* also is the name of a mythological ogress with a *vagina dentata*, that is, who has both female and male (aggressive) characteristics. In the ritual, the figure of the *kwod* represents a strongly negative idea, the confusion of male and female traits. His/her red paint is associated with female sexuality (or else the half-formed sexuality of children and neophytes) and the dancer's penis is bound (sexuality negated); at the same time the *kwod* carries a spray of leaves with which, like a prudish female, he attempts to cover the genital area (men are often and shamelessly naked). He/she carries a bow, and creeps about on the periphery of the arena, threatening people until chased away.

The termites show domesticity and reproductivity taking its normal course, with a comic but inevitable reduction in phallic exuberance consequent upon reproductivity (copulation and nurture of children being regarded as mutually exclusive, complementary activities in the Umeda scheme of things); the *kwod* is a sardonic representation of this reduction in phallicism carried to its logical conclusion. Fig. 4.4 shows the triple relation cassowary/termite/*kwod* as a sequence of reductions: just as the *kwod* dance is a reduction of the termite dance, so also is the *kwod* mask, the *kwod* genital ornament, and the *kwod* body paint. I have also included in this figure a drawing of another intersexual ogre, *sogwa naina*, who obviously forms a pair with *kwod*. Both these (admittedly minor) ritual figures represent witty variations on the basic theme of the ritual, hinting at the ultimate identity of the role of the separate sexes in relation to common reproductive tasks. But this subversive neutralization of sexual stereotypes is introduced into the ritual only to be crushingly rejected, as the intersexual ogres/ogresses are chased off. The creeping *kwod* is a figure from a collective nightmare.

To return to Fig. 4.3, our final graph represents the dance of the *ipele* bowmen. This dance is relatively restrained, but not furtive or ignoble, like the *kwod*. It is true that the *ipele* are sexually repressed (bound penis) but here elements of masculinity are again dominant,

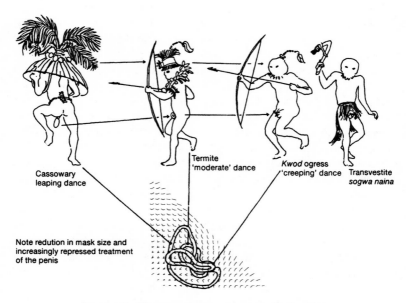

Cassowary
leaping dance

Termite
'moderate' dance

Kwod ogress
'creeping' dance

Transvestite
sogwa naina

Note redution in mask size and
increasingly repressed treatment
of the penis

Figure 4.4   Ida step cycles as a sequence of reductions

154

though under strict control. The exaggerated follow-through has disappeared, and instead we find an emphasis not on the back foot, but on the front foot, which is sharply extended forwards at the beginning of each stride (marked *F* on the graph). This trait bears a certain similarity to the dance of the fish at the analogous point in the step cycle, and in general the *ipele* dance can be seen as a highly compressed version of the fish dance, though without the same upward spring.

The *ipele* are hunters, and in their dance one recognizes more than a hint of ordinary hunting technique. They advance forwards stealthily, bent forwards, keeping a low profile, avoiding unnecessary movement. This gait is like a hunter stalking game in the forest. Most notable is the absence of display elements in the *ipele* dance; where the fish or even the termites seem to be self-consciously showing themselves off before the female audience, the brief *ipele* dance is unwitnessed by women (who turn their backs and hide their eyes) and has more the character of an instrumental act than an expressive display. Here, at the culmination of the ritual, it ceases to be a pretence; the imaginary frame of reference of the ritual drama and the real world in which the actors' vital interests are embedded suddenly fuse and intermingle, metaphors and reality become one. The very simplicity and understatement of the *ipele* dance contribute powerfully to this categorical sleight of hand whereby the ritual achieves its profoundest effects; the dance that is no longer a dance concludes the ritual that is perhaps no longer a ritual.

CONCLUSION

I would like to return briefly, in these concluding remarks, to the question of the relation between dance and nondance. In the preceding sections I have tried to show two things: (*a*) that all Umeda dances can be seen as variants on a common pattern; and (*b*) that the significant differences that distinguish them can often be seen as stemming from the incorporation into the dance of elements drawn from nondance motor programmes. My overall argument would be, therefore, that Umeda dance has two sides to it, style, which is the aspect of the dance that separates it from the nondance world, and meaning, which is the aspect of the dance that refers back to the nondance world. What I want to focus on now is the problem of style. It would be easy to suppose, but I think misleading, that each culture has a set of motor performances that, in and of themselves, communicate the message 'this is dance'. It would be difficult to imagine the elaborate features of Polynesian dance (Kaeppler 1972) or the stereotyped calisthenics of Melpa dance being produced outside the dance context; but none the less they all might be, and moreover it would be difficult to specify anything about these movements that made them purely and totally dances, as opposed to movements of some other kind. What gives dance movements style – and hence what separates them from nondance movements – is not their individual form, as movements, but the relationship in which they stand to (*a*) related nondance motor programmes, and (*b*) other dance movements in the same system. It is here, I think, that the idea I have developed in the preceding analysis that is, that dances can be viewed as members of a transformation set can be particularly useful. If dance style is essentially a product of the deformation or modulation of embedded motor patterns, then it can only be described by setting the dance movement against the template of the underlying nondance schema. The situation, in fact, is not very different in poetry. The meaning of a poem is its paraphrase (what it says about the world, just as the meaning of a dance is what the dancer would be doing in the world were he not dancing), but what dignifies a poem is the difference between the paraphrase and the poem itself, and it is with this that the translator will have problems. With dance – at least with rather transparent kinds of dance, such as that seen at *ida* – we can perhaps make better progress, because the variables are simpler and fewer in number, and can be analysed in physical, concrete terms. Let me recapitulate the essence of what I have been saying by making use of a classic method that dates from the archaeology of structuralism, D'Arcy Thompson's method of coordinates. Fig. 4.5 shows the normal Umeda step cycle inscribed in a rectangular grid, like the rectangular grid D'Arcy Thompson used in his well-known comparison of the skulls of man, chimpanzee, and baboon (Thompson 1969: 318). Next to this I have drawn the deformed grids that correspond to generalized versions of (*a*) the cassowary dance, (*b*) the fish dance. The transformational relation that exists between the coordinates in each case are stylistic relations in the sense defined above, whereas the mappings of the actual movements on to the master graph of Fig. 4.2 and thence onto nondance motor programmes correspond to meaning relations. Dance is thus finally interpretable as a stylized deformation of nondance mobility, just as poetry is a deformation or modulation of language, a deviation from the norm of expression that enhances expressiveness.

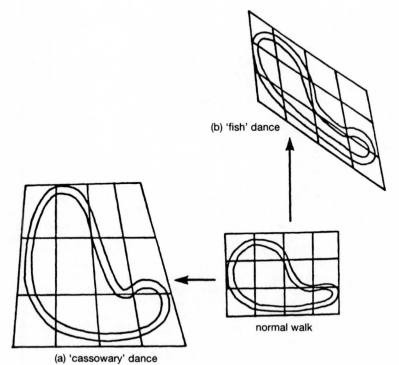

(b) 'fish' dance

normal walk

(a) 'cassowary' dance

Figure 4.5 *Ida* step cycles as transformations of normal walking (after Thompson 1969)

We understand dances, as communicative displays, by working back from the surface manifestation of motor behaviour to the underlying motor schema: that is to say, we read a dance by undoing the process of stylization that makes a dance a dance; in effect, by reversing the transformations. But what we value in the dance is not the surface motor behaviour, nor the underlying schema that gives it its meaning, but the gap that separates the two.

NOTE

1. My title and much else in my approach to the anthropological study of nonverbal communication is a borrowing from Anthony Forge (cf. Forge 1973). The group referred to herein as Umeda also includes the population of the neighbouring village of Punda, where, in fact, the *ida* ritual was filmed. The style of dancing I will describe is also found elsewhere in the Amanat-Imonda region of the West Sepik Province, and doubtless

also across the border in adjoining parts of West Irian. Its distribution is coterminous with the distribution of the kind of globular penis gourd characteristic of this cultural region (cf. Gell 1971), which plays such an important part in the dance.

2. A video version of the film 'The Red Bowman' is being made available for sale (internationally) and/or loan (within the UK) through application to the Royal Anthropological Institute's Film Officer. The Institute's address is: RAI, 50 Fitzroy Street, London W1P 5HS UK.

REFERENCES

Bateson, G. (1972) *Steps to an Ecology of Mind* (New York: Chandler).

Carlsöö, S. (1972) *How Man Moves: Kinesiological Studies and Methods*, trans. B. Michael (London: Heineman).

Forge, A. (1973) 'Style and meaning in Sepik art', in A. Forge, (ed.) *Primitive Art and Society* (London: Oxford University Press).

Gell, A. (1971) 'Penis sheathing and ritual status in a West Sepik village', *Man*, n. s. 6: 165–81.

Gell, A. (1975) *Metamorphosis of the Cassowaries* (London: Athlone).

Hoenkamp, E. (1978) 'Perceptual cues that determine the labeling of human gait', *Journal of Human Movement Studies*, 4: 59–69.

Kaeppler, A.L. (1972) 'Method and theory in analysing dance structure with an analysis of Tongan dance', *Ethnomusicology*, 16: 173–217.

Leach, E.R. (1961) *Rethinking Anthropology* (London: Athlone).

Owen, C. (1977) *The Red Bowman*, Film, Abridged 1979, (Boroko: Institute of Papua New Guinea).

Thompson, D.A.W. (1969) *On Growth and Form*, (Cambridge: Cambridge University Press).

CHAPTER 5

THE TECHNOLOGY OF ENCHANTMENT AND THE ENCHANTMENT OF TECHNOLOGY

INTRODUCTION: METHODOLOGICAL PHILISTINISM

The complaint is commonly heard that art is a neglected topic in present-day social anthropology, especially in Britain. The marginalization of studies of primitive art, by contrast to the immense volume of studies of politics, ritual, exchange, and so forth, is too obvious a phenomenon to miss, especially if one draws a contrast with the situation prevailing before the advent of Malinowski and Radcliffe-Brown. But why should this be so? I believe that it is more than a matter of changing fashions in the matter of selecting topics for study; as if, by some collective whim, anthropologists had decided to devote more time to cross-cousin marriage and less to mats, pots and carvings. On the contrary, the neglect of art in modern social anthropology is necessary and intentional, arising from the fact that social anthropology is essentially, constitutionally, anti-art. This must seem a shocking assertion: how can anthropology, by universal consent a Good Thing, be opposed to art, also universally considered an equally Good Thing, even a Better Thing? But I am afraid that this is really so, because these two Good Things are Good according to fundamentally different and conflicting criteria.

When I say that social anthropology is anti-art, I do not mean, of course, that anthropological wisdom favours knocking down the National Gallery and turning the site into a car park. What I mean is only that the attitude of the art-loving public towards the contents of the National Gallery, the Museum of Mankind, and so on (aesthetic awe bordering on the religious) is an unredeemably ethnocentric attitude, however laudable in all other respects.

Our value-system dictates that, unless we are philistines, we should attribute value to a culturally recognized category of art objects.

This attitude of aestheticism is culture-bound even though the objects in question derive from many different cultures, as when we pass effortlessly from the contemplation of a Tahitian sculpture to one by Brancusi, and back again. But this willingness to place ourselves under the spell of all manner of works of art, though it contributes very much to the richness of our cultural experience, is paradoxically the major stumbling-block in the path of the anthropology of art, the ultimate aim of which must be the dissolution of art, in the same way that the dissolution of religion, politics, economics, kinship, and all other forms under which human experience is presented to the socialized mind, must be the ultimate aim of anthropology in general.

Perhaps I can clarify to some degree the consequences of the attitude of universal aestheticism for the study of primitive[1] art by drawing a series of analogies between the anthropological study of art and the anthropological study of religion. With the rise of structural functionalism, art largely disappeared from the anthropological bill of fare in this country, but the same thing did not happen to the study of ritual and religious belief. Why did things happen this way? The answer appears to me to lie in an essential difference between the attitudes towards religion characteristic of the intelligentsia of the period, and their attitudes towards art.

It seems to me incontrovertible that the anthropological theory of religion depends on what has been called by Peter Berger 'methodological atheism' (Berger 1967: 107). This is the methodological principle that, whatever the analyst's own religious convictions, or lack of them, theistic and mystical beliefs are subjected to sociological scrutiny on the assumption that they are not literally true. Only once this assumption is made do the intellectual manoeuvres characteristic of anthropological analyses of religious systems become possible, that is, the demonstration of linkages between religious ideas and the structure of corporate groups, social hierarchies, and so on. Religion becomes an emergent property of the relations between the various elements in the social system, derivable, not from the condition that genuine religious truths exist, but solely from the condition that societies exist.

The consequences of the possibility that there are genuine religious truths lie outside the frame of reference of the sociology of religion. These consequences – philosophical, moral, political, and so on – are the province of the much longer-established intellectual discipline of theology, whose relative decline in the modern era derives from exactly the same changes in the intellectual climate as have produced the current efflorescence of sociology generally and of the sociology of religion in particular.

It is widely agreed that ethics and aesthetics belong in the same category. I would suggest that the study of aesthetics is to the domain of art as the study of theology is to the domain of religion. That is to say, aesthetics is a branch of moral discourse which depends on the acceptance of the initial articles of faith: that in the aesthetically valued object there resides the principle of the True and the Good, and that the study of aesthetically valued objects constitutes a path toward transcendence. In so far as such modern souls possess a religion, that religion is the religion of art, the religion whose shrines consist of theatres, libraries and art galleries, whose priests and bishops are painters and poets, whose theologians are critics, and whose dogma is the dogma of universal aestheticism.

Unless I am very much mistaken, I am writing for a readership which is composed in the main of devotees of the art cult, and, moveover, for one which shares an assumption (by no means an incorrect one) that I too belong to the faith, just as, if we were a religious congregation and I were delivering a sermon, you would assume that I was no atheist.

If I were about to discuss some exotic religious belief-system, from the standpoint of methodological atheism, that would present no problem even to non-atheists, simply because nobody expects a sociologist of religion to adopt the premises of the religion he discusses; indeed, he is obliged not to do so. But the equivalent attitude to the one we take towards religious beliefs in sociological discourse is much harder to attain in the context of discussions of aesthetic values. The equivalent of methodological atheism in the religious domain would, in the domain of art, be *methodological philistinism*, and that is a bitter pill very few would be willing to swallow. Methodological philistinism consists of taking an attitude of resolute indifference towards the aesthetic value of works of art – the aesthetic value that they have, either indigenously, or from the standpoint of universal aestheticism. Because to admit this kind of value is equivalent to admitting, so to speak, that religion is true, and just as this admission makes the sociology of religion impossible, the introduction of aesthetics (the theology of art) into the sociology or anthropology of art immediately turns the enterprise into something else. But we are most unwilling to make a break with aestheticism – much more so than we are to make a break with theology – simply because, as I have been suggesting, we have sacralized art: art is really our religion.

We cannot enter this domain, and make it fully our own, without experiencing a profound dissonance, which stems from the fact that our method, were it to be applied to art with the degree of rigour and objectivity which we are perfectly prepared to contemplate when it comes to religion and politics, obliges us to deal with the phenomena of art in a philistine spirit contrary to our most cherished sentiments. I continue to believe, none the less, that the first step which has to be taken in devising an anthropology of art is to make a complete break with aesthetics. Just as the anthropology of religion commences with the explicit or implicit denial of the claims religions make on believers, so the anthropology of art has to begin with a denial of the claims which objects of art make on the people who live under their spell, and also on ourselves, in so far as we are all self-confessed devotees of the Art Cult.

But because I favour a break with the aesthetic preoccupations of much of the existing anthropology of art, I do not think that methodological philistinism is adequately represented by the other possible approaches: for instance, the sociologism of Bourdieu (e.g. 1968), which never actually looks at the art object itself, as a concrete product of human ingenuity, but only at its power to mark social distinctions, or the iconographic approach (e.g. Panofsky 1962) which treats art as a species of writing, and which fails, equally, to take into consideration the presented object, rather than the represented symbolic meanings. I do not deny for an instant the discoveries of which these alternative approaches are capable; what I deny is only that they constitute the sought-after alternative to the aesthetic approach to the art object. We have, somehow, to retain the capacity of the aesthetic approach to illuminate the specific objective characteristics of the art object as an object, rather than as a vehicle for extraneous social and symbolic messages, without succumbing to the fascination which all well-made art objects exert on the mind attuned to their aesthetic properties.

ART AS A TECHNICAL SYSTEM

In this essay, I propose that the anthropology of art can do this by considering art as a component of technology. We recognize works of art, as a category, because they are the outcome of technical process, the sorts of technical process in which artists are skilled. A major deficiency of the aesthetic approach is that art objects are not the only aesthetically valued objects around: there are beautiful horses, beautiful people, beautiful sunsets, and so on; but art objects are the only objects around which are *beautifully made*, or *made beautiful*. There seems every justification, therefore, for considering art objects initially as those objects which demonstrate a certain technically achieved level of excellence, 'excellence' being a function, not of their characteristics simply as objects, but of their character-istics as *made* objects, as products of techniques.

I consider the various arts – painting, sculpture, music, poetry, fiction, and so on – as components of a vast and often unrecognized technical system, essential to the reproduction of human societies, which I will be calling the technology of enchantment.

In speaking of 'enchantment' I am making use of a cover-term to express the general premiss that human societies depend on the acquiescence of duly socialized individuals in a network of inten-tionalities whereby, although each individual pursues (what each individual takes to be) his or her own self-interest, they all contrive in the final analysis to serve necessities which cannot be comprehended at the level of the individual human being, but only at the level of collectivities and their dynamics. As a first approximation, we can suppose that the art-system contributes to securing the acquiescence of individuals in the network of intentionalities in which they are enmeshed. This view of art, that it is propaganda on behalf of the status quo, is the one taken by Maurice Bloch in his 'Symbols, song, dance, and features of articulation' (1974). In calling art the technol-ogy of enchantment I am first of all singling out this point of view, which, however one refines it, remains an essential component of an anthropological theory of art from the standpoint of method-ological philistinism. However, the theoretical insight that art pro-vides one of the technical means whereby individuals are persuaded of the necessity and desirability of the social order which encompasses them brings us no closer to the art object as such. As a technical system, art is orientated towards the production of the social consequences which ensue from the production of these objects. The power of art objects stems from the technical processes they objectively embody: the *technology of enchantment* is founded on the *enchantment of technology*. The enchantment of technology is the power that technical processes have of casting a spell over us so that we see the real world in an enchanted form. Art, as a separate kind of technical activity, only carries further, through a kind of involution, the enchantment which is immanent in all kinds of technical activity. The aim of my essay is to elucidate this admittedly rather cryptic statement.

PSYCHOLOGICAL WARFARE AND MAGICAL EFFICACY

Let me begin, however, by saying a little more about art as the technology of enchantment, rather than art as the enchantment of technology. There is an obvious prima-facie case for regarding a great deal of the art of the world as a means of thought-control. Sometimes art objects are explicitly intended to function as weapons in psychological warfare: as in the case of the canoe prow-board from the Trobriand Islands (Fig. 5.1) – surely a prototypical example of primitive art from the prototypical anthropological stamping-ground. The intention behind the placing of these prow-boards on Kula[2] canoes is to cause the overseas Kula partners of the Trobrianders, watching the arrival of the Kula flotilla from the shore, to take leave of their senses and offer more valuable shells or necklaces to

Figure 5.1 Trobriand canoe-prow, Kitava Island, Milne Bay Province, Papua New Guinea; photographer: Shirley F. Campbell, May 1977. The prow assembly is adorned with Kula shell valuables (see Campbell 1984).

the members of the expedition than they would otherwise be inclined to do. The boards are supposed to dazzle the beholder and weaken his grip on himself. And they really are very dazzling, especially if one considers them against the background of the visual surroundings to which the average Melanesian is accustomed, which are much more uniform and drab than our own. But if the demoralization of an opponent in a contest of will-power is really the intention behind the canoe-board, one is entitled to ask how the trick is supposed to work. Why should the sight of certain colours and shapes exercise a demoralizing effect on anybody?

The first place one might seek an answer to such a question is in the domain of ethology, that is, in innate, species-wide dispositions to respond to particular perceptual stimuli in predetermined ways. Moreover, were one to show such a board to an ethologist, they would, without a doubt, mutter 'eye-spots!' and immediately start pulling out photographs of butterflies' wings, likewise marked with bold, symmetrical circles, and designed to have much the same effect on predatory birds as the boards are supposed to have on the Trobrianders' Kula partners, that is, to put them off their stroke at a critical moment. I think there is every reason to believe that human beings are innately sensitive to eye-spot patterns, as they are to bold tonal contrasts and bright colours, especially red, all of them features of the canoe-board design. These sensitivities can be demonstrated experimentally in the infant, and in the behavioural repertoire of apes and other mammals.

But one does not have to accept the idea of deep-rooted phylogenetic sensitivity to eye-spot patterns and the like to find merit in the idea that the Trobriand canoe-board is a technically appropriate pattern for its intended purpose of dazzling and upsetting the spectator. The same conclusion can follow from an analysis of the *Gestalt* properties of the canoe-board design. If one makes the experiment of attempting to fixate the pattern for a few moments by staring at it, one begins to experience peculiar optical sensations due to the intrinsic instability of the design with its opposed volutes, both of which tend to lead the eye off in opposite directions.

In the canons of primitive art there are innumerable instances of designs which can be interpreted as exploiting the characteristic biases of human visual perception so as to ensnare us into unwitting reactions, some of which might be behaviourally significant. Should we, therefore, take the view that the significance of art, as a component of the technology of enchantment, derives from the power of certain stimulus arrays to disturb normal cognitive functioning? I recall that Ripley's *Believe It Or Not* (at one time my favourite book) printed a design which was claimed to hypnotize sheep: should this be considered the archetypal work of art? Does art exercise its influence via a species of hypnosis? I think not. Not because these disturbances are not real psychological phenomena; they are, as I have said, easily demonstrable experimentally. But there is no empirical support for the idea that canoe-boards, or similar kinds of art objects, actually achieve their effects by producing visual or cognitive disturbances. The canoe-board does not interfere seriously, if at all, with the intended victim's perceptual processes, but achieves its purpose in a much more roundabout way.

The canoe-board is a potent psychological weapon, but not as a direct consequence of the visual effects it produces. Its efficacy is to be attributed to the fact that these disturbances, mild in themselves, are interpreted as evidence of the magical power emanating from the board. It is this magical power which may deprive the spectator of his reason. If, in fact, he behaves with unexpected generosity, it is interpreted as having done so. Without the associated magical ideas, the dazzlingness of the board is neither here nor there. It is the fact that an impressive canoe-board is a physical token of magical prowess on the part of the owner of the canoe which is important, as is the fact that he has access to the services of a carver whose artistic prowess is also the result of his access to superior carving magic.

THE HALO-EFFECT OF TECHNICAL 'DIFFICULTY'

And this leads on to the main point that I want to make. It seems to me that the efficacy of art objects as components of the technology of enchantment – a role which is particularly clearly displayed in the case of the Kula canoe – is itself the result of the enchantment of technology, the fact that technical processes, such as carving canoe-boards, are construed magically so that, by enchanting us, they make the products of these technical processes seem enchanted vessels of magical power. That is to say, the canoe-board is not dazzling as a physical object, but as a display of artistry explicable only in magical terms, something which has been produced by magical means. It is the way an art object is construed as having come into the world which is the source of the power such objects have over us – their becoming rather than their being.

Let me turn to another example of an art object which may make this point clearer. When I was about eleven, I was taken to visit Salisbury Cathedral. The building itself made no great impression on me, and I do not remember it at all. What I do remember, though, very vividly, is a display which the cathedral authorities had placed in some dingy side-chapel, which consisted of a remarkable model of Salisbury Cathedral, about two feet high and apparently complete in every detail, made entirely out of matchsticks glued together; certainly a virtuoso example of the matchstick modeller's art, if no great masterpiece according to the criteria of the salon, and calculated to strike a profound chord in the heart of any eleven-year-old. Matchsticks and glue are very important constituents of the world of every self-respecting boy of that age, and the idea of assembling these materials into such an impressive construction provoked feelings of the deepest awe. Most willingly I deposited my penny into the collecting-box which the authorities had, with a true appreciation of the real function of works of art, placed in front of the model, in aid of the Fabric Fund.

Wholly indifferent as I then was to the problems of cathedral upkeep, I could not but pay tribute to so much painstaking dexterity in objectified form. At one level, I had perfect insight into the technical problems faced by the genius who had made the model, having myself often handled matches and glue, separately and various combinations, while remaining utterly at a loss to imagine the degree of manipulative skill and sheer patience needed to complete the final work. From a small boy's point of view this was the ultimate work of art, much more entrancing in fact than the cathedral itself, and so too, I suspect, for a significant proportion of the adult visitors as well.

Here the technology of enchantment and the enchantment of technology come together. The matchstick model, functioning essentially as an advertisement, is part of a technology of enchantment, but it achieves its effect via the enchantment cast by its technical means, the manner of its coming into being, or, rather, the idea which one forms of its coming into being, since making a matchstick model of Salisbury Cathedral may not be as difficult, or as easy, as one imagines.

Simmel, in his treatise on the *Philosophy of Money* (1979: 62 ff.), advances a concept of value which can help us to form a more general idea of the kind of hold which art objects have over us. Roughly, Simmel suggests that the value of an object is in proportion to the difficulty which we think we will encounter in obtaining that particular thing rather than something else. We do not want what we do not think we will ever get under any set of circumstances deemed realizable. Simmel (ibid.: 66) goes on to say:

> We desire objects only if they are not immediately given to us for our use and enjoyment, that is, to the extent to which they resist our desire. The content of our desire becomes an object as soon as it is opposed to us, not only in the sense of being impervious to us, but also in terms of its distance as something not yet enjoyed, the subject aspect of this condition being desire. As Kant has said: the possibility of experience is the possibility of objects of experience – because to have experiences means that our consciousness creates objects from sense-impressions. In the same way, the possibility of desire is the possibility of objects of desire. The object thus formed, which is characterised by its separation from the subject, who at the same time establishes it and seeks to overcome it by his desire, is for us a value.

He goes on to argue that exchange is the primary means employed in order to overcome the resistance offered by desired objects, which makes them desirable, and that money is the pure form of the means of engaging in exchange and realizing desire.

I am not here concerned with Simmel's ideas about exchange value and money; what I want to focus on is the idea that valued objects present themselves to us surrounded by a kind of halo-effect of resistance, and that it is this resistance to us which is the source of their value. Simmel's theory, as it stands, implies that it is difficulty of access to an object which makes it valuable, an argument which obviously applies, for example, to Kula valuables. But if we suppose that the value which we attribute to works of art, the bewitching effect they have on us, is a function, at least to some extent, of their characteristics as objects, not just of the difficulties we may expect to encounter in obtaining them, then the argument cannot be accepted in unmodified form. For instance, if we take up once again the instance of the matchstick model of Salisbury Cathedral, we may observe that the spell cast over me by this object was independent of any wish on my part to gain possession of it as personal property. In that sense, I did not value or desire it, since the possibility of possessing could not arise: no more am I conscious today of any wish to remove from the walls and carry away the pictures in the National Gallery. Of course, we do desire works of art, the ones in our price bracket, as personal property, and works of art have enormous significance as items of exchange. But I think that the peculiar power of works of art does not reside in the objects *as such*, and it is the objects as such which are bought and sold. Their power resides in the *symbolic* processes they provoke in the beholder, and these have *sui generis* characteristics which are independent of the objects themselves and the fact that they are owned and exchanged. The value of a work of art, as Simmel suggests, is a function of the way in which it resists us, but this 'resistance' occurs on two planes. If I am looking at an old master painting, which, I happen to know, has a saleroom value of two million pounds, then that certainly colours my reaction to it, and makes it more impressive than would be the case if I knew that it was an inauthentic reproduction or forgery of much lesser value. But the sheer incommensurability between my purchasing power and the purchase price of an authentic old master means that I cannot regard such works as significant exchange items: they belong to a sphere of exchange from which I am excluded. But none the less such paintings are objects of desire – the desire to possess them in a certain sense, but not actually to own them. The resistance which they offer, and which creates and sustains this desire, is to being possessed in an intellectual rather than a material sense, the difficulty I have in mentally encompassing their coming-into-being as objects in the world accessible to me by a technical process which, since it transcends my understanding, I am forced to construe as magical.

THE ARTIST AS OCCULT TECHNICIAN

Let us consider, as a step up from the matchstick model of Salisbury Cathedral, J. F. Peto's *Old Time Letter Rack* (Fig. 5.2), sometimes known as *Old Scraps*, the notoriously popular *trompe-l'oeil* painting, complete with artfully rendered drawing-pins and faded criss-cross ribbons, letter with still-legible addressed envelopes to which lifelike postage stamps adhere, newspaper cuttings, books, a quill, a piece of string, and so on. This picture is usually discussed in the context of denunciations of the excesses of illusionism in nineteenth-century painting; but of course it is as beloved now as it ever was, and has actually gained prestige, not lost it, with the advent of photography, for it is now possible to see just how photographically real it is, and all the more remarkable for that. If it was, in fact, a colour photograph of a letter rack, nobody would give tuppence for it. But just because it is a painting, one which looks as real as a photograph, it is

Figure 5.2 John F. Peto, *Old Time Letter Rack*, 1894; oil on canvas; 30 × 25 in. (76.2 × 63.5 cm); Manoogian Collection.

a famous work, which, if popular votes counted in assigning value to paintings, would be worth a warehouse full of Picassos and Matisses.

The popular esteem in which this painting is held derives, not from its aesthetic merit, if any, since nobody would give what it represents (that is, a letter rack) a second glance. The painting's power to fascinate stems entirely from the fact that people have great difficulty in working out how coloured pigments (substances with which everybody is broadly familiar) can be applied to a surface so as to become an apparently different set of substances, namely, the ones which enter into the composition of letters, ribbons, drawing-pins, stamps, bits of string, and so on. The magic exerted over the beholder by this picture is a reflection of the magic which is exerted inside the picture, the technical miracle which achieves the transubstantiation of oily pigments into cloth, metal, paper and feather. This technical miracle must be distinguished from a merely mysterious process: it is miraculous because it is achieved both by human agency but at the same time by an agency which transcends the normal sense of self-possession of the spectator.

Thus, the letter rack picture would not have the prestige it does have if it were a photograph, visually identical in colour and texture, could that be managed. Its prestige depends on the fact that it is a painting; and, in general, photography never achieves the popular prestige that painting has in societies which have routinely adopted photography as a technique for producing images. This is because the technical processes involved in photography are articulated to our notion of human agency in a way which is quite distinct from that in which we conceptualize the technical processes of painting, carving, and so on. The alchemy involved in photography (in which packets of film are inserted into cameras, buttons are pressed, and pictures of Aunt Edna emerge in due course) are regarded as uncanny, but as uncanny processes of a natural rather than a human order, like the metamorphosis of caterpillars into butterflies. The photographer, a lowly button-presser, has no prestige, or not until the nature of his photographs is such as to make one start to have difficulties conceptualizing the processes which made them achievable with the familiar apparatus of photography.

In societies which are not over-familiar with the camera as a technical means, the situation is, of course, quite different. As many anthropologists who have worked under such conditions will have occasion to know, the ability to take photographs is often taken to be a special, occult faculty of the photographer, which extends to having power over the souls of the photographed, via the resulting pictures. We think this is a naïve attitude, when it comes to photography, but the same attitude is persistent, and acceptable, when it is expressed in the context of painting or drawing. The ability to capture someone's likeness is an occult power of the portraitist in paint or bronze, and when we wish to install an icon which will stand for a person – for example, a retiring director of the London School of Economics – we insist on a painted portrait, because only in this form will the captured essence of the no-longer-present Professor Dahrendorf continue to exercise a benign influence over the collectivity which wishes to eternalize him and, in so doing, derive continuing benefit from his *mana*.

Let me summarize my point about Peto's *Old Scraps* and its paradoxical prestige. The population at large both admire this picture and think that it emanates a kind of moral virtue, in the sense that it epitomizes what painters 'ought' to be able to do (that is, produce exact representations, or rather, occult transubstantiations of artists' materials into other things). It is thus a symbol of general moral significance, connoting, among other things, the fulfilment of the painter's calling in the Protestant-ethic sense, and inspiring people at large to fulfil their callings equally well. It stands for true artistry as a power both in the world and beyond it, and it promotes the true artist in a symbolic role as occult technician. Joined to this popular stereotype of the true artist is the negative stereotype of the false ('modern') artist of cartoon humour, who is supposed not to know how to draw, whose messy canvases are no better than the work of a child, and whose lax morality is proverbial.

Two objections can be made to the suggestion that the value and moral significance of works of art are functions of their technical excellence, or, more generally, to the importance of the fact that the spectator looks at them and thinks, 'For the life of me, I couldn't do that, not in a million years.' The first objection would be that *Old Scraps*, whatever its prestige among *hoi polloi*, cuts no ice with the critics, or with art-cultists generally. The second objection which might be raised is that, as an example of illusionism in art, the letter rack represents not only a particular artistic tradition (our own) but also only a brief interlude in that tradition, and hence can have little general significance. In particular, it cannot provide us with any insight into primitive art, since primitive art is strikingly devoid of illusionistic trickery.

The point I wish to establish is that the attitude of the spectator towards a work of art is fundamentally conditioned by his notion of the technical processes which gave rise to it, and the fact that it was created by the agency of another person, the artist. The moral significance of the work of art arises from the mismatch between the spectator's internal awareness of his own powers as an agent and the conception he forms of the powers possessed by the artist. In reconstructing the processes which brought the work of art into existence, he is obliged to posit a creative agency which transcends his own and, hovering in the background, the power of the collectivity on whose behalf the artist exercised his technical mastery.

The work of art is inherently social in a way in which the merely beautiful or mysterious object is not: it is a physical entity which mediates between two beings, and therefore creates a social relation between them, which in turn provides a channel for further social relations and influences. This is so when, for instance, the court sculptor, by means of his magical power over marble, provides a physical analogue for the less easily realized power wielded by the king, and thereby enhances the king's authority. What Bernini can do to marble (and one does not know quite what or how) Louis XIV can do to you (by means which are equally outside your mental grasp). The man who controls such a power as is embodied in the technical mastery of Bernini's bust of Louis XIV is powerful indeed. Sometimes the actual artist or craftsman is quite effaced in the process, and moral authority which works of art generate accrues entirely to the individual or institution responsible for commissioning the work, as with the anonymous sculptors and stained-glass artists who contributed to the glorification of the medieval church. Sometimes the artists are actually regarded with particular disdain by the power elite, and have to live separate and secluded lives, in order to provide ideological camouflage for the fact that theirs is the technical mastery which mediates the relation between the rulers and the ruled.

I maintain, therefore, that technical virtuosity is intrinsic to the efficacy of works of art in their social context, and tends always towards the creation of asymmetries in the relations between people by placing them in an essentially asymmetrical relation to things. But this technical virtuosity needs to be more carefully specified; it is by no means identical with the simple power to represent real objects illusionistically; this is a form of virtuosity which belongs, almost exclusively, to our art tradition (though its role in securing the prestige of old masters, such as Rembrandt, should not be underestimated). An example of virtuosity in non-illusionistic modern western art is afforded by Picasso's well-known *Baboon and Young* (Fig. 5.3), in which an ape's face is created by taking a direct cast from the body-shell of a child's toy car. One would not be much impressed by the toy car itself, nor by the verisimilitude of Picasso's ape just as a model of an ape, unless one were able to recognize the technical procedure Picasso used to make it, that is, commandeering one of his children's toys. But the witty transubstantiation of toy car into ape's face is not a fundamentally different operation from the transubstantiation of artists' materials into the components of a letter rack, which is considered quite boring because that is what artists's materials are for, generically. No matter what avant-garde school of art one considers, it is always the case that materials, and the ideas associated with those materials, are taken up and transformed into something else, even if it is only, as in the case of

Figure 5.3 Pablo Picasso, *Baboon and Young*, 1950, Vallauris; bronze (cast 1955); $21\frac{1}{8} \times 14 \times 7\frac{3}{8}$ in. (53.6 × 35.7 × 18.8 cm); collection, The Museum of Modern Art, New York (Mrs Simon Guggenheim Fund). © Succession Picasso/DACS 1999

Duchamp's notorious urinal, by putting them in an art exhibition and providing them with a title (*Fountain*) and an author ('R. Mutt', alias M. Duchamp, 1917). Amikam Toren, one of the most ingenious contemporary artists, takes objects like chairs and teapots, grinds them up, and uses the resulting substances to create images of chairs and teapots. This is a less radical procedure than Duchamp's, which can be used effectively only once, but it is an equally apt means of directing our attention to the essential alchemy of art, which is to make what is not out of what is, and to make what is out of what is not.

THE FUNDAMENTAL SCHEME TRANSFER BETWEEN ART PRODUCTION AND SOCIAL PROCESS

But let us focus our attention on art production in societies without traditions and institutions of 'fine art' of the kind which nurtured Picasso and Duchamp. In such societies art arises particularly in two domains. The first of these is ritual, especially political ritual. Art objects are produced in order to be displayed on those occasions when political power is being legitimized by association with various supernatural forces. Secondly, art objects are produced in the context of ceremonial or commercial exchange. Artistry is lavished on objects which are to be transacted in the most prestigious spheres of exchange, or which are intended to realize high prices at market. The kind of technical sophistication involved is not the technology of illusionism but the technology of the radical transformation of materials, in the sense that the value of works of art is conditioned by the fact that it is difficult to get from the materials of which they are composed to the finished product. If we take up the example of the Trobriand canoe-board once more, it is clear that it is very difficult to acquire the art of transforming the root-buttress of an iron-wood tree, using the rather limited tools which the Trobrianders have at their disposal, into such a smooth and refined finished product. If these boards could be simply cast in some plastic material, they would not have the same potency, even though they might be visually identical. But it is also clear that in the definition of technical virtuosity must be included considerations which might be thought to belong to aesthetics.

Let us consider the position of a Trobriand carver, commissioned to add one more to the existing corpus of canoe-boards. The carver does not only have the problem of physically shaping rather recalcitrant material with inadequate tools: the problem is also one of visualizing the design which he mentally follows in carving, a design which must reflect the aesthetic criteria appropriate to this art genre. He must exercise a faculty of aesthetic judgement, one might suppose, but this is not actually how it appears to the artist in the Trobriands who carves within a cultural context in which originality is not valued for its own sake, and who is supposed by his audience, and himself, to follow an ideal template for a canoe-board, the most magically efficacious one, the one belonging to his school of carving and its associated magical spells and rites. The Trobriand carver does not set out to create a new type of canoe-board, but a new token of an existing type; so he is not seeking to be original, but, on the other hand, he does not approach the task of carving as merely a challenge to his skill with the materials, seeing it, instead, primarily as a challenge to his mental powers. Perhaps the closest analogy would be with a musician in our culture getting technically prepared to give a perfect performance of an already existing composition, such as the 'Moonlight' Sonata.

Carvers undergo magical procedures which open up the channels of their minds to that the forms to be inscribed on the canoe-board will flow freely both in and out. Campbell, in an unpublished study of Trobriand (Vakuta) carving (1984), records that the final rite of carving initiation is the ingestion of the blood of a snake famed for its slipperiness. Throughout the initiation the emphasis is placed on ensuring free flow (of magical knowledge, forms, lines, and so on) by means of the metaphoric use of water and other liquids, especially blood and bespelled betel-juice. It is, of course, true that the Melanesian curvilinear carving style is dominated by an aesthetic of sinuous lines, well-represented in the canoe-board itself; but what for us is an aesthetic principle, one which we appreciate in the finished work, is from the carver's point of view a series of technical difficulties (or blockages of the flow) which he must overcome in order to carve well. In fact, one of the carver's initiatory rites represents just this: the master carver makes a little dam, behind which sea-water is trapped. After some magical to-do, the dam is broken and the water races back to the sea. After this, the initiate's mind will become quick and clear, and carving ideas will flow in similarly unimpeded fashion into his head, down his arms, out through his fingers, and into the wood.

We see here that the ability to internalize the carving style, to think up the appropriate forms, is regarded as a matter of the acquisition of a kind of technical facility, inseparable from the kind of technical facility which has to be mastered in order for these imagined forms to be realized in wood. Trobriand carving magic is technical-facility magic. The imaginative aspect of the art and the tool-wielding aspect of the art are one and the same. But there is a more important point to be made here about the magical significance of the art and the close relationship between this magical significance and its technical characteristics.

It will be recalled that these boards are placed on Kula canoes, their purpose being to induce the Kula partners of the Trobrianders to disgorge their best valuables, without holding any back, in the most expeditious fashion. Moreover, these and the other carved components of the Kula canoe (the prow-board, and the wash-board along the side) have the additional purpose of causing the canoe to travel swiftly through the water, as far as possible like the original flying canoe of Kula mythology.

Campbell, in her iconographic analysis of the motifs found on the carved components of canoes, is able to show convincingly that slipperiness, swift movement, and a quality glossed as 'wisdom' are the characteristics of the real and imaginary animals represented, often by a single feature, in the canoe art. A 'wise' animal, for instance, is the osprey, an omnipresent motif: the osprey is wise because it knows when to strike for fish, and captures them with unerring precision. It is the smooth, precise efficiency of the osprey's fish-getting technique which qualifies it to be considered wise, not the fact that it is knowledgeable. The same smooth and efficacious quality is desired for the Kula expedition. Other animals, such as butterflies and horseshoe bats, evoke swift movement, lightness and similar ideas. Also represented are waves, water, and so on.

The success of the Kula, like the success of the carving, depends on unimpeded flow. A complex series of homologies, of what Bourdieu (1977) has called 'scheme transfers', exists between the process of overcoming the technical obstacles which stand in the way of the achievement of a perfect 'performance' of the canoe-board carving and the overcoming of the technical obstacles, as much psychic as physical, which stand in the way of the achievement of a successful Kula expedition. Just as carving ideas must be made to flow smoothly into the carver's mind and out through his fingers, so the Kula valuables have to be made to flow smoothly through the channels of exchange, without encountering obstructions. And the metaphoric imagery of flowing water, slippery snakes and fluttering butterflies applies in both domains, as we have seen.

We saw earlier that it would be incorrect to interpret the canoeboard ethologically as an eye-spot design or, from the standpoint of the psychology of visual perception, as a visually unstable figure, not because it is not either of these things (it is both) but because to do so would be to lose sight of its most essential characteristic, namely, that it is an object which has been made in a particular way. That is, it is not the eye-spots or the visual instabilities which fascinate, but the fact that it lies within the artist's power to make things which produce these striking effects. We can now see that the technical activity which goes into the production of a canoe-board is not only the source of its prestige as an object, but also the source of its efficacy in the domain of social relations; that is to say, there is a fundamental scheme transfer, applicable, I suggest, in all domains of art production, between technical processes involved in the creation of a work of art and the production of social relations via art. In other words, there exists a homology between the technical processes involved in art, and technical processes generally, each being seen in the light of the other, as, in this instance, the technical process of creating a canoe-board is homologous to the technical processes involved in successful Kula operations. We are inclined to deny this only because we are inclined to play down the significance of the technical domain in our culture, despite being utterly dependent on technology in every department of life. Technique is supposed to be dull and mechanical, actually opposed to true creativity and authentic values of the kind art is supposed to represent. But this distorted vision is a by-product of the quasi-religious status of art in our culture, and the fact that the art cult, like all other cults, is under a stringent requirement to conceal its real origins, as far as possible.

THE ENCHANTMENT OF TECHNOLOGY: MAGIC AND TECHNICAL EFFICACY

But just pointing to the homology between the technical aspect of art production and the production of social relations is insufficient in itself, unless we can arrive at a better understanding of the relation between art and magic, which in the case of Trobriand canoe art is explicit and fundamental. It is on the nature of magical thought, and its relation to technical activity, including the technical activity involved in the production of works of art, that I want to focus in the last part of this essay.

Art production and the production of social relations are linked by a fundamental homology: but what are social relations? Social relations are the relations which are generated by the technical processes of which society at large can be said to consist, that is, broadly, the technical processes of the production of subsistence and other goods, and the production (reproduction) of human beings by domesticating them and breeding them. Therefore, in identifying a homology between the technical processes of art production and the production of social relations, I am not trying to say that the technology of art is homologous to a domain which is not, itself, technological, for social relations are themselves emergent characteristics of the technical base on which society rests. But it would be misleading to suggest that, because societies rest on a technical base, technology is a cut-and-dried affair which everybody concerned understands perfectly.

Let us take the relatively uncontentious kind of technical activity involved in gardening – uncontentious in that everybody would admit this is technical activity, an admission they might not make if we were talking about the processes involved in setting up a marriage. Three things stand out when one considers the technical activity of gardening: firstly, that it involves knowledge and skill, secondly, that it involves work, and thirdly, that it is attended by an uncertain outcome, and moreover depends on ill-understood processes of nature. Conventional wisdom would suggest that what makes gardening count as a technical activity is the aspect of gardening which is demanding of knowledge, skill and work, and that the aspect of gardening which causes it to be attended with magical rites, in pre-scientific societies, is the third one, that is, its uncertain outcome and ill-understood scientific basis.

But I do not think things are as simple as that. The idea of magic as an accompaniment to uncertainty does not mean that it is opposed to knowledge, that is, that where there is knowledge there is no uncertainty, and hence no magic. On the contrary, what is uncertain is not the world but the knowledge we have about it. One way or another, the garden is going to turn out as it turns out; our problem is that we don't yet know how that will be. All we have are certain more-or-less hedged beliefs about a spectrum of possible outcomes, the more desirable of which we will try to bring about by following procedures in which we have a certain degree of belief, but which could equally well be wrong, or inappropriate in the circumstances. The problem of uncertainty is, therefore, not opposed to the notion of knowledge and the pursuit of rational technical solutions to technical problems, but is inherently a part of it. If we consider that the magical attitude is a by-product of uncertainty, we are thereby committed also to the proposition that the magical attitude is a by-product of the rational pursuit of technical objectives using technical means.

MAGIC AS THE IDEAL TECHNOLOGY

But the relationship between technical processes and magic does not only come about because the outcome of technical endeavours is doubtful and results from the action of forces in nature of which we are partially or wholly ignorant. Work itself, mere labour, calls into being a magical attitude, because labour is the subjective cost incurred by us in the process of putting techniques into action. If we return to Simmel's ideas that 'value' is a function of the resistance which has to be overcome in order to gain access to an object, then we can see that this 'resistance' or difficulty of access can take two forms: *(a)* the object in question can be difficult to obtain, because it has a high price at market or because it belongs to an exalted sphere of exchange; or *(b)* the object can be difficult to obtain because it is hard to produce, requiring a complex and chancy technical process and/or a technical procedure which has high subjective opportunity costs, that is, the producer is obliged to spend a great deal of time and energy producing that particular product, at the expense of other things he might produce or the employment of his time and resources in more subjectively agreeable leisure activities. The notion of 'work' is the standard we use to measure the opportunity cost of activities such as gardening, which are engaged in, not for their own sake, but to secure something else, such as an eventual harvest. In one sense, gardening for a Trobriander has no opportunity cost, because there is little else that Trobriander could conceivably be doing. But gardening is still subjectively burdensome, and the harvest is still valuable because it is difficult to obtain. Gardening has an opportunity cost in the sense that gardening might be less laborious and more certain in its outcome than it actually is. The standard for computing the value of a harvest is the opportunity cost of obtaining the resulting harvest, not by the technical, work-demanding means that are actually employed, but effortlessly, by magic. All productive activities are measured against the magic-standard, the possibility that the same product might be produced effortlessly, and the relative efficacy of techniques is a function of the extent to which they converge towards the magic-standard of zero work for the same product, just as the value to us of objects in the market is a function of the relation between the desirability of obtaining those objects at zero opportunity cost (alternative purchases forgone) and the opportunity costs we will actually incur by purchasing at the market price.

If there is any truth in this idea, then we can see that the notion of magic, as a means of securing a product without the work-cost that it actually entails, using the prevailing technical means, is actually built into the standard evaluation which is applied to the efficacy of techniques, and to the computation of the value of the product. Magic is the baseline against which the concept of work as a cost takes shape. Actual Kula canoes (which have to be sailed, hazardously, laboriously and slowly, between islands in the Kula ring) are evaluated against the standard set by the mythical flying canoe, which achieves the same results instantly, effortlessly, and without any of the normal hazards. In the same way, Trobriand gardening takes place against the background provided by the litanies of the garden magician, in which all the normal obstacles to successful gardening are made absent by the magical power of words. Magic haunts technical activity like a shadow; or, rather, magic is the negative contour of work, just as, in Saussurean linguistics, the value of a concept (say, 'dog') is a function of the negative contour of the surrounding concepts ('cat', 'wolf', 'master').

Just as money is the ideal means of exchange, magic is the ideal means of technical production. And just as money values pervade the world of commodities, so that it is impossible to think of an object without thinking at the same time of its market price, so magic, as the ideal technology, pervades the technical domain in pre-scientific societies.[3]

It may not be very apparent what all this has got to do with the subject of primitive art. What I want to suggest is that magical technology is the reverse side of productive technology, and that this magical technology consists of representing the technical domain in enchanted form. If we return to the idea, expressed earlier, that what really characterizes art objects is the way in which they tend to transcend the technical schemas of the spectator, his normal sense of self-possession, then we can see that there is a convergence between the characteristics of objects produced through the enchanted technology of art and objects produced via the enchanted technology of magic, and that, in fact, these categories tend to coincide. It is often the case that art objects are regarded as transcending the technical schemas of their creators, as well as those of mere spectators, as when the art object is considered to arise, not from the activities of the individual physically responsible for it, but from the divine inspiration or ancestral spirit with which he is filled. We can see signs of this in the fact that artists are not paid for 'working' for us, in the sense in which we pay plumbers for doing so. The artists' remuneration is not remuneration for his sweat, any more than the coins placed in the offertory plate at church are payments to the vicar for his praying on behalf of our souls. If artists are paid at all, which is infrequently, it is as a tribute to their moral ascendancy over the lay public, and such payments mostly come from public bodies or individuals acting out the public role of patrons of the arts, not from selfishly motivated individual consumers. The artist's ambiguous position, half-technician and half-mystagogue, places him at a disadvantage in societies such as ours, which are dominated by impersonal market values. But these disadvantages do not arise in societies such as the Trobriands, where all activities are simultaneously technical procedures and bound up with magic, and there is an insensible transition between the mundane activity which is necessitated by the requirements of subsistence production and the most overtly magico-religious performances.

THE TROBRIAND GARDEN AS A COLLECTIVE WORK OF ART

The interpenetration of technical productive activity, magic and art is wonderfully documented in Malinowski's *Coral Gardens and Their Magic* (1935). Malinowski describes the extraordinary precision with which Trobriand gardens, having been cleared of scrub, and not only scrub, but the least blade of grass, are meticulously laid out in squares, with special structures called 'magical prisms' at each corner, according to a symmetrical pattern which has nothing to do with technical efficiency, and everything to do with achieving the transcendence of technical production and a convergence towards magical production. Only if the garden looks right will it grow well, and the garden is, in fact, an enormous collective work of art. Indeed, if we thought of the quadrangular Trobriand garden as an artist's canvas on which forms mysteriously grow, through an occult process which lies partly beyond our intuition, that would not be a bad analogy, because that is what happens as the yams proliferate and grow, their vines and tendrils carefully trained up poles according to principles which are no less 'aesthetic' then those of the topiarist in the formal gardens of Europe.[4]

The Trobriand garden is, therefore, both the outcome of a certain system of technical knowledge and at the same time a collective work of art, which produces yams by magic. The mundane responsibility for this collective work of art is shared by all the gardeners, but on the garden magician and his associates more onerous duties are imposed. We would not normally think of the garden magician as an artist, but from the point of view of the categories operated by the Trobrianders, his position is exactly the same, with regard to the production of the harvest, as the carver's position is with regard to the canoe-board, that is, he is the person magically responsible, via his ancestrally inherited *sopi* or magical essence.

The garden magician's means are not physical ones, like the carver's skill with wood and tools, except that it is he who lays out the garden originally and constructs (with a good deal of effort, we are told) the magic prisms at the corners. His art is exercised through his speech. He is master of the verbal poetic art, just as the carver is master of the use of visual metaphoric forms (ospreys, butterflies, waves, and so on). It would take too long, and introduce too many fresh difficulties, to deal adequately with the tripartite relationship between language (the most fundamental of all technologies), art and magic. But I think it is necessary, even so, to point out the elementary fact that Trobriand spells are poems, using all the usual devices of prosody and metaphor, about ideal gardens and ideally efficacious gardening techniques. Malinowski (1935: i. 169) gives the following ('Formula 27'):

I

Dolphin here now, dolphin here ever!
Dolphin here now, dolphin here ever!
Dolphin of the south-east, dolphin of the north-west.
Play on the south-east, play on the north-west, the dolphin plays!
The dolphin plays!

II

The dolphin plays!
About my *kaysalu*, my branching support, the dolphin plays.
About my *kaybudi*, my training stick that leans, the dolphin plays.
About my *kamtuya*, my stem saved from the cutting, the dolphin plays.
About my *tala*, my partition stick, the dolphin plays.
About my *yeye'i*, my small slender support, the dolphin plays.
About my *tamkwaluma*, my light yam pole, the dolphin plays.
About my *kavatam*, my strong yam pole, the dolphin plays.
About my *kayvaliluwa*, my great yam pole, the dolphin plays.
About my *tukulumwala*, my boundary line, the dolphin plays.
About my *karivisi*, my boundary triangle, the dolphin plays.
About my *kamkokola*, my magical prism, the dolphin plays.
About my *kaynutatala*, my uncharmed prisms, the dolphin plays.

III

The belly of my garden leavens,
The belly of my garden rises,
The belly of my garden reclines,
The belly of my garden grows to the size of a bush hen's nest,
The belly of my garden grows like an ant-hill,
The belly of my garden rises and is bowed down,
The belly of my garden rises like the iron-wood palm,
The belly of my garden lies down,
The belly of my garden swells,
The belly of my garden swells as with a child.

and comments (1935: ii. 310–11):

> the invocation of the dolphin . . . transforms, by a daring simile, the Trobriand garden, with its foliage swaying and waving in the wind, into a seascape . . . Bagido'u [the magician] explained to me . . . that as among the waves the dolphin goes in and out, up and down, so throughout the garden the rich garlands at harvest will wind over and under, in and out, of the supports.

It is clear that not only is this hymn to superabundant foliage animated by the poetic devices of metaphor, antithesis, arcane words, and so on, all meticulously analysed by Malinowski, but that it is also tightly integrated with the catalogue of sticks and poles made use of in the garden, and the ritually important constructions, the magic prisms and boundary triangles which are also found there. The garden magician's technology of enchantment is the reflex of the enchantment of technology. Technology is enchanted because the ordinary technical means employed in the garden point inexorably towards magic, and also towards art, in that art is the idealized form of production. Just as when, confronted with some masterpiece, we are fascinated because we are essentially at a loss to explain how such an object comes to exist in the world, the litanies of the garden magician express the fascination of the Trobrianders with the efficacy of their actual technology which, converging towards the magical ideal, adumbrates this ideal in the real world.

NOTES

1 'Non-western' has been suggested to me as a preferable alternative to 'primitive' in this context. But this substitution can hardly be made, if only because the fine-art traditions of oriental civilizations have precisely the characteristics which 'primitive' is here intended to exclude, but cannot possibly be called 'western'. I hope the reader will accept the use of 'primitive' in a neutral, non-derogatory sense in the context of this essay. It is worth pointing out that the Trobriand carvers who produce the primitive art discussed in this essay are not themselves at all primitive; they are educated, literate in various languages, and familiar with much contemporary technology. They continue to fabricate primitive art because it is a feature of an ethnically exclusive prestige economy which they have rational motives for wishing to preserve.

2 The Kula is a system of ceremonial exchanges of valuables linking together the island communities of the Massim district, to the east of the mainland of Papua New Guinea (see Malinowski 1922; Leach and Leach 1983). Kula participants (all male) engage in Kula expeditions by canoe to neighbouring islands, for the purpose of exchanging two types of traditional valuable, necklaces and arm-shells, which may only be exchanged for one another. The Kula system assumes the form of a ring of linked island communities, around which necklaces circulate in a clockwise direction. Kula men compete with other men from their own community to secure profitable Kula partnerships with opposite numbers in overseas communities in either direction, the object being to maximize the volume of transactions passing through one's own hands. Kula valuables are not hoarded; it is sufficient that it should become public knowledge that a famous valuable has, at some stage, been in one's possession. A man who has succeeded in 'attracting' many coveted valuables becomes famous all around the Kula ring (see Munn 1986).

3 In technologically advanced societies where different technical strategies exist, rather than societies like the Trobriands where only one kind of technology is known or practicable, the situation is different, because different technical strategies are opposed to one another, rather than being opposed to the magic-standard. But the technological dilemmas of modern societies can, in fact, be traced to the pursuit of a chimera which is actually the equivalent of the magic-standard: ideal 'costless' production. This is actually not costless at all, but the minimization of costs to the corporation by the maximization of social costs which do not appear on the balance sheet, leading to technically generated unemployment, depletion of unrenewable resources, degradation of the environment, etc.

4 In the Sepik, likewise, the growing of long yams is an art-form, and not just metaphorically, because the long yam can be induced to grow in particular directions by careful manipulation of the surrounding soil: it is actually a form of vegetable sculpture (see Forge 1966).

REFERENCES

Berger, Peter (1967) *The Social Reality of Religion* (Harmondsworth: Penguin).

Bloch, Maurice (1974) 'Symbols, song, dance, and features of articulation: is religion an extreme form of traditional authority?', *Archives Européennes de Sociologie*, 15(1): 55–81.

Bourdieu, Pierre (1968) 'Outline of a sociological theory of art perception', *International Social Science Journal*, 20(4): 589–612.

Bourdieu, P. (1977) *Outline of a Theory of Practice* (Cambridge: Cambridge University Press).

Campbell, Shirley (1984) 'The art of the Kula', PhD thesis, Australian National University, Canberra.

Forge, Anthony (1966) 'Art and environment in the Sepik', *Proceedings of the Royal Anthropological Institute for 1965* (London: Royal Anthropological Institute), 23–31.

Leach, Jerry W., and Leach, Edmund (1983) *The Kula: New Perspectives on Massim Exchange* (Cambridge: Cambridge University Press).

Malinowski, Bronislaw (1922) *Argonauts of the Western Pacific: An Account of Native Enterprise and Adventure in the Archipelagoes of Melanesian New Guinea* (London: Routledge).

Malinowski, B. (1935) *Coral Gardens and their Magic: A Study of the Methods of Tilling the Soil and of Agricultural Rites in the Trobriand Islands*, 2 vols (London: Allen & Unwin).

Munn, Nancy (1986) *The Fame of Gawa: A Symbolic Study of Value Transformation in a Massim (Papua New Guinea) Society* (Cambridge: Cambridge University Press).

Panofsky, Erwin (1962) *Studies in Iconology: Humanistic Themes in the Art of the Renaissance* (New York: Harper & Row).

Simmel, Georg (1979) *The Philosophy of Money* (Boston: Routledge & Kegan Paul).

CHAPTER 6

VOGEL'S NET

TRAPS AS ARTWORKS AND ARTWORKS AS TRAPS

A good deal of discussion in the philosophy of art, visual art particularly, at the present time, has to do with the problem of defining
the idea of an 'artwork'. When is a fabricated object a 'work of art'
and when is it something less dignified, a mere 'artefact'? There are
(at least) three possible answers to this question. It may be said that a
work of art can be defined as any object that is aesthetically superior,
having certain qualities of visual appealingness or beauty. These
qualities must have been put there intentionally by an artist, because
artists are skilled in activating a capacity present in all human beings,
that is, the capacity to respond aesthetically to something. This
theory is not one I propose to discuss here, although it is still widely
held, especially by the general public, who tend to think that visual
attractiveness, or beauty, is something they can recognize
automatically.

The second theory holds that artworks are not, as the 'aesthetic'
theory holds, distinguished by any external quality. A work of art
may not be at all 'beautiful' or even interesting to look at, but it will
be a work of art if it is interpreted in the light of a system of ideas
that is founded within an art-historical tradition. Call this the
'interpretive' theory. The great critical merit of the interpretive
theory over the 'aesthetic' theory is that it is much more attuned to
the realities of the present-day art world, which has long abandoned
the making of 'beautiful'-looking pictures and sculptures in favour
of 'concept' art, for example, of the exhibition of gallery
assemblages like Damien Hirst's dead shark in a tank of formaldehyde (Fig. 6.1, to be discussed later) – not an object that could be
called appealing, nor a work of any excellence in terms of craftsman-
ship. But Hirst's shark is a highly intelligible gesture in terms of
contemporary art-making, not a stunt or a symptom of insanity. It is

Figure 6.1 Damien Hirst's shark: *The Impossibility of Death in the Mind of Someone Living*, 1992

a work thoroughly grounded in the post-Duchampian tradition of 'concept' art and, as such, is capable of being evaluated as good art, bad art, middling art, but definitely art of some kind. Proponents of the 'aesthetic' theory have difficulties with this kind of work, to say the least, and may be inclined to deny that it is art at all, but in that case they may be accused by critics and artists, rightly to my way of thinking, of reactionary tendencies.

Finally, there is a more radical version of the 'interpretation', theory, which provides the third possible answer to the question 'what is an artwork?'. This theory, known as the 'institutional' theory, claims, like the 'interpretive' theory, that there is no quality in the art object, as material vehicle, that definitively qualifies it to be, or not be, an artwork. Whether it is or not is dependent on whether or not it is taken to be one by an art world, that is, a collectivity interested in making, sharing and debating critical judgements of this type. The difference between the interpretive theory and the institutional theory is that the institutional theory does not presuppose the historical coherence of interpretations. A work may be in origin unconnected with the mainstream of art history, but if the art world co-opts the work, and circulates it as art, then it *is* art, because it is the living representatives of this art world, namely artists, critics, dealers and collectors, who have the power to decide these matters, not 'history'. This view is the one put forward by a noted American philosopher of aesthetics, George Dickie (1974; 1984). It is a theory that does not seem to have the support of anything like a majority of Dickie's philosophical colleagues, but that is perhaps, because it is a sociological theory rather than a truly philosophical one – a theory about what is (really) considered art, rather than what ought (rationally) to be considered art. But the objectionableness of Dickie's theory from the standpoint of traditional aesthetics is precisely what constitutes its appeal to the anthropologist, since it bypasses aesthetics entirely in favour of a sociological analysis much of the kind this discipline would provide anyway (Bourdieu 1984). None the less, the merits of the 'institutional' theory of art as a contribution to philosophical aesthetics must be assessed independently of its usefulness as a starting point for sociological study of the art world.

The points at issue between these various theories were brought very much into focus at an exhibition, 'ART/ARTIFACT', mounted at the Center for African Art, New York, in 1988, under the direction of the anthropologist Susan Vogel. (I never saw this exhibition, but it received a detailed review in *Current Anthropology* outlining its contents and layout; see Faris [1988], who makes certain critical comments that I take up later.) The first exhibition space was entitled 'The Contemporary Art Gallery' (whitewashed walls, spotlights) and the star item on display was a striking object (Fig. 6.2) – a Zande hunting net, tightly rolled and bound for transport. Susan Vogel presumably displayed this item in this way because New York gallery-visitors would be spontaneously able to associate this 'artefact' with the type of artwork that they would have looked at in other

Figure 6.2   Zande hunting net, bound up for transport (central Africa)
Source: By courtesy of the American Museum of Natural History (negative no. 3444(2)). Photo J.L. Thompson

galleries, or at least seen illustrated in newspapers and magazines. (The closest immediate analogy is with the string-bound sculptures of Jackie Windsor, see Fig. 6.3. Faris [1988: 776] mentions Nancy Graves and Eva Hesse as further parallels.) Vogel's choice of this particular item was a curatorial masterstroke, for which she deserves much praise, and the 'net' provoked an equally masterly catalogue essay by the American critic and philosopher of art, Arthur Danto (1988), which was published in the exhibition catalogue. What Vogel wanted to do was to break the link between African art and modern art 'Primitivism' (the Picasso of *Les Demoiselles d'Avignon*, pseudo-African masks by Modigliani, Brancusi, etc.) and suggest instead that African objects were worthy of study in a more expanded perspective, including the dominant art style in New York in the 1980s, that is, concept art, represented by the likes of Jackie Windsor and others. Vogel's catalogue essayist, Danto, had reasons for wishing to resist this move, inasmuch as he was not persuaded that the hunting net was, or could ever become, art. 'Institutionally' speaking, the net had indeed become art in the sense that it had been exhibited as such by Vogel, and we may be sure it was received as such by a significant, and very gallery-educated, segment of the visiting public. I would hazard that had Dickie, rather than Danto, written the catalogue essay, the 'net' would have been celebrated precisely as an instance of the way in which an art world creates its artworks by labelling them as such. But Danto, on the other hand, devoted his essay to proving that the 'net's' affinities with contemporary concept art were only superficial.

In this essay I want to do two things: first, to consider Danto's

Figure 6.3   Bound Square by Jackie Windsor, 1972

proposed distinction between 'artefacts' and true works of art; and, second, to mount a little exhibition of my own (unfortunately consisting only of text and illustrations) of objects that Danto would consider artefacts but which I consider candidates for circulation as works of art, even if they were not intended to be 'works of art' by their originators, who indeed probably lacked this concept altogether. If I persuade my public, and if the institutional theory is true, that is, art is what I and enough like-minded people say it is, then a new category of art objects is about to be born. Or not, as the case may be. . . . And especially not according to Danto, to whose arguments I must now turn.

Danto is responsible for both the interpretive and institutional theories of art, in that it was he, originally, who introduced the expression 'art-world' into philosophical aesthetics (Danto 1964). But whereas Dickie (1974) developed Danto's ideas in the sociological direction outlined above, so that being a 'work of art' becomes a matter of social consensus among the art public, Danto tends towards a more idealist view of art, with many explicit references to Hegel in his later work. Danto's position is that art objects are such by virtue of their interpretation, and that interpretation is historically grounded. He has written two very important and well-received studies on the philosophy of modern art along these lines (1981; 1986). I agree with Danto's output in many, probably most, respects; but I am forced to say that the weaker points in Danto's version of interpretive theory emerge rather visibly in the anthropological, cross-cultural context of his 'ART/ARTIFACT' essay.

According to Danto, there are no characteristics that an object can have which make that object a work of art; the 'objective' difference between a real Brillo box and a mock Brillo box by Warhol is not what is responsible for the fact that only the latter is a work of art. Indistinguishably similar objects could be differentiated such that one would be an artwork and the other not. (This is exhaustively discussed in Danto 1981.) But there is a big difference between the kind of interpretation, context, symbolic significance, and so on, that an object must have if it is to be an artwork, compared to that attached to a non-artwork or 'mere' artefact. The interpretation must relate to a tradition of art-making that has internalized, reflects on and develops from its own history, as western art has done since Vasari, and maybe before. According to Danto (and I am entirely persuaded by this), modern 'concept' art corresponds to the total take-over of the 'image-making' side of art by the 'reflecting on history' side of art: concept art is the final convergence of art-making, art history, art philosophy and art criticism in a single package. However, the key concept here is the notion of a progressive, cumulative tradition (*Geist*, spirit, etc.). What is Danto to do when New York gallery-goers seem to want to enthuse over a hunting net as if it was the latest production of *Geist* in the person of Jackie Windsor or her ilk? Can contemporary art swallow extraneous objects in this way? Is the absence of an identifiable maker, and any recognizable 'artistic' intention on his or her part, an obstacle? Danto cannot but assume a critical position because intention, meaning and groundedness in a discrete, self-reflexive tradition is essential to his understanding of contemporary art, and indeed all western post-Renaissance art. The Zande hunter who made or commissioned the net did not participate in the historic frame of reference to which Windsors similiar-looking work refers, so the analogy between them is misleading. Nor could it be alternatively argued (Danto does not even consider this possibility) that the 'artist' here is Vogel, who is presenting the 'net' as a 'ready-made' in the tradition of such Duchamp prototypes as the shovel, coat rack, urinal, and so on, because Vogel is not presenting herself as a second Duchamp, but as a museum curator, offering us something to admire made in Africa, by an anonymous 'artist' who is certainly not Vogel herself.

Danto's dilemma is, essentially, that his interpretive theory of art is constructed within the implicit historical frame of western art, as was its Hegelian prototype. If he says that nothing that comes from without the historical stream of western art (which is certainly a broad stream) is 'art' in his sense, then he is certainly open to an unwelcome charge of Euro-centricity; but if he admits that exotic objects that do not participate in the *Geist* of western art are nonetheless art, how is he to exclude the 'net'? And if he allows the 'net' to be included, what is left of the explanatory value of the historically grounded interpretation, and the art/artefact distinction that is founded on it? The philosopher is truly ensnared in Vogel's net, fulfilling, at long last, its function, if not in the originally intended way.

There is only one way out for the idealist under these circumstances; he must assume that there are underlying interpretive or symbolic affinities between all true works of art in all traditions. The Zande net is to be excluded in Zande terms, because in Zande culture, as in all possible cultures, art objects have to have a particular type of symbolic significance, which a mere hunting net could safely be assumed to be lacking. Having been excluded (presumptively) by the Zande, it cannot be included by the New Yorkers, because to do so is to contradict their own principle of 'no interpretation – no art'; having agreed that not just any Brillo box but only a Warhol Brillo box is 'art', they have to accept that this net, in Zande terms, is no Warhol, but just any old net.

But how to specify the basis of the affinity between (qualifying) African artworks and western artworks, and the non-affinity between the Zande net and either of these? Danto argues that 'great' African sculpture was recognized as on a par with Donatello, Thorwaldsen, and so on, by a process of 'discovery' that he likens to scientific discovery, carried out by Picasso, Brancusi, Roger Fry and their contemporaries; this greatness was always there but had been obscured by prejudicial canons of taste associated with colonialism. But this kind of African art was produced, it is implied, by individual, highly talented and discriminating sculptors, who had specific artistic (aesthetic) intentions that they carried through in their work, which ultimately became accessible to the non-African public via the efforts of sympathetic westerners. However, this approach to the incorporation of African art into the Danto scheme of things carries with it a certain risk of aestheticism – and is not Danto the one responsible for telling us that what makes art art, is not any external (aesthetic) characteristic it may possess? So Danto is obliged to change tack, and consider an instance in which there might be African 'art' that would not be obviously different, in any external or visible respect, from African non-art, a stipulation not applicable to famous examples of African sculptural art, whose art-object status is never in doubt, for Danto at least.

Danto is a philosopher, so he does not take the obvious course of turning to the tomes upon tomes that have been written on material culture in Africa – instead he obeys his disciplinary imperative and indulges in a *Gedankexperiment*, in which he happens to be a particularly skilled practitioner. He imagines that there are two related, contiguous, but historically divergent African tribes, whom he names the Pot People and the Basket Folk, respectively. To outward observation the material productions of these two tribes, which include both pots and baskets, are pretty much identical. But the Pot People revere Pot makers, who are their priests and wise men, and the making of pots is a sacred activity that recapitulates cosmogeny, since God was a potter who formed the earth out of mud. The Pot People also make baskets, for utilitarian purposes, but they do not regard basket-making as a particularly noble activity. On the other side of the hill, among the Basket Folk, things are otherwise; here God was a basket-maker who wove the world from grass, and it is pots that are considered merely utilitarian. So here the basket-makers are the wise men of the tribe and the potters are mere technical specialists, artisans.

Danto maintains that even if only the most minute examination enables the museum experts to distinguish the pots and baskets of the Pot People from the pots and baskets of the Basket Folk, the difference in the spirit in which potting is engaged in among the Pot People is sufficient to ensure that their pots are works of art, as opposed to the Basket Folk's pots, which are not (and vice versa for their respective baskets). The pots of the Pot People and the baskets of the Basket Folk belong in the prestigious *Kunsthistorisches Museum*; the baskets of the Pot People and the pots of the Basket Folk in a quite different collection, the *Naturhistorisches Museum*. The works in the Art History Museum emanate from Absolute Spirit, they are vehicles of complete ideas, stemming from, and illuminating, the human condition in its full historic density and fatefulness, whereas the objects in the Natural History Museum are means towards ends, implements that help human beings to live out their material lives – they are, in another Hegelian expression, only part of 'the Prose of the World'.

Danto, by implication, excludes the hunter's net on the grounds that it is 'prose' in object form, and it will be seen that he draws a particularly sharp distinction, on the basis of his thought-experiment, between art objects and artefacts. But, as with all such experiments, one is entitled to ask whether it is realistic. Anthropology ought to be able to pronounce on these matters, since Danto's experiment is clearly meant to evoke real ethnography as the proto-type for useful expository fictions. According to Faris, in his review of the exhibition, anthropology is only too willing to oblige with copious corroborating instances of wise men uttering Dantoesque things – and that is the problem. He roundly denounces Danto's piece for promoting tainted orthodoxy, both art-historical and anthropological. Modernists like Danto are

> paralysed by the acceptance of all cultural tyrannies and the con-
> sequent blindness to specific tyrannies [so that] they frequently
> fall into the most banal of humanist sentiment and idle gush

about expressive and emotive power. . . . [T]hey do so largely in acceptance of the anthropological enterprise – the notion that, for example, African objects cannot be fully understood without indigenous Africans in the specific cultural setting that produced them. . . . Danto might agree, and while it is trivially true that context is relevant to meaning, it cannot be accorded axiomatic value, particularly as such context and such meaning have been structured by anthropology.

(Faris 1988: 778)

Faris argues that this kind of liberalism ostensibly receives the productions of the ethnographic Other on the Other's terms, but in fact only does so if the Other comes up with something acceptable – consistent with an existing concept of Absolute Spirit, perhaps. Danto's imaginary ethnographies of Pot- and Basket-cosmogeny reveal exactly what kind of anthropological story-telling he would find congenial, but in reality anthropologists and indeed their informants have never been slow in providing just this sort of thing. Faris's Foucauldian point is that the whole anthropological enterprise is slanted towards finding the sort of wise men Danto endows with the power to distinguish between art and non-art, because we want to pin these objects down and attribute to them fixed, controllable meanings. I agree with Faris that Danto's (fictional) wise men are palpably projections of authority, and that they deserve to be unmasked. But unfortunately Faris does not really grapple with the 'art object' vs. 'artefact' distinction, except to indicate that it is subject to continuous redefinition (cf. Clifford 1988: 224) and can be hardly disentangled from issues of ideology and power.

Danto himself has more to say on the subject than simply that wise men can provide the interpretations that make true artworks fragments of Absolute Spirit. In the second half of his essay he dwells on the idea that artefacts are 'incomplete' whereas artworks embody complete, self-sufficient ideas. Citing Heidegger, he remarks that an artefact is always part of a *Zeugganzes* – a system of tools, a technical system forming a whole. There cannot be a hammer by itself; a hammer implies nails to be hammered, wood to hammer them into, saws to shape the wood, and so forth. The net (implicitly) is only a component of the Zande hunting *Zeugganzes*, and has no meaning in itself. However finely crafted, an object like a net, a hammer, or even a very decorative door-hasp or other example of applied art, is incapable of conveying the kind of idea that distinguishes the art object, which always addresses the universal:

> It would be baffling were someone to say such things [pertaining to universal truths] about knives or nets or hairpins, objects whose meaning is exhausted in their utility. Universality belongs after all to thoughts or propositions, and no one would have supposed that knives or nets or hairpins express universal content. They are what they are used for, but artworks have some higher role, putting us in touch with higher realities: they are defined through the possession of meaning. They are to be explained through what they express. Before the work of art we are in the presence of something we can grasp only through it, much as only through the medium of bodily actions we have access to the mind of another person.
>
> (Danto 1988: 31)

But even Danto is forced to qualify this, since it is obviously the case that the bulk of the art comprising the western art tradition was not produced to be appreciated by an art public, but to fulfil instrumental purposes. Religious pictures serve liturgical functions (as altarpieces, aids to piety), portraits convey likenesses, statues dignify public spaces and glorify rulers, and so forth. The same is even more glaringly true of African products of the kind Danto is prepared to concede artwork status to; not one of them was made to be admired as an independent artwork rather than as an adjunct to public ceremony – ceremonies that cannot be exported when the artworks are exported. In short, not just nets but things like African masks are part of *Zeugganzes*, too. Danto deals with this problem by admitting that

> until very recent times [and even now, presumably, in Africa] artworks enjoyed double identities, both as objects of use and praxis, and as vessels of spirit and meaning. African art, once exported, loses its former functions, but retains its latter ones. One does not want to make placelessness one of the defining attributes of art, because that would disenfranchise as art the artworks of Primitive cultures. In their own societies these works have a place, but it would not be the *kind* of place they have in the *Zeugganzes*, in their dimensions as tools in system of tools. The important point is that the whole practical life of those societies could go forward if the

society had in fact no works of art . . . granted that works of art play roles in ritual that are believed to have practical efficacy.

(Danto 1988: 29)

This is surely a puzzling statement, even for a philosopher. Danto wishes to say that artworks have meaning apart from their use, and in so far as they are art they are not useful but meaningful. The self-same objects do have uses, though, in rituals of presumed efficacy. Now we could subtract the artworks and 'practical life' would still be able to continue, minus artworks, because the self-same objects, in their guise as tools or artefacts, would still be there to fulfil their previous extra-artistic functions. This is surely casuistry. How could African masks be deployed in a ritual context as instruments of efficacy and not simultaneously have whatever cultural-interpretative significance they would have to have, according to Danto's own theory, to qualify as artworks? The proposed separation between instrumentality and spirituality is not feasible. And if artworks are implements of a kind (which would not I think be disputed by African carvers) then is it not also conceivable that implements might also be artworks of a kind?

When you come down to it, the reason that Danto excludes the 'net' as art is that he cannot imagine a wise man who might be able to tell him a tale sufficiently compelling to induce him to think otherwise; he assumes that because it is a net, and nets are used for hunting, and hunting is a means of obtaining food, ergo, the net is a mere tool, like a cheese-grater. In this he reveals lack of familiarity with African ethnography where most of the hunting is described as taking place either as part of specific rituals (initiations, annual festivals, etc.) or at the very least in a highly ritualized manner, certainly not as a routine means of obtaining the staff of life. So had the 'net' been properly documented at the time of its collection (c. 1910) it is most likely that it would have figured ritually as an attribute of the 'hunter' role in the collective drama of the ritual hunt – or at least one cannot exclude this possibility – in which case it would be functioning in a way not too different from any other item of ritual paraphernalia, such as a mask.

Meanwhile, one is able to know that wise men in Africa are prepared to tell stories to anthropologists that reveal not only that hunting is ritually important (as a source of augury, an ordeal for the youth, and so on) but that the means of hunting, namely, nets, or in this case, traps, are metaphysically significant. The source I use here is Boyer's (1988) account of wise men, chanters of magical epics, *mvet*, among the Fang of West Africa. Boyer is explicitly trying to understand the nature of 'traditional' wisdom, and in the course of his enquiries he comes to know a certain expert chanter, Ze, with whom he holds long discussions on the nature of wisdom:

> Like wild animals, and like *evur* (wisdom/magical power), *mvet* (epic) is a thing of the forest, in that it is evanescent; you think you can get hold of it, but it escapes, and it is you who gets caught. It was with Ze that I pointed out that at a certain point the complexities of *mvet* were often being compared to traps. In response, he told me the following story:
>
> 'In my youth I got to know the Pygmies well. The Pygmies belong to the forest, they are not village people like us. . . . I often went hunting with the Pygmies, they have special traps for every kind of animal, that is why they obtain so much game. They have a special trap for chimpanzees, because chimpanzees are like human beings: when they have a problem, they stop and think about what to do, instead of just running off and crying out. You cannot catch a chimpanzee with a snare because he does not run away [and thus does not pull on the running-knot]. So the Pygmies have devised a special trap with a thread, which catches on the arm of the chimpanzee. The thread is very thin and the chimpanzee thinks it can get away. Instead of breaking the thread, it pulls on it very gently to see what will happen then. At that moment the bundle with the poisoned arrow falls down on it, because it has not run away like a stupid animal, like an antelope would.'
>
> (Boyer 1988: 55–6, my translation)

This is not a dumb hunting anecdote, but Ze's way of communicating to Boyer (among other things) the basic Faustian problem about knowledge, a problem that is no less salient for the Fang of the Cameroonian rain forest than it is for the Professors at MIT.

It seems unquestionable, on the basis of this testimony, that for this Fang wise man the idea of a 'trap' is a master metaphor of very deep significance, a refraction of Absolute Spirit if ever there was one. But let us bear in mind Faris's strictures against wise men, who may be considered not to be talking about utilitarian traps, traps in prose, but about imaginary, spiritual traps, traps as tropes, not common or garden traps. The Fang wise man does not produce any traps for Boyer's inspection. Can we move one step on from Boyer's text, to the point at which we could mount an exhibition, in a gallery, of animal traps, and present this to the public as an exhibition of artworks?

Let us leave wise men out of it for the present and ask ourselves what animal traps reveal about the human spirit, even in the absence of native exegesis. Do animal traps, in their bare, decontextualized presence, tell us no more than that human beings like to consume animal flesh?

In order to allow you to arrive at a judgement, I offer the accompanying illustrations, drawn from the ethnological literature on traps. Take the arrow trap (Fig. 6.4). Remember that Danto says that looking at a work of art is like encountering a person; one encounters a person as a thinking, co-present being by responding to his or her outward form and behaviour – similarly one responds to an artwork as a co-present being, an embodied thought. Now imagine encountering the arrow trap, not (one hopes) as the victim is going to encounter it, but as a gallery-goer encounters an 'installation' by the latest contemporary artist. In those circumstances, and without additional context, what might the sensitive gallery-goer intuit as the thought, or intention, in this artwork?

There would be nothing amiss, I think, should the imaginary visitor to our exhibition see here, in the arrow trap, a representation of human being-in-the-world. It is a representation that the narrow-minded might prefer to censor and repress, were they only aware that the trap *could be* a representation. For it shows being-in-the-world as unthinking, poised violence, which is not perhaps a pretty thought,

Figure 6.4 Arrow trap, central Africa; sketch by Weule

but not for that reason an untrue or inartistic one. Initially, a trap such as this communicates a deadly absence – the absence of the man who devised and set it, and the absence of the animal who will become the victim (the artist has indicated this victim in the background of the illustration). Because of these marked absences, the trap, like all traps, functions as a powerful sign. Not designed to communicate or to function as a sign (in fact, designed to be hidden and escape notice), the trap nonetheless signifies far more intensely than most signs intended as such. The static violence of the tensed bow, the congealed malevolence of the arrangement of sticks and cords, are revelatory in themselves, without recourse to conventionalization. Since this is a sign that is not, officially, a sign at all, it escapes all censorship. We read in it the mind of its author and the fate of its victim.

This trap is a model as well as an implement. In fact, all implements are models, because they have to be adapted to their users' characteristics, and so bear their imprint. An artificial leg is a model of a missing real leg, a representation that functions as a prosthesis. The arrow trap is particularly clearly a model of its creator, because it has to substitute for him; a surrogate hunter, it does its owner's hunting for him. It is, in fact, an automaton or robot, whose design epitomizes the design of its maker. It is equipped with a rudimentary sensory transducer (the cord, sensitive to the animal's touch). This afferent nervous system brings information to the automaton's central processor (the trigger mechanism, a switch, the basis of all information-processing devices) which activates the efferent system, releasing the energy stored in the bow, which propels the arrows, which produce action-at-a-distance (the victim's death). This is not just a model of a person, like any doll, but a 'working' model of a person. What carving, it is surely reasonable to ask, which only shows us our outward lineaments, actually reveals as much about human being as this mechanical device? Much more of what there actually is to a human being is present here than in any carving, but because it is not an obvious instance of an 'art' object, it is never to be looked at in this light.

Moreover, if we look at other traps, we are able to see that each is not only a model of its creator, a subsidiary self in the form of an automaton, but each is also a model of its victim. This model may actually reflect the outward form of the victim, as in the comical giraffe trap shown in Fig. 6.5, which delineates, in negative contour, the outlines of the lower half of a giraffe. Or the trap may, more

Figure 6.5   Giraffe trap drawn by Wood

subtly and abstractly, represent parameters of the animal's natural behaviour, which are subverted in order to entrap it. Traps are lethal parodies of the animal's *Umwelt* (Figs. 6.6, 6.7). Thus the rat that likes to poke around in narrow spaces has just such an attractive cavity prepared for its last, fateful foray into the dark (Fig. 6.6). Of course, it is not really the case that the trap is clever or deceitful; it is the hunter who knows the victim's habitual responses and is able to subvert them. But once the trap is in being, the hunter's skill and knowledge are truly located in the trap, in objectified form, otherwise the trap would not work. This objective knowledge would survive even the death of the hunter himself. It would also be (partially) 'readable' to others who had only the trap, and not the animal lore

Figure 6.6   Rat trap, Vanuatu; sketch by Bell

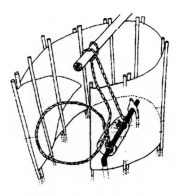

Figure 6.7 Trap from Guyana; sketch by Roth

that was reflected in its design. From the form of the trap, the dispositions of the intended victim could be deduced. In this sense, traps can be regarded as texts on animal behaviour.

The trap is therefore both a model of its creator, the hunter, and a model of its victim, the prey animal. But more than this, the trap embodies a scenario, which is the dramatic nexus that binds these two protagonists together, and which aligns them in time and space. Our illustrations cannot show this because they either show traps awaiting their victims, or victims who have been already entrapped; they cannot show the 'time structure' of the trap. This time structure opposes suspended time, the empty time of 'waiting', to the sudden catastrophe that ensues as the trap closes. This temporal structure varies with the kind of trap employed, but it is not hard to see in the drama of entrapment a mechanical analogue to the tragic sequence of hubris-nemesis-catastrophe. Consider the doomed hippopotamus (Fig. 6.8) lulled into a sense of false security by sheer bulk and majesty. How many tragic heroes have suffered from the same hubristic illusions and have invited the same fate? If the chimpanzee who falls for Boyer's trap is Faust, perhaps this hippopotamus is Othello. The fact that animals who fall victim to traps have always brought about their downfall by their own actions, their own complacent self-confidence, ensures that trapping is a far more poetic and tragic form of hunting than the simple chase. The latter kind of hunting equalizes hunters and victims, united in spontaneous action and reaction, whereas trapping decisively hierarchizes hunter and victim. The trapper is God, or the fates, the trapped animal is man in his tragic incarnation.

Figure 6.8 Hippopotamus trap drawn by Boteler

It therefore seems to me that, even without ethnographic context, without exegesis from any wise men, animal traps such as these might be presented to an art public as artworks. These devices embody ideas, convey meanings, because a trap, by its very nature, is a transformed representation of its maker, the hunter, and the prey animal, its victim, and of their mutual relationship, which, among hunting people, is a complex, quintessentially social one. That is to say, these traps communicate the idea of a nexus of intentionalities between hunters and prey animals, via material forms and mechanisms. I would argue that this evocation of complex intentionalities is in fact what serves to define artworks, and that, suitably framed, animal traps could be made to evoke complex intuitions of being, otherness, relatedness. The impact of these traps, now being presented as artworks, might however be increased if they were exhibited in conjunction with western artworks (of which it is easy to find numerous examples) that seem to occupy the same semiological territory.

The work of Damien Hirst, the most media-exposed of younger British artists in recent times, seems to be a case in point. In fact, it was Hirst's notorious Turner Prize exhibit at the Tate Gallery in 1992 that first induced me to start thinking about traps as art objects. Consider Hirst's shark in a tank of formaldehyde (Fig. 6.1). This work captivates because of the profound contrast between the gigantic, ultra-biological fish and its aseptic glass cage, or trap (recalling Eichmann at his trial, trapped in a glass box) whose reflective walls project virtual images of the equally aseptic surrounding gallery into the shark's biological domain. A distant echo of the upper (biological) and lower (mechanical) halves of Duchamp's *Large Glass*? – no doubt – but also a reflection on our power to immobilize elemental forces, which none the less always seem potentially liable to escape. Even Hirst's shark, as dead as a dead thing can be, is still residually alive, watching and thinking, or seems to be, because it keeps its eyes open and stares at us. One day it is going to get out.

It would be appropriate to place the shark alongside this bark-painting scene from Morphy's *Ancestral Connections* (Fig. 6.9) showing the painting of a trapped shark, visually nearly identical to Hirst's installation in the Tate. The Yolnngu produce this painting during funerary rituals, and it refers to the up-river journey of a mythical ancestral shark, which was temporarily trapped on the way, but which escaped. This painting refers to the deceased's clan affiliations, and metaphorizes the journey of the spirit towards the ancestral country, and the need to transfer power to it (via funerary ceremonies) so that it, like the ancestral shark, can burst out of the 'traps' that threaten to impede its progress. The episode of the shark being trapped, and escaping, is enacted by the participants. These eschatological ideas are, of course, specifically Yolnngu, but I would submit that the surface similarity between Hirst's work and the Yolnngu work are not just superficial, and that a metaphor is being deployed here that is accessible cross-culturally in a highly transformed, but still readable, way.

Meanwhile, to reinforce the point that Hirst's work is in a rather deep way about traps, and the network of complex intentionalities that the notion of entrapment sets up, I should simply describe another of Hirst's works in the same exhibition, which actually incorporated a working trap device. I refer to the installation consisting of a decaying sheep's head in a glass box, which breeds maggots, which turn into flies, which then become victims of a butchers'-shop type fly trap, which attracts the flies by violet light on to high-voltage

Figure 6.9 Coffin lid being painted with the image of a trapped shark
Source: Morphy 1991, fig. 7.4 and pp. 125–6, by courtesy of Howard Morphy;
Photo Howard Morphy

electrified wires, on which they die. A trap within a trap, victims within a victim: as anthropologists we should be the first to recognize redundancy within the mythological code as a means of underlining the dialectical message, which in this case is to induce the spectator to identify him- or herself with the victims in this assemblage (the dead animal, the maggots, the flies) and at the same time with the vicious God who has set this rigmarole of a world in motion, the maker of traps, Hirst, you, me . . .

Hirst would not be the only western contemporary artist whose work would be on display at the exhibition of traps. Next to the arrow trap, for instance, I might install the work by the concept artist Judith Horn (Fig. 6.10), consisting of two shotguns suspended from the gallery ceiling, which periodically blast one another with red, blood-resembling liquid, drawn off from tanks above them. Evidently, at one level, this is a commentary on the senselessness of war, but the key to this work is not so much the theme of mutual violence as the marked absence of its perpetrators – precisely the theme I

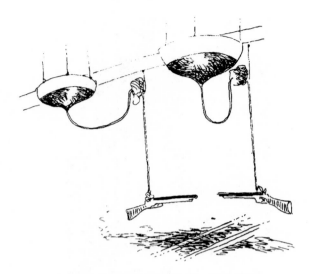

Figure 6.10   High Noon by Judith Horn

identified earlier in relation to the arrow trap. In fact, Horn's installation directly relates to the type of 'class war' man-traps (shotguns
triggered by tripwires) that were set to deter poaching on shooting
estates in times past.

Additional examples of post-Duchampian artworks (even work
by Duchamp himself, such as the *Trébuchet* of 1917) that could
figure in this exhibition could easily be selected, but Hirst and Horn
will do for now. It is not that I would insist that a trap from Africa
and the latest work of Damien Hirst are instances of the same kind
of thing at all, but only that each is capable, in the context of an
exhibition, of synergizing and drawing meaning out of the other.
They are not the same, and are not entirely different or incommensurable either; they are, in Marilyn Strathern's (1991) phrase
'partially connected'.

Nor do I suppose that for an African trap, or a trap from any other
exotic part of the world, to function as an artwork it is actually
necessary or desirable for the ethnographic context to be stripped
away. The artistic meaning of certain traps can often only be established ethnographically, and this makes essential a textual component to any satisfactory exhibition of 'trap' artworks – but there is no
need to apologize for this; since Duchamp it has gone without saying
that written notes and commentary in the form of interviews and

suchlike are necessary for the comprehension of contemporary art-works – just as a knowledge of neo-Platonic philosophy is necessary for a true appreciation of Renaissance art, I would say (Wind 1957). I simply happen to have no exegesis for the arrow trap, for instance, but this trap is so graphic it hardly needs any. With certain other traps it is essential.

Take, for instance, the angling trap from Guyana, illustrated in Roth (1924), see Fig. 6.11. I would hardly have regarded it as a particularly artistic trap unless Stephen Hugh-Jones had informed me (pers. comm.) that the equivalent type of fishing trap among the Barasana (in neighbouring Colombia) is known as the trap 'which turns fish into fruit'. Given this information, one sees at once how wittily metaphysical and magical this trap is. One moment the fish is placidly swimming along belonging (so it thinks) to the animal king-dom and then, bang, before it knows what has happened it is a vegetable, dangling from the branches of a tree, to be plucked like any other fruit by a passing Indian. What a come-uppance, in more senses than one! This transubstantiation recalls the (dead) sheep's head/maggot/fly/(dead) fly transubstantiations in Hirst's installation discussed above, but more radically, in that the fish moves between kingdoms, while the sheep's head, rather more literally, only moves between orders. Certainly, this point would not occur to a non-Barasana art public without textual clues – but once the clue is pro-vided one does not need a PhD in anthropology to enjoy the joke, nor, I think, to be led to reflect on its deeper implications.

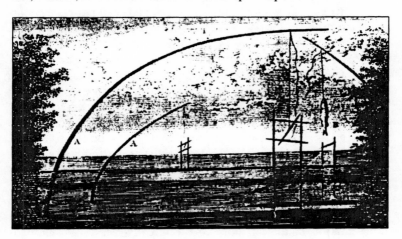

Figure 6.11 Spring-hook fishing trap, Guyana; sketch by Stedman

Another instance (which must be the last) of a trap that can function as an artwork only with the assistance of a certain degree of exegetical material is the Anga eel-trap described in a recent paper by Pierre Lemonnier (1992). This trap consists of a long cylinder of rolled-up tree-bark, bound together with numerous coils of rattan, reinforced with wood and provided with an ingenious sprung trapdoor. Eels are trapped in elongated traps like this in many parts of New Guinea and, indeed, elsewhere. What is significant about the Anga trap is the context in which it is made, and the care which is lavished on it, which could not be apparent to the uninstructed. Lemonnier's Anga trap eels in traps like these in the context of mortuary ritual, specifically, at the end of the period of mourning, when the mourners must be revived in preparation for their return to ordinary life. Feasting on eels is efficacious at this time, not just because eels are excellent, valued food; but also because eels are associated with the penis of the founding ancestor, detached because it was superfluously long. They are thus a source of spiritual vitality as well as superior nourishment, not that these categories can be completely dissociated in local terms. Were this all, the traps themselves might still be considered mere implements, because the fact that eels are sacred to the Anga does not necessarily also mean that the means of obtaining eels are sacred, or in any way extraordinary. Even the fact that the traps are constructed in the course of a ritual, with much magical attention being given to them, might not suffice to take them outside the ruck of common objects. But what Lemonnier can show – and this, very probably, would only be apparent to an anthropologist, poised between the Anga world and the western one, not a native – is that it is actually in the fabrication of the traps that the Anga construct their notion of the 'power' inherent in eels. The traps are made of strips of bark bound together with hoops of cane and provided with a trapdoor at the wider end. What Lemonnier notices is that the cane 'binding' hoops are far stronger, more numerous and more carefully made than would be needed to restrain a few eels, and, similarly, the trapdoor is much sturdier than strictly necessary. Thus it is the trap, rather than the real eel, that carries the message of eel-power. As a symbolic artefact that captures and contains eel-power, it functions, metonymically, to empower the eel, by virtue of its own sturdiness and strength. Indeed the trap, which is shaped to accommodate and attract eels, is a representation of an eel, both in the already-mentioned sense of being an objectification of eel behavioural lore, but also more directly, in that it is itself eel-like (eel-ongated), phallic, ingestive and reproductive.

There could not be a clearer refutation of the thesis that would consign things like animal traps to the status of 'mere' artefacts, by comparison to ancestor-carvings and the like (which the Anga, incidentally, do not make) as candidates for artwork status. If the Anga embody their ancestors in fabricated form, it is surely in the form of traps such as these (as well as other artefacts, such as initiation temples). These traps are 'images of the ancestors' in the sense that they contain, embody and communicate ancestral power. Moreover, they make possible its realization of ancestral presence in the here and now as few conventional images may be said to, not 'in spite of' the fact that they are also useful implements for catching eels, but *because* of this fact. We in the west have longed for (and fantasized about) statues or images that would move, or bless, or make love, but, for centuries, always in vain. The Anga, by contrast, have 'images' of ancestral power that actually accomplish work, actually nourish those who make them, and so achieve a goal that has always eluded our artists, waylaid as they have been by the need for realistic representation of (surface) forms.

CONCLUSION

Suppose, then, that such a hybrid exhibition of animal traps from far and wide, interspersed with relevant western artworks, were to be presented to the gallery public. What might that imply for the problem with which I began this essay – the dispute concerning the criteria for artwork status? I hope that I might have said enough to convince at least some people that such a conjunction would not be wholly inopportune. The institutional theory of art would at this point immediately 'enfranchise' a large array of artefacts – hithero consigned to the *Naturhistorisches Museum* – to a place in the *Kunsthistorisches Museum*, assuring them a quite different audience and reception, since by being successfully circulated as artworks, these works would become nothing less. Would that be a retrograde step?

Speaking as an anthropologist concerned with art, rather than as an art critic or a mouthpiece for Absolute Spirit, I believe that this would be a welcome development. The worst thing about the 'anthropology of art' as at present constituted is precisely the way in which it has inherited a reactionary definition of art, so that it more

or less has to concern itself with objects that would have been classified as 'art' or, more likely, 'craft' at the beginning of this century, but
has little or nothing to do with the kinds of objects (installations,
performances) that are characteristically circulated as 'art' in the late
twentieth century.

In effect, 'art' for the anthropology of art consists of those types
of artefacts one might find on display as 'art' only in a very sleepy
provincial town which (as most of them do) boasts a 'gallery' where
one finds folksy ceramics, carvings and tufted woollen tapestries, not
to mention innumerable still-lives and Palmeresque rural idylls. The
tradition of middle-brow art that produces and consumes these
things is of course indestructible, but why should the ethnographic
Other be deemed a producer of 'art' only if he or she produces work
that is generically analogous to such reactionary dross, even if individual works of 'primitive art', so circumscribed, are actually of the
highest quality. The reason for the persistence of this state of affairs
– which may, however, be unravelling as I write (see Weiner 1994) –
lies in the continuing hold of the 'aesthetic' notion of artworks over
the anthropological mind (Maquet 1986), since it is this definition of
artworks that ensures that only 'aesthetically pleasing' carvings,
paintings, pots, cloths, and so on, are to count as 'art'.

The move I advocate is the abandonment of the aesthetic notion
of artworks by the anthropology of art (Gell 1992), which alone
would permit the kind of direct confrontation described above,
between the artefacts of non-western peoples and the productions of
post-Duchampian artmaking, that is, the central tradition of contemporary art, properly speaking, not the *ersatz* to be seen in
provincial arts-and-crafts galleries. One should accept the essentially
liberating premiss of the institutional theory of art, which has arisen
precisely to accommodate the historic fact that western artworks no
longer have an aesthetic 'signature' and can consist of entirely arbitrary objects, like dead sharks in tanks of formaldehyde, and so on.

Do I mean that any object of human manufacture whatsoever can
be circulated as an artwork? Is this what is implied by the 'institutional' theory of art? Potentially, perhaps, yes; but this has been
trivial, in terms of contemporary art theory, since 1917, when
Duchamp exhibited his notorious urinal (or *Fountain*). That was in
the time of my grandfather, and the time of the great-grandfathers
of today's artists, such as Damien Hirst. So if selecting and exhibiting arbitrary objects as 'art' were all that defined the post-
Duchampian tradition, there would be little left to expect from it by

this late stage. Actually, things are otherwise; Duchamp's ready-mades were carefully selected and thematically tightly integrated to his two major projects (the *Large Glass* (1915–23) and the *Waterfall* (1944–66)). What is interesting about Duchamp's ready-made art objects was never the objects themselves, but Duchamp's reasons for selecting them (divulged in the course of a life-long strip-tease performance) and the same is true for the art produced by his many followers. The apparently 'arbitrary' objects of concept art are only *apparently* arbitrary, and they all work, if they do work, because they have complex (Dantoesque) historic and iconographic resonances, of which the gallery public is, to a greater or lesser extent, made aware. They are objects that are scrutinized as vehicles of complicated ideas, intended to achieve or mean something interesting, difficult, allusive, hard to bring off, and so on. I would define as a candidate artwork any object or performance that potentially rewards such scrutiny because it embodies intentionalities that are complex, demanding of attention and perhaps difficult to reconstruct fully (cf. Kant's notion of the 'free play of cognitive powers').

Thus it takes more to make a post-Duchampian artwork than merely exhibiting it in a gallery – an interpretive context also has to be developed and disseminated. In this respect the purely institutional theory of the artwork is less than satisfactory because it has nothing to say about the criteria that govern the creation of the kinds of contextual resonances to which the educated gallery public are sensitive. To this extent Danto is right to insist on the priority of interpretability in the constitution of the artwork. What is wrong with his theory, at least so far as the artwork vs. artefact distinction is concerned, is its dependence on an over-idealized distinction between 'functional' artefacts and 'meaningful' artworks. This is a legacy of post-Enlightenment philosophers such as Hegel, but it obscures the view of any art world other than the one Hegel had specifically in mind. Perhaps contemporary gallery artworks do nothing but evoke meaning; but most artworks have political, religious and other functions which are 'practical' in terms of local conceptions of how the world is and how humans may intervene in its workings to their best advantage. Artworks can also trap eels, as we have seen, or grow yams (Gell 1992: 60). The 'interpretation' of such 'practically' embedded artworks is intrinsically conjoined to their characteristics as instruments fulfilling purposes other than the embodiment of autonomous 'meaning'.

A half-way house between the 'institutional' and 'interpretive' theories therefore seems to me the best option. The institutional theory of art is amenable to the idea that artworks can be 'arfefacts' securing a range of human purposes, so long as they are simultaneously deemed interesting as art to an art public. But the institutional theory has a problem in that it is less clear about the kinds of criteria that dictate whether candidate objects will or will not be selected as artistically 'interesting'. The Danto–Hegelian conception of an autonomous art '*Geist*' will not enfranchise any but a narrow and unrepresentative range of human productions, and fails to account for the rather successful artwork candidacy of Vogel's 'net' except as the result of a category mistake on the part of the art public. A broader notion of interpretability, encompassing the objectification of 'complex intentionalities' in pragmatic and technical modes, as well as the project of communicating autonomous symbolic meaning, seems to me to overcome the problems contained in both the 'interpretive' and 'institutional' theories of art.

What the 'anthropology of art' ought to be about, in my opinion, is the provision of a critical context that would enfranchise 'artefacts' and allow for their circulation as artworks, displaying them as embodiments or residues of complex intentionalities. Anthropology should be part of art-making itself, in so far as art-making, art history and art criticism are a single enterprise nowadays. Partly this would consist of the provision of relevant ethnography (such as provided by Boyer, Hugh-Jones, Lemmonnier, mentioned earlier) and partly the discovery of connections between complex intentionalities in western artworks and the kind of intentionalities embodied in artworks and artefacts (now recontextualized as artworks) from elsewhere. This would be a one-sided transaction in art-making, in the sense that essentially metropolitan concepts of 'art' would be in play, not indigenous ones; but objects, as Thomas (1991) has shown are 'promiscuous' and can move freely between cultural/ transactional domains without being essentially compromised. This they can do because they have indeed no essences, only an indefinite range of potentials.

So was Vogel's net an artwork? I believe that the New York gallery-goers who took it for one were not mistaken. Nor were they entirely swayed by the mere fact that they were institutionally invited to see it as one, by the gallery setting and the chance rhymes between the Zande net and the work of well-known western concept artists such as Jackie Windsor. They were also, I am sure, responding to the very notion of a 'net' and the paradoxical way in which this net had been itself caught, and tightly bound, within a second net. This recursive metaphor of capture and containment would have been itself enough to give them pause, halt them in their passage, and induce them to stand and stare, like Boyer's fated chimpanzee. Every work of art that works is like this, a trap or a snare that impedes passage; and what is any art gallery but a place of capture, set with what Boyer calls 'thought-traps', which hold their victims for a time, in suspension? Vogel's net was set with care, and in it she captured, besides sundry philosophers and anthropologists – including this one – a large part of the question 'what is art?'.

REFERENCES

Bourdieu, Pierre (1984) *Distinction: A Social Critique of the Judgement of Taste*, (London: Routledge & Kegan Paul).

Boyer, Pascal (1988) *Barricades mystérieuses et pièges à penséé: introduction à l'analyse des épopées Fang* (Paris: Société d'Ethnologie).

Clifford, James (1988) *The Predicament of Culture* (Cambridge, MA: Harvard University Press).

Danto, Arthur (1964) 'The Artworld', *Journal of Philosophy* 61: 571–84.

Danto, Arthur (1981) *The Transfiguration of the Commonplace* (Cambridge MA: Harvard University Press).

Danto, Arthur (1986) *The Philosophical Disenfranchisement of Art* (New York: Columbia University Press).

Danto, Arthur (1988) 'Artifact and Art', in *ART/ARTIFACT: African Art in Anthropology Collections*, Exhibition Catalogue (New York: Center for African Art).

Dickie, George (1974) *Art and the Aesthetic: An Institutional Analysis* (Ithaca, NY: Cornell University Press).

Dickie, George (1984) *The Art Circle: A Theory of Art* (New York: Havens).

Faris, James (1988) 'ART/ARTIFACT: on the museum and anthropology', *Current Anthropology*, 29 (5): 775–9.

Gell, Alfred (1992) 'The technology of enchantment and the enchantment of technology', in Jeremy Coote and Anthony Shelton (eds) *Anthropology, Art and Aesthetics* (Oxford: Oxford University Press).

Lemonnier, Pierre (1992) 'The eel and the Ankave-Anga: material and symbolic aspects of trapping', draft article, unpublished.

Maquet, Jaques (1986) *The Aesthetic Experience: An Anthropologist Looks at the Visual Arts* (New Haven, CT: Yale University Press).

Morphy, Howard (1991) *Ancestral Connections: Art and an Aboriginal System of Knowledge* (Chicago: Chicago University Press).

Roth, Walter (1924) *38th Annual Report of the American Bureau of Ethnology*.

Strathern, Marilyn (1991) *Partial Connections* (Savage, MD: Rowman & Littlefield).

Thomas, Nicholas (1991) *Entangled Objects* (Cambridge, MA: Harvard University Press).

Weiner, J. (ed.) (1994) 'Aesthetics is a cross-cultural category', Group for Debates on Anthropological Theory, Manchester University, Department of Anthropology.

Wind, Edgar (1980) *Pagan Mysteries in the Renaissance* (Oxford: Oxford University Press).

CHAPTER 7

ON COOTE'S 'MARVELS OF EVERYDAY VISION'

Jeremy Coote's contribution to the volume jointly edited by himself and Anthony Shelton (Coote 1992) has exactly the characteristics which a paper needs to possess in order to be eminently discussable. It is economically short. It has a straightforward argument, lucidly set forth. It makes use of ethnography which is mostly familiar and, if not familiar, easily assimilated. It is original and thought-provoking. In fact, I would say that Coote's paper raises what ought to be considered the fundamental problems of the anthropology of art at the present. Naturally, I am going to disagree with Coote about certain aspects of his position, as outlined in his paper. But I entirely agree with his basic contention that the relation between art, anthropology and aesthetics is highly problematic, and that various solutions to it may be devised and canvassed. Even more, I am indebted to him for his basic methodological insight, which is, that if one wants to get to grips with art as an anthropological problem, it is precisely to societies which ostensibly 'don't have any art' that one should turn one's attention. Are members of these cultures without any aesthetic sensibilities? Surely not. As Kant pointed out long ago, and as many have reiterated since, by discussion of aesthetic values has a universalizing tendency, and the same goes for any discussion of art as an expression of aesthetic values. In principle, aesthetic judgements are communicable and intelligible in the light of the psychic unity of mankind. One who says 'this is beautiful' expects to be understood subject only to the stipulation that the addressee is aware of the features of the world to which attention is being drawn in the making of this aesthetic evaluation. But clearly there is nothing universal about artefacts or artworks of the kind which end up in collections. Some societies produce them in great abundance, others do not. This fact seems to drive a wedge between the domain of aesthetics and the domain of artwork production. According to this line of reasoning, the universal disposition towards aesthetic awareness, stimulation and evaluation is prior to, and encompasses the production of artworks. Accordingly the study of the anthropology of art must be preceded, and be unpinned, by an anthropology of aesthetics.

Treating anthropological aesthetics as prior to the anthropology of art dictates a turning away from artefacts and art-making. This is a liberating step, in that it marks a break between the old-style anthropology of art which betrays all too evidently its roots in the eighteenth- and nineteenth-century practice of collecting exotic 'curios'. Ethnological museums are interesting institutions but they do not tell one much about anybody's aesthetics except our own. While I do not agree with Coote's treatment of anthropological aesthetics, I support the move away from an object-centred, museological anthropology of art, towards a more conceptual or philosophical approach, but a rather different one, as I will explain shortly.

Coote's problem, in a word, is the problem of 'art' in ostensibly 'art'-less societies. His solution is the proposal that such societies have 'aesthetics' without having 'art' as such. His paper consists of a demonstration that the Sudanese Dinka, who do not produce art, have a pronounced and distinctive visual aesthetic of their own, which is culturally coded and transmitted, analogously to any other component of transmissible culture, that is, morality, kinship attitudes, religious beliefs, and so forth. The Dinka have inculcated into them a cultural set of categorizations regarding colour, pattern, shape, and so on, which dictate their attitudes towards all things visual, the objects or artefacts which they admire or spurn, the features of their ambience and landscape which they find sublime or deplorable, and so forth.

Needless to say, given the ethnographic setting, much of the discussion centres on the aesthetics of cattle, with which Nilotic cultures of southern Sudan, who include the Nuer, are notoriously obsessed. The key to Coote's argument is the Dinka aesthetic preference for cattle marked in particular ways. Most cattle are a dull greyish white colour, but some beasts are white, black, brown, reddish or yellowish. Occasionally, calves are born with multicolour, piebald or spotted markings, and of these the most admired are those which have large, distinct, blotches of colour on a white background. (Hopkins' 'Glory be to God for dappled things' is the Dinkas' aesthetic watchword as well.) Such animals, if they are male, will most likely be castrated to make them tractable, and will become show-oxen, or as they are called in the literature, 'personality-oxen', owned and cared for by ambitious youths, who accompany them to their pasture, decorate them, make much of them, and compose songs about them (Deng 1972). Ox and youth become an inseparable pair; the ox is the bovine counterpart of his owner, and vice-versa, each is an exponent of the person of the other.

Coote contends that the Dinka preoccupation with 'pied' beasts, and with the minute classification of variation in bovine colour and marking, is fundamental to a more inclusive set of visual-aesthetic categories. Indeed, Coote repeats the observation, made by many ethnographers of Nilotic people, that any visual appearance is likely to be referred to the extensive vocabulary which has been developed in order to classify bovine markings. This prototypically bovine vocabulary is their vocabulary of the visible generally. And although it may be true, for instance, that a certain type of spotted cattle are called 'leopard', so far as the average Dinka (or Nuer, etc.) are concerned, the prototype of a 'leopard-marked' (*makuak*) beast is not the leopard itself – which is rarely seen, if at all – but the bovine equivalent (Coote 1992: 257).

This cattle-derived visual schema does more than classify the world; it also imposes a hierarchy of value upon it. The Dinka like to make their own bodies resemble those of the admired type of ox; by holding ox-postures in the dance, by selecting adornments which emphasize light/dark contrast, and by covering themselves with ash, which recalls the whitish colour of oxen. They construct shrines to ancestors and divinities from tree-branches which seem to be selected to resemble horned cattle, and they may paint these horned shrines with contrasting stripes, evoking desirable ox-markings. God himself is described as piebald, at least occasionally, and his white head is likened to that of an old man and/or a well marked ox of the category *majok* or *marial* (ibid.: 267–8).

There is no need to continue with further details of Coote's demonstration that the Dinka are, indeed, much preoccupied with the visual characteristics of cattle, especially of the admired types. The evidence is copious. If this were all there was to Coote's paper, only a very foolhardy person would take issue with it. But there is obviously much more at stake here. Let me take up in turn what I see as the main theoretical points made in Coote's paper. In sequence, they seem to me to comprise three linked positions:

(1) The domain of 'aesthetics' (specifically, in this instance, visual aesthetics) is not necessarily associated with 'art'. Art consists of the social practices associated with the production and consumption of identifiable artworks. (Visual) aesthetics is the socially derived practice of categorizing and evaluating visual phenomena, that is, shapes, patterns, forms – whether natural or manmade – according to a cultural scheme of value. Aesthetics can be discussed in the absence of any attempt being made to manufacture objects according to the aesthetic preferences of a culture. And in fact, aesthetic preferences may best be identified outside this domain, as in the Dinka aesthetics of cattle. Here aesthetic evaluation is simply applied to a 'given' object, so one can identify it as a mode of classification and value, without having to consider the complicating factor of artistic (artefactual) creativity. Aesthetics has to do with the perception of aesthetic quality, not the manufacture of objects possessing this quality.

(2) Accordingly, societies may maintain an aesthetic without producing and consuming art. 'Art'-less societies, or the more numerous societies which do not produce 'significant' art, or which are not classified as 'rich' in art according to the standard categories operated by the old-style 'Anthropology of Art', still have to be considered as societies with an 'aesthetic' sensibility of their own. They are misrepresented if this aesthetic bent is concealed in the process of ethnographic description. Coote does not exactly say this, but it is implied in his paper that all societies without exception have an aesthetic of some sort, the possession of which is a universal of culture, stemming from psychic universals of perception and cognition. But each culture has a distinct aesthetic with regard to the selection and evaluation of aesthetically salient features of the visual world.

(3) Aesthetic sensibility is prior to artwork production and consumption, not the other way around. The mistake in previous attempts to discuss non-western or 'primitive' aesthetics was to take artefacts as a starting point, and to infer, or try to infer, an aesthetic from the objects themselves. It would be preferable instead to see the objects as embodying references to a more fundamental 'everyday' aesthetic, a perceptual aesthetic, applied to everything in the world, not just the manufactured bits of it – the pots or carvings or house-façades or whatever. In order to understand the aesthetics of the artefactual world, Coote implies (I am not following him to the letter here, but I am reasonably

sure this implication was intended) that one must first come to grips with the local culture aesthetics of 'seeing'. Only when we have understood how the X-people see, according to their culture of seeing things, can we start to understand what the X-people make, according to their culture of making things.

Before I begin to dissent from certain aspects of Coote's argument, I should like to say that I agree entirely with the critique he makes of the old-style anthropology of art, with its hierarchy of art-rich and art-poor cultures, and its ethos of museums, collections, and the identification of 'masterpieces'. I support his democratic approach, and I concur with the remark that he makes to the effect that western categories of (generic) 'artworks' are inadequate to the task of identifying aesthetic practices even in western societies – including, as they do, the products of every obsolete Sunday painter, but excluding those of the imaginative gardener, home decorator, or budgerigar-breeder. The concept of artwork in the conventional anthropology of art deserves to be criticized and should indeed be completely reformulated, as I will elaborate shortly. He is quite justified in insisting that the Dinka have as much right to be accorded an aesthetic sensibility as any other tribe on the continent of Africa, even if they have not produced much that has attracted the attention of public or private collectors.

The key issue here is the interpretation given to the notion of 'the aesthetic'. Certain very important theorists have based aesthetics on the human propensity to find not art but nature beautiful or sublime. Kant was, I believe, notoriously indifferent to art of any kind; but he was a noted contributer to aesthetic theory nonetheless. Because Kantian aesthetics takes as its starting point the aesthetic appreciation of 'Nature' it ought to provide the appropriate theoretical basis for considering Dinka aesthetics, since the Dinka, according to Coote, take the 'natural' beauty of cattle as the yardstick for all things aesthetic.

Although Coote does not refer to Kant, perhaps out of modesty, there are many reasons for suspecting that the position Coote takes on aesthetics can be traced back to Kantian sources. (For an accessible account of Kant's aesthetics see McCloskey 1987.) Kant belonged to the school of aesthetic theory, originally Greek but revived and codified during the Enlightenment, which considers that aesthetics is the branch of philosophy concerned with judgements about beauty or sublimity (as ethics is the branch of philosophy concerned with judgements about the morally good, logic the branch of philosophy concerned with valid inference and so on). Kant is a 'beauty' aesthetician, and so is Coote, in that what he is concerned to show is that the Dinka consider certain visual presentations beautiful. Beauty-aesthetics is currently opposed to a more recent formulation of philosophical aesthetics, which one can call 'artwork' aesthetics, which is the philosophical study of the status of artworks and their interpretations. Obviously, Coote, who is explicitly separat- ing anthropological aesthetics from the anthropology of artworks, their production, reception and interpretation, has to be aligned with beauty-aesthetics rather than artwork aesthetics.

Although Coote does not mention Kant, the references he does make to the literature on aesthetic theory are to writers in the post-Kantian vein. For instance, he cites Zangwill (1986) who defends the thesis that the analysis of 'beauty' is prior to, and quite independent from, any consideration of art. Diffey (1986) likewise regards 'aes- thetic experience' as *sui generis*, just as Kant did, and linked with religious awe. Further, Coote makes approving mention of Jacques Maquet (1986), the only anthropologist to have explicitly argued the need for an anthropological aesthetics. Reference to Maquet's book reveals that Maquet's ideas on aesthetics are taken from the con- temporary aesthetician Jerome Stolnitz (1960) who is explicitly a Kantian in arguing for the specificity of aesthetic awareness, and the very Kantian stipulation that aesthetic awareness comes only in the absence or abeyance of non-aesthetic, practical or appetitive interest in the object of aesthetic appreciation.

In order to investigate the philosophical basis of Coote's position, it seems worthwhile therefore to summarize the main features of Kantian aesthetics and their Cootian/Dinka applications. Kant (1928) treats aesthetics as the critique of 'taste' which is the faculty of estimating an object or a mode of representation as a source of delight or aversion, apart from any (practical) interest. The object which affords delight is called beautiful.

Secondly, the beautiful object pleases in the absence of a 'concept', by which Kant means that the judgement of beauty does not depend on what one knows about the object, whether it is good for some purpose, or an excellent example of something (a 'beautiful' speci- men of a fossil cockroach, for instance). The sensation of beauty is perceived directly rather than being mediated by discursive thought or reasoning; it cannot be confirmed or refuted by argument of discussion.

Thirdly, although beauty is not a matter of knowledge or reasoning, it is intersubjective. For reasons touched on before, it is implicitly universal. Any person, once made aware of what the other finds beautiful, will find it beautiful also, if it is indeed genuinely beautiful. (Cootian/Maquetian anthropological aesthetics, it would be fair to say, has this ambition, that is, telling us what other people find beautiful so that we are in a position to find the same things beautiful too. Coote would have failed to communicate the 'everyday aesthetic' of the Dinka were we not able ourselves to see as beautiful what the Dinka allegedly see as beautiful.)

Finally, potentially universalizable judgements of beauty cohere around objects which possess certain formal properties which are recognized by aesthetic awareness if awareness is pointed in the right direction. This property Kant calls 'the form of finality' (Kant 1928). The simplest example of this, discussed at length in Maquet (1986), is the aesthetic appreciation of the human body. According to Kantian aesthetics, the body is an object of beauty inasmuch as it is possible to see at least some bodies, under some conditions, as adumbrating an 'end', a final purpose towards which all bodies tend, without any simultaneous consideration of inhabiting or confronting another human body in a practical sense. Such a body may be seen as strong, without any reference to the use or exploitation of human strength, desirable without any sexual motive, and so on. We find this body beautiful in that, through perfection of form, it adumbrates the finality or purpose present in nature and elicits the free play of our cognitive powers. This aesthetic appreciation is sharply distinct from the delight motivated by utilitarian considerations, the delight a miser might take in contemplating his gold. The beauty of finality is present only to a free, disinterested, contemplative consciousness. It is worth noting that Kant thought that artworks such as pictures were beautiful only in that they were faithful representations of objects which were themselves beautiful, and discounted the possibility of a beautiful representation of a repulsive subject. Hence all beauty was originally natural for him (as for the Dinka) and artworks as artefacts only had, so to speak, derivative beauty. Kant thus proposes a theory of aesthetics which identifies the aesthetic not with perception as such, but with a distinct attitude towards that which is perceived, that is, disinterested contemplation.

Coote is an implicit rather than an explicit Kantian. As I have noted, he thinks that aesthetics has to do with beauty, essentially 'natural' beauty viewed through a cultural lens. Secondly, Coote agrees with Kant in linking notions of beauty to perception, rather than discourse or interpretation. In fact, it is to psychic universals of perception that he finally makes appeal, indicating that each 'local' perceptual aesthetic is a refraction of a general aesthetic of seeing in which all humans ultimately participate. Thirdly, he is anti-functional, and hence aligns himself with the Kantian stipulation that the perception of beauty, the affordance of visual delight, is not a simple transcription of material interest or the possibility of the realization of individual desire. Cattle are beautiful to the Dinka independently of considerations as to who owns which beast and what practical use any animal might serve. Their beauty is cognitive/contemplative rather than practical, and the possibility of the extrapolation of bovine beauty to a more general notion of harmony in the human and divine world, on which Coote lays considerable stress, indicates that it is indeed towards order or Kantian 'finality' that the everyday aesthetics of the Dinka seem to converge.

Now let me turn to my criticisms. The question is whether there can be an aesthetic which is independent of the existence of art-works. Coote's position draws its strength from the fact that we must all be aware of having been visually stimulated by, or having found appealing, visual presentations other than those made for us by artists. Animals are often very beautiful – so are sunsets, mountains, shimmering leaves, and so forth. These things are aesthetically appealing, but also subject to the vicissitudes of taste and culture (witness the declining popularity of typically 'Victorian' house-plants, such as Aspidistras and their substitution by modernist houseplants such as Yuccas, or the decline of the Spaniel and the rise of the Saluki). Obviously, it is possible to construct an aesthetic theory around the elementary Boasian observation that each culture selects certain features of its ambience for appreciation and celebra-tion, and that, as we pursue our ordinary existence, we often have occasion to evaluate our visual surroundings without reference, however remote, to the concept of an artwork.

When Coote says that the Dinka have an aesthetic attitude towards cattle, does he mean that the Dinka are culturally prone to find, in cattle, a source of moral enlightenment, divorced from utili-tarian considerations, as Kant's aesthetic theory proposes? I think this is partly what Coote has in mind. But the Kantian linkage of aesthetics with a special 'disinterested' moral attitude does not seem to fit very well with Coote's otherwise 'populist' line which locates the aesthetic within the everyday life-world. This world is dominated precisely by self-interested competitive striving, not disinterestedness. Could one ever really say that the Dinka were 'disinterestedly' appreciative of the natural beauty of cattle, even if they might agree that excellent cattle are a gift of God? The Dinka youth glorifying his ox is surely not prone to regard it as 'the embodiment of a purpose without the purpose itself' – the regard taken in Kantian aesthetics (Kant 1928). On the contrary, it is the fitness of the ox for a specific purpose, that of embodying him, and glorifying him – and helping him to marry the girl of his dreams – which makes him think it beautiful. Would Kant have thought that the regard taken by Lord Godolphin for his racehorse 'Eclipse' was an instance of aesthetic appreciation? I do not think so. But in the Dinka case this is surely the closest analogy. Dinka admiration for oxen is intrinsically linked to the possibility of ownership and control. They admire the oxen they own and they covet the ones they do not.

So, on the basis of his chosen example, Coote cannot be a Kantian, associating the beautiful in nature, disinterestedly contemplated, with the universal moral good. Oxen are good for a purpose and well-marked oxen are especially good for the purpose of becoming a young man's personality-ox. In so far as Dinka have an aesthetic attitude towards oxen, this attitude cannot be dissociated from their practical interest in oxen as mediating elements in social praxis, tending towards the realization of their social ambitions. The ox is beautiful because, in the phrase Blake coined in his decidedly non-Kantian celebration of beautiful women, it has 'the lineaments of gratified desire'.

But at this point the whole matter of identifying the 'aesthetic' component in the Dinka–ox relations seems to become rather shaky. Let us admit that a Dinka youth prefers his ox to be large, generously humped, long-horned and piebald, rather than thin and plain. What is added to this by calling his preference an 'aesthetic' preference, rather than an ox which meets certain practical specifications? To cite an analogous instance from our own society: does a man who wants a Ferrari (a personality-ox is a bovine Ferrari) want one for 'aesthetic' reasons or practical reasons? Clearly, practical reasons – prestige, attractiveness to women, and so on – dictate this choice of car, but a Ferrari is a good choice of car for these purposes because it has certain visual characteristics, being long and low, probably red, having fat tyres, multiple exhausts, and so on, which contribute to the devastating image a Ferrari can project. These visual characteristics are largely dictated by functional engineering considerations, and even the red colour is semiotic rather than aesthetic, in that it indicates, to the sports-car lover, the Ferrari's Italian origins.

Desire can be realized through the possession of such objects, which manifest certain visual characteristics. In so far as these visual characteristics are preferred or chosen, they are chosen because they are associated with the realization of desire, not because they have abstract properties of form or contrast which can be considered in isolation from utilitarian motives. So, in saying that piebald oxen are chosen for aesthetic reasons, we are not saying that oxen are chosen on the basis of 'looks' but on the basis of their contribution to the performance of a social function, the performance of that social function being associated with the possession of those looks.

At this point it will be seen that the notion of a cultural scheme of pure aesthetic preferences has broken down. It is the way in which objects (such as the oxen or Ferraris) are inserted as means into sequences of instrumental actions which accounts for the preferences shown for their visual appearance. But is this a chicken-and-egg argument about which comes first, the piebaldness of the ox, or its fitness to realize desire? In some cases appearances and function may be arbitrarily related, so that theoretically, appearance could be 'chosen' first, and only subsequently appreciated in the light of the fitness of objects having such an appearance to fulfil a certain function. But this is certainly not the case in the present instance. Piebald animals are suited to fulfil the requirements of personality-oxen for two very obvious practical reasons, firstly their distinctiveness and recognizability, and secondly their relative rarity. Given the distribution of colour-types in the Dinka herd, and the fact that no effort is made to increase the number of piebalds (the best-marked bulls are castrated, as we have seen) then it would be very odd indeed were common grey animals selected as show oxen and distinctly marked animals neglected.

I am sceptical that Dinka preferences with regard to oxen can be attributed to an aesthetic sensibility for form and colour as such. I do not think that there is a 'cultural eye' which singles out visual appearances as pleasing or unpleasing, independently of the non-visual, non-aesthetic characteristics of objects. It might be felt that I am taking a functionalist line here. It might also be felt that I am simply saying that the Dinka have no aesthetics and no art, but are just interested in stock-raising to the exclusion of all else. On the contrary, I think the Dinka do have art and, in that they have art, they have aesthetics. But what I would deny is that they have aesthetics without, or prior to, art.

Let us agree, for argument's sake, that I have disposed of the idea that Dinka have a visual aesthetic which can be dissociated from the utilitarian role which objects (which always have to have *some* appearance) play in their lives. Are there any objects in the Dinka world which are artworks? What difference would it make to our understanding of Dinka aesthetics if there were?

Coote, as we have seen, has based his Dinka aesthetics on the supposition that there are no artworks in Dinkaland. But although Coote is very much against the old-style, collection-based discipline of art-anthropology, it is curious to observe that his definition of what constitutes an artwork is directly derived from this rightly disparaged discipline. There are no artworks in Dinkaland because there is nothing to collect there. There are only the Dinka, their cattle, and nothing else much, nothing worth exhibiting beside the best that the rest of Africa can provide. Accordingly, Coote says the Dinka have aesthetics but no art.

I reject completely the idea that the Dinka do not have artworks, including art objects. They just don't come in the collectible form of artefacts like carvings, cloths or pots. But one would be foolish to expect people of such a nomadic habitus to encumber themselves with excess baggage in the form of artefacts, collectible or otherwise. Dinka art is incarnate or inanimate, consisting of the bodies of the Dinka themselves and their cattle, and their expressive behaviour – their music, singing, oratory, dance, body-decoration and so forth. It is only by looking for the *wrong kind of art* that Coote can maintain that the Dinka do not produce artworks. Despite what Coote (and Zangwill, the philosopher cited by him) say, there is nothing wrong with the assumption that artworks and aesthetics are intrinsically connected. What is wrong is the assumption that artworks necessarily consist of objects of the kind that can be placed in museums.

This must seem a simple point, but if it is true, the proposed independence of 'anthropological aesthetics' and 'the anthropology of art (objects)' collapses. I am going to argue the contrary case; namely, that the Dinka have aesthetics only in so far as they have art and produce artworks. I think that it can be shown ethnographically that all the evidence which bears on the Dinkas' aesthetic dispositions, including the evidence cited by Coote, stems from their artistic practice. The 'everyday', untutored, aesthetic vision is a myth.

Let me back-track a bit to the situation we had reached *vis-à-vis* the Dinka youth and his piebald ox. Coote is saying that the ox is selected because it is aesthetically valued on the basis of its appearance. I am saying that there is no evidence for it being aesthetically valued which is not also evidence for it being valued instrumentally, as a means of realizing desire. But I also want to say that this ox is an artwork, in fact, it is *the* characteristic artwork Dinka society produces. And I also seem to be intent on saying that, *qua* art object, the ox is a focus of aesthetic concern. So it is an aesthetic ox after all.

I could be accused of falling into evident self-contradiction at this point. But there is no contradiction here, because what makes the Dinka ox an artwork is not what it looks like, its visual appearance as such, but what the Dinka think, say, or more precisely, sing, about it.

The principle I am invoking here is one which has many supporters among contemporary philosophers of art, namely, the principle that what makes an artwork an artwork is what members of an art world say about it, or think about it, that is, the way in which it is interpreted as such (Danto 1964; Dickie 1974). Coote thinks that an aesthetic is a set of culturally transmitted visual preferences ontologically prior to the production of artworks. But the crucial thing to note is that his *evidence* for this all comes in the form of the social cult surrounding certain objects in the Dinka world, notably, well-marked personality-oxen. If this social cult did not exist, Dinka would have no occasion to manifest their 'intrinsic' visual preference for contrastive colour combinations, or strikingly curved horn-shapes. In fact, Coote's primary source of evidence for the Dinka aesthetic is the published material on Dinka sung poetry, particularly the songs composed by youths praising their own personality-oxen (Deng 1972; 1973; Burton 1982). These songs are artworks in themselves, addressed to the Dinka art public or art world. The effect of these songs is to aestheticize the personality-ox so that it, too, becomes an artwork displayed before that art public by means of its owner's song. This makes it impossible to claim that there is evidence for a Dinka aesthetic which is independent of the existence of Dinka artworks; since the evidence for the aesthetic is these very artworks, that is, the poetic discourse surrounding the personality-ox, the ox as the embodiment of this discourse and the fact that this discourse is directed towards a discriminating public.

I will leave the question of Dinka poetic aesthetics aside for the moment, in order to concentrate on the idea that the Dinka ox is an artwork and on what that might mean. My proposition is that the

Dinka ox is a non-artefactual artwork, by virtue of what is said, thought or sung about it in the Dinka art world. The possibility that artworks might be non-artefactual, animate or vegetable, is one that Coote should readily accept, given that he has praised the activity of suburban gardeners as practitioners of popular art (Coote 1992: 246). I hope we are past the point at which conventional displays of manual dexterity are regarded as the *sine qua non* of art-object pro-duction, to the exclusion of art objects which are simply selected, like Duchamp's ready-mades, or nurtured, like these oxen, or the long yams which are placed beside carvings in Sepik ceremonial, with no sense that these are entities belonging to quite distinct orders of being (Forge 1966).

The special care which these oxen receive from their owners, including their castration, must contribute substantially to their size and condition, and the attention given to training, sharpening and decorating their horns means that to a certain extent these oxen are artefacts rather than pure products of nature. But it is not really this bodily shaping which turns them into artworks. An ox which lacks an owner capable of publicizing its true quality through an appropriately composed song is no artwork, however magnificent in other respects. It is a potential, rather than an actual artwork. It is the song, or rather, the public nexus created by the song, between the owner and his animal, which creates the ox as artwork, just as it is the interpretation, poised between artwork and recipient, which brings into existence the artworks of the western art world.

The personality-ox is at once the pretext and product of the poetic imagination, and it is in this poetic imagination, which is also an academy of taste in matters bovine, that the aesthetic resides. That is to say, the aesthetic is verbal, or conceptual, although the animal itself is visible. The aesthetic, in other words, is not a way of 'seeing' but a mode of discursive thought. Aesthetics is the form of discursive thought which intervenes to turn mere objects into art-works. It is for this reason that it is senseless to find 'aesthetic' thought anywhere other than in the creation and reception of artworks.

Dinka aesthetics is a poetic discourse which evokes cattle, humans, their environments, interactions and histories, in their fullness and confusion, as may be readily seen by reading the translated texts of the ox-songs which have been published (especially Deng 1973). Coote cites these ox-songs only in so far as they support his conten-tion that the Dinka are overwhelmingly concerned with the visual characteristics of oxen and that the Dinka assess all things visual, so to speak, according to categories of shape and colour derived from prototypical oxen. It is true that visible features of oxen are frequently mentioned, especially colours, patterns and the forms of the animals' humps and horns. But only a small proportion of the text of these poems is actually devoted to the direct evocation of the visible features of oxen. Their acoustic attributes and, even more so, their behaviour, are just as important, not to mention where they came from, how they were stolen and recaptured, pawned and redeemed, and so on. These are poems about every aspect, not just of the ox but of the owner and the surrounding society and its history. It is misleading to single out the references to visual features of oxen as constituting 'the' Dinka aesthetic as represented in Dinka poetry.

The artistry which is displayed in these poems is not directed towards the delineation of oxen for their own sake. Oxen are primarily evoked in order to provide a pivot for metaphorical conceits which take in every aspect of Dinka experience. The ox, in these poems, is a lay-figure, like 'the beloved' addressed in so much western poetry, who is there only to provide an excuse for displays of poetic wit. Take, for instance, these lines:

On the back of my Mijok are four spots, close together
But they will never meet,
They will miss each other like the sun and the moon.

(Deng 1973: 100)

Rather than read this as evidence that the Dinka are so ox-obsessed that they can see the heavenly bodies only as so many spots on an ox's rump, I prefer to read this as a sophisticated trope, designed to elicit an 'aaah' response, from an audience who appreciate metaphors which are daring but apt. One of the longest poems in Deng's collection (no. 8 pp. 106–12), is built on the following conceit: the singer's ox is Mijok and Mijak, colour terms which refer to the plumage of geese and pelicans. The poem begins by mentioning the ox drinking at a pool ruffled by the wind, and then the geese who fly before a storm. This leads into an extended passage which praises the ox indirectly, via an account of the 'war' waged by the pelican against fish. The pelican spears a balloon-fish which, lying on the bank, becomes a football 'stuffed with grass' by the pelican for the amusement of the 'schoolboys':

> Hopelessly rolling on the ground
> He is the ball of the schoolboys
> The schoolboys of the pelican

There follows a passage in which the people are warned to beware the attack of the 'pelican', whose outstretched wings resemble the horns of the oxen of the feared enemies of the Dinka, the Falata and the Nuer. A curious circularity has been created here: the pelican is metaphorized as a fearsome Nuer ox, while itself being the chosen metaphor for a Dinka one. The horns of the Nuer ox (and/or the outstretched wings of the pelican) are then darkly metaphorized in their turn:

> The Great One whose horns have grown exceedingly high
> Like the poles on which the Government hangs people
> The poles of the judge
> With which he is finishing the people of the south (109).

And so the poem continues, alluding to ancient and contemporary political events, before culminating in a display of artistry in which the poet openly boasts of his own skill:

> I, Mithiang, may rush my songs,
> But even if a man is a famous composer
> I can defeat him;
> Those with whom we bang our heads bang in competition
> Even is a man is a famous composer
> I can defeat him

before making his peroration:

> His head (the ox's) is white like the animal which grows horns in
>   the place of teeth,
> The elephant grows his horns in his mouth
> My Mijok grows horns in his mouth

This poem and many others like it, reveal the virtuoso characteristic of Dinka poetry, and the fact that it is composed in order to flatten the (poetic) opposition. This is important because it shows that it would be wrong to suppose that these poems reflect the 'natural' or 'everyday' thought processes of the Dinka. On the contrary, these poems must be difficult to compose, otherwise there would be no competition to produce the finest ones, and may also be hard to follow, even for the Dinka themselves, unless they are 'learned' enough to follow the recondite allusions and metaphors with which these poems bristle. It is no part of the Dinkas' 'everyday vision' to see their oxen as elephants, pelicans or lions, and I doubt whether – unless inspired to do so by the poem cited above – they all spontaneously see the hangman's gibbet as the horns of an ox. And if the Dinka, as reportedly they do, tend to compare all manner of objects to features of oxen, and classify all patterned and coloured surfaces by reference to an ox-colour vocabulary, that is evidence not of an 'everyday' aesthetic standing prior to artistic practice, but simply to the effects of the dominant role that aesthetic display (especially sung poetry) has in their lives. The search for ox-metaphors and ox-analogies is second nature because it is the basis of a poetic practice in which all are implicated, as producers, audiences and critics and, moreover, which they enter in a competitive spirit, so that the form becomes more and more elaborate and arcane.

The Dinka preoccupation with oxen is indeed an aesthetic preoccupation, but it is not one which should be understood as the direct transcription of the material centrality of cattle in securing physical livelihood to the plane of aesthetic sensibility and values. What makes oxen 'aesthetic' is the role they play in a locally dominant form of social competition, the competition for symbolic, rather than or as well as material capital, which accrues to a singer and composer of repute. The aesthetic importance of oxen is a function of the scope they give to imagination and creativity within the canons of Dinka poetic traditions. It is not the case, as Coote argues, that the Dinka 'see' the world in terms of the visible properties of admired oxen, that they 'see the ox in the world', as it were. On the contrary, the Dinka 'see the world in the ox', because that is what is demanded of the Dinka poet, that is the basic conceit the ox-song elaborates. One might be tempted to call this poetic aesthetic 'everyday' in the sense that it is quite likely that Dinka routinely think about things in a poetic way, just as I routinely recall bits of Haydn and Beethoven, and think about pictures, novels, and so forth. But just because the poetic may be a very quotidian feature of Dinka life and experience, that does not cause it to cease to be poetic, nor sever its connection with the 'prestige' arena of poetic competition for prestige. The 'marvels of everyday vision' of which Coote speaks are marvels produced by art.

The task of the anthropology of art is to understand the sometimes very dominant role that competition in the realm of aesthetic expression (underwritten by sophisticated artistic techniques) plays in many societies, even to the possible detriment of their material productivity. My criticisms of Coote have been aimed at showing that there cannot – at least where the Dinka are concerned – be an anthropology of aesthetics which is not also an anthropology of art, or more precisely, of artworks. I find unsatisfactory the idea that any society can be said to just 'have' an aesthetic simply by virtue of having preferences that things should look one way rather than another. It always turns out that if people want things to look one way rather than another, it is for reasons which cannot be stated in terms just of how things look. Coote's search for a quintessential 'cultural' aesthetic seems to me to lead towards a dead end, just as the aesthetician's search for universal definitions of 'beauty' led to a philosophical dead end.

REFERENCES

Burton, J. (1982) 'Figurative language and the definition of experience: the role of ox-songs in Atuot social theory', *Anthropological Linguistics*, 24 (3): 263–79.

Coote, J. (1992) '"Marvels of everyday vision": the anthropology of aesthetics and the cattle-keeping Nilotes', in J. Coote and A. Shelton (eds) *Anthropology, Art and Aesthetics* (Oxford: Clarendon).

Danto, A. (1964) 'The Artworld', *Journal of Philosophy*, 61: 571–84.

Deng, F. (1972) *The Dinka of the Sudan* (New York: Holt Rinehart & Winston).

Deng, F. (1973) *The Dinka and their Songs* (Oxford: Clarendon).

Dickie, G. (1974) *Art and the Aesthetic: An Institutional Analysis* (Ithaca: Cornell University Press).

Diffey, T. (1986) 'The idea of aesthetic experience', in M. Mitias (ed.) *Possibility of Aesthetic Experience* (Dordrecht: Nijhoff).

Forge, A. (1966) 'Art and environment in the Sepik', *Proceedings of the Royal Anthropological Institute for 1965* (London: Royal Anthropological Institute).

Kant, I. (1928) [1790] *The Critique of Judgement* (Oxford: Clarendon).

Maquet, J. (1986) *The Aesthetic Experience: An Anthropologist Looks at the Visual Arts* (New Haven: Yale University Press).

McCloskey, M. (1987) *Kant's Aesthetic* (London: Macmillan).

Stolnitz, J. (1960) *Aesthetics and Philosophy of Art* (Boston: Houghton Mifflin).

Zangwill, N. (1986) 'Aesthetics and art', *British Journal of Aesthetics*, 26 (3): 257–69.

CHAPTER 8

THE LANGUAGE OF THE FOREST

LANDSCAPE AND PHONOLOGICAL ICONISM IN UMEDA

It might seem odd to raise the question of linguistic iconicity – the diagram-like or mimetic attributes of language – in the context of a work on landscape and culture. But I hope to show that my choice of subject-matter is not as arbitrary as it might appear, and that there may be, indeed, an intimate relationship between the cultural factors shaping the phonology of certain natural languages, and the particularities of the landscape setting within which the speakers of these languages live. My thesis is that people who live in dense, unbroken jungle, such as the New Guinean peoples I shall discuss, speak languages that are unusually rich in phonological iconisms, and that this association between forest habitats and iconic languages can be theoretically accounted for. Phonological iconisms are instances in which there are interpretable relationships between speech sounds or articulatory 'gestures', and the semantic meanings conveyed by words in speech.

The simplest form of phonological iconism is onomatopoeia, which motivates such common English forms as 'hiss', 'buzz', 'crunch', and so on, a device which is also present in the New Guinean languages I am dealing with; but in these languages intelligible sound–meaning relationships are carried much further, into semantic domains in which there is no obvious relationship between 'natural' sounds and speech sounds, and the force of the iconisms involved is only apparent in the light of a much more complex cultural analysis. Our culture, for instance, supplies no answer to the question, 'What is the sound a mountain makes?' English mountains make no sounds, and consequently, there is no basis for linking the concept 'mountain' to the specific speech-sounds which have to be enunciated in order to say the word 'mountain'. English 'mountain' is an 'arbitrary sign' conforming to the general principle of the arbitrary nature of all spoken signs proposed by de Saussure (1966) and overwhelmingly accepted by linguists, with only sporadic murmurs of dissent (Sapir 1929, Jakobson and Waugh 1979). I believe that in Umeda, things are otherwise, and that the Umeda word for 'mountain' (*sis*) should be understood precisely as 'the sound that a mountain makes', or more precisely, 'the shape in articulatory/ acoustic space' made by a mountain.

The ethnographic material I shall explore in this paper is the articulatory symbolism of Umeda 'landscape' concepts (such as 'mountain') in the context of Umeda culture, which is keyed to sound-symbolism at a very basic level, as I have attempted to show more than once already (1975; 1979). But I also have in mind to do rather more than describe an interesting (questionable) linguistic phenomenon; my primary objective is to explain just why it is that it is the Umeda (and other people who live in an Umeda-like landscape) who resort to expression in the phonological-iconic mode, and why other people, who inhabit different landscapes, do not do so.

It would be a hopeless proposition to attempt to demonstrate a clear 'statistical' correlation between the New Guinea forest habitat and phonological iconism, even if one suspects, as I do personally, that such a correlation exists. I shall attempt no such demonstration, whose hopelessness resides in the fact that most ethnographers simply do not consider the possibility of a profound relationship between landscape, cognition and language, and do not construct indigenous 'culture' in the light of this unexamined possibility. Nor do linguists commonly describe languages with this in mind, even in those instances in which they are simultaneously interested in the cultural context of the language they are studying. It was mere accident which led me to devote as much attention as I did to iconism in Umeda while I was in the field; and I never explicitly focused attention on 'sounds' in Umeda culture, apart from speech sounds (Gell 1975: 120). Because of this methodological deafness, I could not advance my study of Umeda sound-symbolism beyond the point I reached in 1979, which was only to show to my own satisfaction that the pervasive presence of articulatory/phonological iconism in Umeda constituted a unique 'poetic language', so that to speak Umeda was to speak poetry, as envisaged by Rousseau (Gell 1979: 61). I had no positive explanation whatsoever to offer for this marvellous state of affairs, though I thought I could explain why Umeda had not ceased to be poetic, as most languages have.

Subsequent developments in Melanesian anthropology have altered the situation. Two ethnographies have now been published which specifically seek to reveal the auditory domain, including natural sounds, language and song, as cultural systems in their own right, and not just as adjuncts to culture at large, but as foundations, thematic at every level of cultural experience. I refer to Steve Feld's (1982: 3) path-breaking study dealing with 'sound as a cultural system' among the Kaluli of the Great Papuan Plateau and the more recent and theoretically elaborated work of James Weiner (1991) on Foi language and ethno-poetics. Both of these 'ethnographies of sound' (dealing with different language-groups, hundreds of miles from Umeda, and separated by the central highlands of New Guinea) come independently to similar conclusions about phonological iconism to those advanced by me. I draw some encouragement from this convergence of opinion, which, it seems to me, supports the inference that phonological iconism in New Guinea languages is probably widespread, but that it requires a particular ethnographic approach, that is, sensitivity to the acoustic domain as a fundamental constituent of culture, to reveal it. But this also means, unfortunately, that for a 'statistical' demonstration of the pervasiveness of phonological iconism in New Guinea languages, one would have to envisage a large cohort of Felds and Weiners committed to providing particularistic studies of the iconic systems of each of New Guinea's multitudinous cultures, since languages can be equally 'iconic' – in the sense here discussed – without bearing the least mutual resemblance one to another (see below). Similarity of landscapes does not imply 'surface' similarity of languages, because the landscape–language relationship is crucially mediated by cultural factors which may vary extensively. Extracting the in-built 'poetics' of languages (at every level, including the phonological, morphosyntactic, etc.) is in every case a new enterprise. But what may be emerging is that the enterprise is, at least with respect to a delimited category of languages, theoretically feasible and analytically fruitful.

The aim now is to delimit the kind of parameters which circumscribe the languages which are likely to show pronounced phonological iconicity. I exclude from consideration the other kind of iconicity which all languages probably do manifest, namely syntactic iconicity. Syntactic iconicity covers the kinds of relationships which exist between syntax (the rules governing the arrangement of main and subsidiary clauses within the sentence, and other grammatical features) and semantics or sentence meaning. A paradigm case of syntactic iconism is Caesar's famous sentence 'Veni, vidi, vici,' where the order of verbs mirrors the order of Caesar's actions, and the terseness of the entire construction figures the ease and rapidity of his successful military operations (Jakobson 1965). Syntactic iconicity in New Guinea languages has been examined recently by Haiman (1985), and this work has been incorporated into ethnopoetics by Weiner (1991: 87). This kind of iconicity does not breach the principle of the arbitrariness of the spoken sign, which applies not to sentences but to words and morphemes. Phonological iconism is much more problematic, since it depends on tracing connections between the sound-substance of individual words and morphemes and their meanings. As a culturally elaborated expressive mode it is probably quite rare, if only because the regular processes of sound-shift which all languages undergo would ensure, other things being equal, that phonologically iconic forms evolved into non-iconic ones after a lapse of time. Only where things are not equal, that is, where there are specific cultural vectors tending to preserve, generalize and intensify expressivity against the countervailing forces of morphological change, should one expect to encounter elaborate phonological iconism as opposed to sporadic onomatopoeia.

Now I do not think it is a matter of chance that the New Guinea languages which have seemed susceptible to analysis as systems of phonological symbolism (so far, Umeda, Kaluli and Foi) are situated in 'marginal' areas, away from the more populous and socially dynamic central highlands and maritime/riverain belts. Kaluli and Foi are in the sparsely inhabited and thickly forested slopes to the south of the central highlands (where lowland forest cover gives way to more open grassland) and Umeda occupies a similar niche in the hill country to the north of the Sepik bend, where, once again, population is very thin and livelihood depends on exploiting the forest and only minimal horticulture. What I have to say depends crucially on this common factor of forest habitat, as opposed to grassland/riverain/coastal habitats. I propose that the primary forest environment imposes a reorganization of sensibility, such that the world is perceived in a manner which gives pride of place to the auditory sense (and another sense we hardly use, olfaction: Gell 1977), and that this transformed sensibility has manifold consequences in the domain of cognition, tending to promote phonological iconicity in language.

Nor is this all. The value systems of New Guinea 'forest' cultures seem to emphasize sentiment, or (a better word, perhaps) 'sympathy', more than the cultures of the open plains and the coastal and river flats. Here, in the vibrant, tactile, scented gloom is the landscape of nostalgia and abandonment, so well described by the ethnographers of Kaluli and nearby societies (Feld 1982; Schieffelin 1976; Wagner 1972; Weiner 1988; 1991). I suspect that there is an intrinsic connection between the cultural bias towards the expression of heightened sympathy towards community members (see below on Foi/Kaluli poetics) and the predominance of hearing over seeing, which, I argue, also distinguishes these cultures. Hearing is (relatively) intimate, concrete and tactile, whereas vision promotes abstraction; iconic language is, likewise, 'concrete' (in the sense of Goldstein and Scheerer 1971; cf. Merleau-Ponty 1962) whereas arbitrary language, in which sign and meaning belong to entirely separate codes, is abstract. Forest habitat, language iconism, and the 'culture of sympathy' I will touch on later, all seem to be linked together in a way I hope to clarify as I proceed. The Umeda share some features of this cultural pattern, though I placed little emphasis on 'sympathy' in my account of Umeda culture (1975) partly because of my visualist bias, and partly because emotionality was of little theoretical interest to me in the early 1970s. At this stage it suffices to say that my argument is not just about language and the forest habitat, but also raises the question of the relationship between language and 'sociality', as it has come to be known.

Briefly, I define my problem as follows: there are, in New Guinea – and perhaps also beyond New Guinea, wherever suitable natural and cultural environments coexist – certain languages which show marked phonological iconism (of a type to be specifically described below). I propose that these languages correspond to certain forest habitats and lifestyles which privilege audition and olfaction and which de-emphasize vision, especially long-range vision. These are 'auditory' cultures which also show certain ideological continuities (i.e. sympathy). I have, first of all, to sketch in the phenomenology underlying these claims. Having done so, I will attempt to explain these facts cognitively, by arguing that where signs and their signifieds are coded in the same sensory modality, there is an in-built tendency towards iconic expressions.

UMEDA: AN AUDITORY CULTURE

Let me introduce my subject-matter by means of a brief autobiographical reflection. During my fieldwork in Umeda (West

Sepik district, now Sandaun Province, Papua New Guinea) in 1969–70, I suffered from many forms of frustration. One of the most annoying and insurmountable problems I encountered was my inability ever to obtain a decent view of the country in which Umeda is situated. In the end, I spent fourteen months in visual surroundings limited to tens of metres, and at most, half a kilometre or so. (There was one exception to this which I will go into later.) I found these restricted horizons profoundly unsatisfactory. Like all middle-class Britishers, I share our national obsession with views and panoramas, despite having to peer at them through ever-thickening spectacles. No hill is too rocky, jungly, sun-baked or windswept to deter me if I fancy that I can indulge my craving for distant prospects by ascending it. But Umeda was purgatory in this respect. The surrounding country is by no means flat and there are a number of hills in the vicinity over which I passed frequently on hunting trips or on my way to the patrol post. But on none of these hills was the forest cleared in such a way as to afford a 'view' despite my best efforts to find a suitable spot. To this day, I do not know what Umeda village looks like from a distance.

At the time, I endured my unconsummated craving for a view of Umeda as just one more of the many trials which constitute an ethnographer's lot. I was not aware that this problem had any deeper significance, though in the light of subsequent developments, it certainly had. My inability to encompass Umeda as a visualizable totality offered a direct challenge, at an experiential level, to my theoretical ambition which was to 'encompass' Umeda as an intellectually constructed whole. Please remember that this was long ago, before 'visualism' had been made a culpable offence in enlightened circles. I was perfectly confident that the objective of anthropological research was to make visible, in the form of a predominantly geometric/spatial model, the totality of Umeda social relations. Because I happen to be a pronouncedly visual thinker, I was quite successful at this, but now my self-critical middle age is upon me and I can see that there are certain disadvantages inherent in the notion that anthropological understanding is co-terminous with the provision of a visual/spatial *Gestalt*. Making use of geometrical diagrams and analytical figures, and a descriptive language continually emphasizing visual forms, this is, none the less, what I set out to do, and what, to some extent, I did. I was already in possession of the elements of the visual model of Umeda social relations while I was in the field, and my unavailing efforts to encompass Umeda in a 'view from afar' (Lévi-Strauss 1985) were motivated, not just by cultural predilection, but also by a more ambitious desire to project my intellectual construction of Umeda on to the physical terrain.

The point is that, in hindsight, this preoccupation with the visual and the visualizable may have been misplaced. The very fact that Umeda was invisible and that vision itself was of rather restricted use for a lot of the time ought to have alerted me to the possibility that the balance between vision and other sensory modalities was differently struck where the Umeda were concerned. As it was, there were a number of odd things I could not help noticing.

I was very intrigued, for instance, by a story I was told by a young man who had been a member of the first group of Umeda to visit the coast, where they had been imprisoned for a period, returning to Umeda shortly before I arrived there myself. On arrival at Vanimo (on the coast, where the prison was located) the Umeda were lined up on the sloping beach, facing out to sea. Between the Umeda and the shoreline stood a policeman. The Umeda had never seen the sea before, or any large body of water, and they had never seen a distant, flat, horizon. So rather than perceive the sea receding in the horizontal plane, they perceived it as a huge vertical wall of water, sticking up into the sky and clearly higher, from their point of vantage, than the head of the policeman facing them on the foreshore. They were afraid that he was about to be engulfed by an immense wave, and would be rapidly followed by themselves. They could not understand why the expected wave did not come.

I think that, for Umeda, whatever was visible was, *ipso facto*, relatively close. This may explain their extraordinary courage, not to say foolhardiness, in attempting to walk from Wewak (a coastal town about 150km away) to Umeda, after a mass break-out from the labour compound there. This famous escapade (in New Guinea it is an adventure to pass 10 kilometres through enemy territory, let alone 150) was undertaken, so participants told me, because they had been able to see the whole country through the windows of the aeroplane which flew them from Imonda (near Umeda) to Wewak. They had seen the line of the Torricelli mountains and the valley of the Sepik on the other side. These they followed during the return journey, taking many weeks, during which they were mostly captured and one of them was shot as a presumed witch. They had no idea of the actual difficulty of the journey, which they undertook only because they were deluded into thinking that the distance was very much shorter than it was in reality. I believe that this arose from their habitual tendency to assume that the distance between any two intervisible points would be short and easily traversed.

Another line of evidence that the Umeda operated a different perceptual framework from the western norm, was the way in which they were always much more aware of their acoustic and olfactory surroundings than I was. Mostly this goes without saying. Hunting (and also raiding and escaping from raids) in dense forest places a premium on hearing as the main sensory modality for detecting objects and events at some distance, where they are invariably out of sight. Out hunting, I could never find game for myself, because I tended to look for it; the Umeda listened, and of course knew exactly what to listen for. In the bush, they travelled with eyes downcast, looking for thorns and obstacles on the path (and other signs, such as tracks) while they 'surveyed' their surroundings with their ever-receptive ears. Because hearing had such acute functional saliency for them, they observed a discipline about noise which was very marked; either they were very quiet, or they were very noisy, but they did not tolerate intrusive unsocial background noise, which we take for granted. This feature is well brought out in the Umeda origin myth which accounts for the existence of white men, who are defined, characteristically, as producers of noise pollution. The myth begins, as usually for myths of this genre in New Guinea, by relating that there were two brothers, the older one black-skinned and stupid, the younger one white-skinned and intelligent. The elder lived like an Umeda, hunting in the forest, while the younger stayed behind in the village and made things. My informant specified that the things that the younger brother made were kettles, spoons, knives, tin plates and saucepans. He made them by bashing metal with a hammer. The elder brother came back from hunting weary and wishing to sleep, but the younger brother persisted with his metal-bashing operations. The elder brother found the clatter unbearable so he rose up in his wrath and drove his brother from the village. The younger brother took his metal objects and descended into a hole which led to the interior of the earth. That is where white men live to this day, underground, bashing metal, and making a terrible noise.

Of course, vision as well as hearing is necessary in hunting and raiding, especially at the climax of events. But the point I am making here is not that the Umeda did not see things, or relied on hearing to the exclusion of all else, but that the relationship between the visual and auditory components of their ambience was differently evaluated than it is with us. For an Umeda an audible but invisible object was entirely 'present' in a way difficult for us to grasp, in that for us such an object is 'hidden', however perceptible. The concept of 'hiding' in Umeda culture was, in fact, quite different from our own. The Umeda term for 'hidden(ly)', *maksmaks*, implies, not invisibility, but the concealment of auditory clues, as in the silent approach of an assassin. An individual who approached audibly, even if concealed the while in thick bush, would not be 'hidden' at all in their terms. The Umeda expression applies to clandestine (silent) movement, and also to concealment of the truth in speech, that is, lying, prevarication, depriving the interlocutor of the auditory information needed to perceive the true state of affairs.

For us, invisible objects are deeply problematic, but not for the Umeda, who defined objective existence in terms of audibility, not visibility. This came out in conflicts over 'evidence' which I often had with my informants. Once an Umeda man I knew well came into my house looking as if he had just had the fright of his life and bursting to tell me about the harrowing experience he had just had. He had been on a forest path leading to the village and he had been chased up and down by a *yawt*, a horrifying kind of ogre in whom all Umeda firmly believe. The dusk had fallen and the forest was plunged in more than the usual darkness, but, yes, the ogre had been there all right, waiting. He had heard it panting, *hu-hu-hu*, and he had raced up the path to escape it, but the ogre had doubled round, hiddenly (*maksmaks*) and before he knew it, the thing was right in front of him, going *hu-hu-hu* again and he had had to cut through the forest to avoid it. Finally, rejoining the path, he had made it home as quick as his legs would carry him. 'Yes, yes,' I said, cutting him off, 'but did you actually see the ogre?' My informant looked at me in perplexity. 'It was dark, I was running away, it was there on the path, going *hu-hu-hu* . . .' I came away from this conversation, and from similar ones, as puzzled as ever about how such sensible people as the Umeda could remain so credulous on the subject of ogres and other terrifying apparitions. When, I wondered, was an Umeda going to admit to actually seeing one of these monsters? But that, of course, was a misapprehension bred of a visually based notion of the real. For Umeda, hearing is believing, and the Umeda really do hear ogres, or what they take to be ogres.

It is relevant here to note that strong emotion makes Umeda 'deaf' rather than 'blind'. Where we would say somebody was 'blind' with rage, or 'could not stand the sight of' some other person, the Umeda say they cease to hear, or wilfully won't hear one another, because they are 'deaf' (*agami*, 'closed ears').

Umeda treat sight, not as a basic evidential sense, but as a climactic sense with connotations of intimacy and danger. As is common in New Guinea, ordinary conversations do not require sustained eye contact, while intimate or confrontational conversations do. Direct sustained eye contact between a man and a woman implies sexual solicitation or complicity. The aim, in dancing, or simply ogling any passing female, is to capture the woman's glance, because everything, depends on seeing and being seen. Besides being the organ of seduction, the eye (especially of a senior kinsman) which gives an angry glance, terrifies and demoralizes the victim of a sorcery attack. This is the Umeda version of the belief in the 'evil eye', but the point is that it works only at close (genealogical) range, between agnatic kin, while lethal sorcery (and actual violence) is carried out invisibly, by means of night attacks from affinal and enemy villages.

The visual world is close-range, intimate, but it is very far from being the whole world, very far from being anything like what we could recognize as a 'landscape' since it is only a sequence of partial glimpses, which do not cohere around any central point of vantage. In the 'village' one sees the hamlet one happens to be in, not the 'village' as a whole. Looking out, one sees the tops of the nearby trees, but not the gardens, paths, streams, hunting tracts, sago-stands, and so on which really constitute 'the bush'; these are hidden below, though one can hear bush activities in progress; chopping, pounding sago, and the standard location-giving 'whoops' uttered by parties of Umeda on the move. In 'the bush' one never sees the village, or indeed, any but the most adjacent surroundings, most of which are irrelevant. There is nothing to bind all this together, no privileged 'domain-viewing' point, like the view from the keep of a castle. Bound together it is, though, but in a quite different way. Lacking a visual landscape, what the Umeda have instead, I would say, is a 'landscape of articulation', a landscape which is accessible, primordially, in the acoustic modality. This landscape is constructed out of the interface between two kinds of experience; distally it comprises a codification of ambient sound, that is, a soundscape, proximally it comprises the basic unifying armature of the body as a sounding cavity, sensitive to sound and, through the autokinetically sensed experience of verbal and mimetic vocalization, productive of sound.

THE ARTICULATORY LANDSCAPE

Merleau-Ponty (1962: 184) says, 'The spoken word is a gesture, its meaning, a world.' One can indeed imagine the Umeda world/ landscape as a series of mappings between articulatory gestures, syllabic shapes moulded within the oral tract (microcosm) and the macrocosm consisting of the body, social relationships mediated through the body, and other natural forms, particularly trees, and the encompassing physical ambience. The oral tract (fulfilling both vocal and gustatory functions, emitting and receiving) is a little landscape in itself (cf. Mimica 1981) but not a stationary one. Moving and shaping, transforming itself from within, its various positions correspond to particular physical and social vectors: constriction and restraint, above and below, centrality and distance.

The Umeda language is richly provided with onomatopoeic words (e.g. *huf*, the name of the wooden trumpets Umeda play, which make a noise exactly like that). Even more so, there is a large class of vocal 'sound-effects' which are used in narratives to punctuate and illustrate the action. These can be used without any additional explanation. For instance, in one myth, the hero has been abandoned at the top of a tall, unclimbable tree. At this point the story goes into pure sound-effects, *w-w-w-ba*. . . One just has to know that this is the noise of the hero's tears dripping softly down from on high, striking leaves as they fall, alerting the friendly snake who will rescue him. But these onomatopoeic words and sound-effects are not what constitutes the basic system, which is not confined to contexts in which sounds are directly represented, albeit in terms which are only transparent to members of the culture.

The fundamental schema of Umeda phonological symbolism can be derived from the following basic mappings. Front (alveolar) consonants are associated with centrality (*edi* = man, *edie* = middle, *edtodna* = male/central moiety) while velar (back) consonants are associated with peripherality (*agwa* = woman, *aga* = ear, *agea* = arm/ branch, *agwatodna* = female/peripheral moiety). This basic opposition is aligned with another, which opposes nasalized front bilabials and alveolars which denote 'soft' nutritive/gustatory objects and experiences (*mo* = fruit, *mol* = daughter/vulva) to hard back consonants associated with hard objects (*ke* = bone) and velar affricates associated with disgust (*ehe*). Umeda lexemes are commonly built up from morphemic elements each of which may be found in diverse combinations. Thus, for instance, an entity which combines, say,

centrality/masculinity with disgustingness must combine an element
featuring one of the alveolar consonants with an element featuring
one of the velar affricates. Such an entity is easily identified: it is the
species of blindworm (actually a legless lizard) which lives inside the
hollow interiors of old palm trees, living on the ants which are to be
found there. The name of this creature, of which the Umeda are
extremely fearful, is *eliehe*, a long, pink, self-propelled phallus which
sometimes emerges when palms are cut down (cf. Gell 1975: 240).
The name *eliehe* decomposes into *eli + ehe*; *eli* being a variant of *edi*
(replacing the alveolar stop with the corresponding glide) plus *ehe*,
which we have already met. *Eliehe* is more than a neutral phonic
sign, it is a 'gesture' delineating its object in articulatory space, which
is simultaneously mapped on to social and emotional space. As
Merleau-Ponty (1962: 179–87) writes:

> the meaning of words must finally be induced from the words
> themselves, or more exactly their conceptual meaning must be
> formed by a kind of deduction from a gestural meaning which is
> immanent in speech . . . The gesture brings certain perceptible bits
> of the world to my notice, inviting my concurrence in them . . . the
> gesture does not make me think of anger, it is anger itself . . . [the
> 'conceptual and delimiting' meanings of words are arbitrary, but
> this] . . . would no longer be the case if we took in the emotional
> content of a word, what we have called above its 'gestural' sense
> which is all-important in poetry for example. It would then be
> found that words, vowels and phonemes are so many ways of
> 'singing' the world, and their function is to represent the world,
> not, as naïve onomatopoeic theory had it, by reason of an object-
> ive resemblance, but because they extract, and literally express,
> their emotional essence.

These remarks of Merleau-Ponty may seriously overstate the role
of phonological iconism in most languages, but I hold them to be
almost literally true of Umeda (serendipitously, *The Phenomenology
of Perception* was among the small collection of books I carried into
the field). Let me examine another example of 'gestural' meaning,
this time specifically to do with 'landscape' in the sense we would
understand. I said, at the outset, that there was no culturally obvious
way in which 'mountain' in English could be phonologically motivated. English mountains are silent and immobile, and it is hard to
imagine that there could be any one vocal 'gesture' which would

communicate the essence of mountainhood better than any other. In Umeda, things are otherwise, though it requires a cultural interpretation to bring this out. The Umeda word for mountain is *sis*. Umeda 'mountains' are really ridges, with sharp tops, and they define the boundaries of territories, particularly to the north and west, where the major enemies of Umeda reside. The sibilant 's' is uniformly associated with (*a*) male power and (*b*) sharp, narrow things like pointed sticks (*sah*). Male power comes from the coconut *sa*, and the ancestors *sa-tod* (village/male/central). Sharp things like bamboo knives are *sai*, *sa* plus the constricted, 'narrow' vowel 'i'. *Sis*, a symmetrical arrangement of sibilants and the narrow 'i', is very appropriate for an Umeda 'mountain', that is, a narrow ridge, associated with masculine pursuits, danger, and so on. As a ridge, it is opposed to *kebe*, a flat-topped knoll of the kind Umeda hamlets are built on, which combines the hardness-implying 'k' sound with *ebe* (bilabial) meaning 'fat' (prosperous).

One can carry the analysis of *sis* as 'a mountain made audible' one stage further. I mentioned that there is one exception to the generalization that no landscape-features distant by more than half a kilometre or so are visible from Umeda. The exception is the *awsis*, a tall ridge to the north of Umeda, marking the boundary between Umeda territory and the territory of the 'Waina-Sowanda' groups who share the same culture and language (the Umeda's 'minor' enemies and affines) and the Wasengla valley people to the north and west, 'major' enemies, who before the imposition of the colonial peace often threatened to overwhelm the Umeda. In traditional times, no Umeda had ventured beyond this ridge into the Wasengla valley. The name *awsis* decomposes into *aw* + *sis*. *Aw* plays an independent role in the language; as the maximally 'open' vowel 'a' followed by the rounded, constricted, or restraining semivowel 'w', *aw* is a component of words indicating encircling limits; thus one has *awda* = a fence, and *popaw* = a river dam: *po* = water + *aw*. (Cf. also *yawt*, the encircling ogre of the forest.) The *awsis* is thus the vertical restraining fence or wall around the Umeda world, perhaps the real progenitor of the vertical wall of water the prisoners saw when they looked out to sea on Vanimo beach.

Umdakebe, the village knoll, and *awsis* mark, respectively, the core and the periphery of the Umeda articulatory landscape; but what stands between foreground and background? The Umeda landscape, formed as it is out of transient sounds and articulations, has to be understood dynamically, rather than as a fixed array of visual/spatial objects. Landscape features are grasped as movements rather than as forms. Take, for instance, a common feature of Umeda country, the kind of pools known as *pwiob* which form where springs emerge through rock. Such a pool consists of a narrow passage from which water emerges (under slight pressure) and the surrounding, swelling, pool itself. As an articulatory gesture, *pwiob* has two parts, *pwi* + *ob*. *Pwi* belongs to the class of words all of which imply upward growth; *wi* = cucurbit (symbol of growth, taboo to children for that reason, cf. Gell 1979), *wis* = moon (growth), *pwi* = growth shoot, pitpit (tall spindly edible cane), *pwie* = tall. This corresponds to the 'forced upward growth' of the water emerging from the rock. *Ob*, on the other hand, belongs to the class of articulatory gestures of 'swelling', usually with 'a' or 'e', thus *ab* = ripe (also *abwi*), *kabwi* = big, fat, *ebe* = fat, *pab* = penile erection, *popab* = highwater, flood. All of these words featuring vowel + b involve an articulatory 'swelling' in that to utter them one must allow the cheeks to distend with air while voicing the bilabial (this resonation is acoustically what is distinctive about this type of consonant). Finally the rounded vowel 'o' seems to mimic round shapes, the round shape of the pool in this instance (cf. *mol* = fruit, *mo* = gullet, vulva, word, etc.). Thus, taken as a whole, the word *pwiob* provides a dynamic moving image of a spring-fed pool as a process rather than a thing; an articulated demonstration of the water spurting up through the rock, and the swelling, rounded pool forming around it.

There is a more encompassing sense of 'movement' in the Umeda acoustic/articulatory landscape which opposes above and below, complementing the axis of centrality/peripherality which has already been described (for further details see Gell 1975: 133–7 and 1979: 46). The above/below axis is linked to the phonological contrast between the low/back vowels 'u' and 'o' and the high/front vowels 'a' and 'i'. If we start at the top, we have the empyrean (*pai*). The stars are *painauf*. Stars are also the penises of the ancestors, the penis itself being *paiha*. Closing off the uppermost realm we have the clouds *awfie* (another of the group of -*aw*- words). *Awfie* means 'on top'.

The element for 'up' is *ap*, Umeda being one of those languages in which the word for 'come' implies upward motion (come up, *idapiav*) and the word for 'go' implies downward motion (*iduiav*). When upward motion is rapid and explosive, *ap* is inverted and becomes *pa*, as in *hotamovie pa*! ('he scrambled up the *hotamov* tree'). In general, superiority expressed by the open/front vowel 'a', as in *sa-tod* = ancestor, mentioned previously. Senior male agnates are *at*, which is also usable as an 'up' deictic. I was occasionally addressed as *at* by Umeda, not because they wanted to claim kinship with me, but because I was taller than them; sometimes kinship term and deictic expression would fuse entirely, as when they were attempting to point me in the right direction to shoot some bird concealed above in the foliage (*at-at-at* . . . 'up there, uncle, up, up . . .'). *Pat* is the roof beam of a house, *asi* senior affines and grand-parents, *na* mother's brother, and so on.

Downward movement is indicated by -u- as in *iduiav* (go down). The bush, which is 'low' in relation to the village, is *sugut*. The lowest part of the bush are swamps: *pud*. 'Inferior' social roles are marked by the same 'u' vowel symbolism; *mugtod* = bachelor, from *mug* = leg, foot; *ipudi* = son; *tuda* = child; *ude* = little sister, dog. But the canonical downward movement is that of water, falling from the skies and flowing down the many streams; all these are *po*. The general down/bush direction is indicated as *pokwie* or *sugwie*. When the *po* falls in quantity, the floods rise, *popab*, from *pab* = erection (cf. above on 'swelling' words). These falling/rising watery motions have the standard sexual/cosmological significance. The earth is female and womb-like; transfixed by earthworms (*subul*) of which the Umeda are extremely afraid, its properties as a womb (*uda*: also 'netbag') are particularly concentrated in the deposits of white kaolin clay hidden underground, which are a prime magical material. The term for this magical kaolin is *urugubwe*, a most magical sound, delivered *sotto voce*.

These notes on the articulatory landscape of Umeda must suffice for the present; I might prolong them, since the entire vocabulary of the Umeda language constitutes a 'landscape' in the sense I am driving at. I have already published much additional material and there seems no point in duplicating it. However, to afford a further glimpse of the system, and for the enjoyment of puzzle addicts, I reproduce an illustration which I devised for the article I published in 1979, which maps a number of the most important Umeda terms on to the composite man/tree/society, forming the 'triple analogy' at the heart of the system (Fig. 8.1). I trust that what I have said here, in conjunction with what I have said in earlier publications, will have been enough to lend plausibility to my basic contention that the Umeda language is pervasively iconic at the level of phonology and articulation. Now, having established my ethnographic point, I want to put forward an explanation for this relatively unusual, or at least unfamiliar, state of affairs.

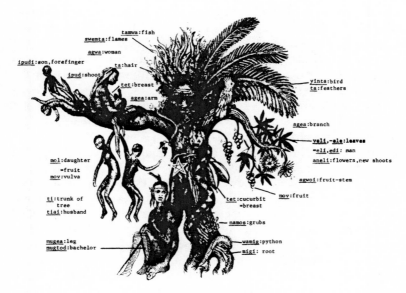

Figure 8.1   The triple analogy

SENSORY MODALITY AND LANGUAGE ICONISM

In the New Guinea forest habitat, I have argued, hearing is relatively dominant (over vision) as the sensory modality for coding the environment as a whole. What I aim to do now is to propose a general principle which would explain why 'acoustic' cultures might be particularly liable to invent, elaborate, and preserve linguistic phonological iconisms, by contrast to speakers of the languages of non-acoustic, or 'visual' cultures. The principle involved is this: where there is uniformity between the dominant sensory modality for registering 'the world', and the sensory modality used in linguistic communication, iconism will tend to prevail; but where this uniformity of sensory modality does not exist, phonological iconism will tend to be less well marked or entirely absent.

The normal sensory modality for language is hearing; language is acoustically coded. But whereas in 'visual' cultures – which for the purposes of argument can be taken to include all cultures in which vision is the main distal sense – there has to be a cross-over between the sense modality of the (visual) world evoked by language, and the (acoustic) code of language, in primarily acoustic cultures there is no such cross-over; the dominantly acoustic 'world' is directly evoked in the same sensory modality, in the acoustic code of language. In other words, Umeda, and languages like Umeda, are phonologically iconic, because they evoke a reality which is itself 'heard' and imagined in the auditory code, whereas languages like English are non-iconic because they evoke a reality which is 'seen' and imagined in the visual code.

Why should uniformity of sensory modality between the sign and signified give rise to iconism? Is this in fact true? Let us consider English, for a start. English has two main kinds of phonologically iconic words, onomatopoeias (squeak, hum, rumble, etc.) and a more problematic category of 'expressive' words like the set of words ending in 'sh' which denote sudden destructive action: bash, crash, crush, smash, and so on (Fudge 1970). Maybe these latter are not motivated at all, but only appear to us to be so, by what I have called elsewhere 'a posteriori iconism', that is, by being associated with their meanings (Gell 1979: 57, 59). Let us say, therefore, that the only indisputable instances of phonological motivation in English are actually onomatopoeias, that is, words which denote sounds, and to some extent actually resemble those sounds (so that one could anticipate that non-English speakers, presented with the words 'squeak' and 'hum' and a selection of actual squeaks and hums, could sort them out correctly according to the English taxonomy of sounds). This is good evidence for my proposition, because it shows that, in a language like English, where, exceptionally, the meaning of a word is actually a sound, then 'the arbitrariness of the sign' is suspended, and the language preserves a thriving subset of phonological iconisms, through all the historical vicissitudes which otherwise beset sound–meaning relationships. But the huge majority of words in English do not denote sounds and are not onomatopoeic, and thus the whole question of onomatopoeia is relegated to the sidelines. It is too obvious and trivial to merit much consideration.

But perhaps the 'obvious' can teach us a lesson. If words for sounds continue to be iconic even where there is no pervasive tendency to phonological iconism elsewhere in the language, then at the very least it suggests that in this domain (i.e. the linguistic ceding of acoustic experience) there is a principle of 'least effort' at work in the deployment of expressive resources; if an onomatopoeic expression is intrinsically feasible (because of the uniformity of the sound-substance of language and the acoustic reality being evoked) then an onomatopoeic form is likely to emerge and be preserved. We only need to expand the scope of what, for any culture, counts as 'acoustic reality' to find the explanation for pervasive phonological iconism, that is, generalized onomatopoeia.

Unfortunately, in the history of attempts to criticize the Saussurean postulate of the 'arbitrariness of the sign' the obvious has been lost sight of. Following the work of Sapir (1929), some linguists and psychologists have sought to explain phonological iconism by means of 'synaesthesia', that is, certain natural propensities we may have to associate qualities in one sensory modality with corresponding qualities in another (Peterfalvi 1970: 47). Thus comparative studies have been carried out to link 'bigness' with open vowels and littleness with narrow vowels, as in the French pairing *grand* versus *petit*. Or we have Köhler's famous experiment in which respondents were invited to decide which of the two forms shown below (Fig. 8.2) was TAKETE and which was MALUMA (Peterfalvi 1970: 33). These studies are predicated on the notion that 'spatial' (visual) qualities are intrinsically associated with acoustic (articulatory) qualities by 'synaesthesia'. This, I think, is a mistake, not because these experiments have failed to demonstrate certain uniformities in human intuitions, but because they have assumed that phonological iconism, above the level of 'mere' onomatopoeia, necessarily involves associative links between vision and hearing, or some other pairing of different sense modalities. I would interpret the Köhler experiment differently. I believe that respondents see the 'takete-object' not as a silent, spiky, thing, but as an object which makes the sound 'takete' (e.g. if one attempted to bowl it along the floor), and ditto the soft, rubbery, maluma-object. So 'takete' and 'maluma' are really onomatopoeic, and respondents tended to identify them correctly, not on the basis of acoustic/visual associations, but because of sedimented (and cross-culturally uniform) knowledge of the kinds of sounds objects make. This analysis also applies to the kinaesthetic sensations generated in the oral tract while articulating, in that

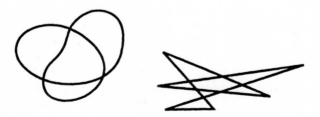

Figure 8.2 Köhler's figures.

auditory awareness is a specialized 'tactile' sense anyway, and 'inside the head' tactile and acoustic sensations are indissociable, not two separate sensory modalities.

One can approach the problem of uniformity and non-uniformity between the sensory modalities of sign and signified from the opposite direction. As is well known, there has been much debate among specialists in the education of the deaf about lip-reading, finger-spelling, and other communicative modes which allow the deaf to access spoken language indirectly (via a visual channel) versus sign-language, which was developed in institutions for the deaf, by the deaf, primarily for the purpose of communicating with one another (the history of the subject is summarized in Sacks 1989). (These deaf-community sign-languages have to be distinguished from sign-languages used by hearing people to communicate unspeakingly, or with deaf individuals in their midst.) The best known of the sign-languages developed within deaf communities, which exclude hearers and have frequently been repressed by well-meaning but insensitive authorities, is American Sign Language (ASL). The world of the deaf is a visual one. ASL, despite what its detractors once said, is a fully functional communication system, capable of transmitting all the semantic representations of spoken language, except, of course, the ones appertaining to acoustic experiences. It is just as 'good', just as 'advanced', as spoken language. But even the briefest study of the standard work on ASL (Klima and Bellugi 1979) suffices to show that (visual) iconisms are not just frequent, but pervasive throughout the entire language.

Klima and Bellugi note that there are some arbitrary signs in ASL, and that the frequency of arbitrary forms seems to be increasing as time goes by, but they are in no doubt that iconicity has been, and remains, a constitutive principle in acquiring, using, and developing ASL, and that this arises from the 'cognitive naturalness' of imitative signing (ibid. 21–6). In terms of the theory being advanced here, the pervasive iconism of ASL is the predictable consequence of the uniformity between the sensory modality used in signing (vision) and the sensory modality which dominates in the deaf world (also vision). That is to say, the principle of least effort (or 'naturalness') in expression, leads to the production of visual iconisms which are easier to interpret, remember, and innovate than arbitrary signs. They also permit greater flexibility of paralinguistic expression (e.g. emphasis, stylization, comic effects, etc.) as is well brought out in Klima and Bellugi's chapter devoted to ASL signed poetry (ibid. ch. 14).

Such, then, is the suggested cognitive explanation for the pervasiveness of phonological iconisms in Umeda. Because, in the forest habitat, there is relative dominance of the acoustic modality as the distal sense in terms of which experience is organized and concepts are formed, it follows that (relatively speaking) there is uniformity in sensory modality between signs and signifieds, and consequently phonological iconisms are favoured on the basis of 'naturalness' in the employment of expressive means.

It would be interesting to enquire further as to whether the pervasive iconicity of ASL as the cognitively most natural mode of communication among the deaf is associated with a specific set of value orientations, as I shall claim below that phonological iconism is associated with a value orientation stressing 'sympathy'. The resilience of ASL over nearly a century of outright suppression (after 1880: Sacks 1989: 27) suggests that it fulfilled an emotional as much as a practical or instrumental need among the deaf in institutions. And the very marked suitability of ASL for the expression of moods and feelings might suggest that this is a language which mediates egalitarian social solidarity particularly well, whatever else it may be able to do with respect to the communication of abstract information. So there may be a deep connection here, but it would require a more extended analysis to do full justice to the problem. Let me return therefore to phonological iconism and landscape in New Guinea, this time in a slightly wider comparative perspective.

CONCLUDING COMMENTS: LANGUAGE AND ETHNO-POETICS

The significance of Feld's Kaluli 'ethnography of sound' in the context of the present discussion lies less in what he says about phonological iconism as such, which I shall come to in due course, than in his original and highly successful attempt to focus on sound as a formative element in culture. Feld is able to do this because of the conjunction of two factors; first of all the Kaluli environment, and secondly certain thematic elements in Kaluli culture, which are equally well brought out by Schieffelin (1976). The Kaluli occupy the slopes of Mount Bosavi, on the Great Papuan Plateau (which is very far from being flat). This is an enormous expanse of very densely forested and thinly settled territory, ecologically not unlike the Border Mountains region where Umeda is situated, and, like the Umeda, the Kaluli exploit sago extensively (and, like the Umeda, sing sad songs while they do so: Feld n.d.). The Kaluli forest is full of voices; these voices are birds, particularly the Muni bird whose song, descending D–C–A–G, is the prototype of Kaluli 'sung-texted-weeping' (Feld 1982: 32–3). Birdsong, Feld shows, is a basic key to Kaluli culture, since it is as birds/mourners that Kaluli seek ritual apotheosis in the Gisaro song ceremonies described in Schieffelin's work (1976), and in fact, after death, they become birds, travelling from place to place and singing, as in life. Birds are simultaneously part of the world of the living and the world of the dead, but not as tangible things, only as disembodied songs. 'To you they are birds, to [us] they are voices in the forest,' as one Kaluli put it to Feld (1982: 45). Bird classification, he goes on to show, is based not on what birds look like, but on the kinds of songs they have (ibid. ch. 2). All this strongly underlines the claim I am making that certain forest cultures are disposed to order reality in the acoustic code, or, to be more precise, it was as a result of reading Feld that this possibility occurred to me.

Birdsong is not the only kind of sound which is thematic in Kaluli culture. The other very important source of acoustic coding of the environment is noise produced by watercourses and particularly waterfalls. The descending movement of Kaluli song is the sung equivalent of a waterfall, and particular streams and falls are perpetually evoked in the texts of Kaluli songs, which are typically 'journeys' through the remembered forest, in search of lost companions (ibid. 107 ff.). Place, sound and social memory are fused together in Kaluli poetics. It would certainly be correct to suppose that the acoustic landscape of Kaluli constitutes their 'world' in the fullest sense; and that their rituals, in which visual display, though present, is subordinated to a cataract of sheer sound, evoke a heard rather than a visible transcendence.

Of the presence of a degree of acoustic dominance in Kaluli there can perhaps be no doubt; what remains to be asked is whether the Kaluli language shows the same pervasive iconism as I have claimed is the case in Umeda. I cannot say whether this is so in relation to the language as a whole, but Feld is quite specific in noting the presence of phonological symbolism in song texts. The device is known as 'sound words', and employs specific vowels to communicate environmental features and qualities (ibid. 144–50). These symbolically employed vowel sounds (in combination with appropriate consonants) evoke birds, water and forest. For instance *gi-ge* 'is the sound of trees turning with the change of season . . . the forest hums and buzzes as some leaves fall dramatically with crisp sounds and others drop softly and continuously' (ibid. 146). Poetic 'sound words' based on -*u*- evoke waterfalls, thunder, falling trees; -*o*- words the flight of birds, and so on.

These forms also play a part in ordinary speech, though they are treated differently from a grammatical point of view in their poetic and ordinary language uses. What is not perhaps clear from the discussion is whether they are a delimited class, or whether many more words in the language employ the same kind of vowel symbolism than the ones particularly used in song texts. It could be that 'sound words' are just that, words for sounds, and more comparable to the 'sound-effects' one finds in Umeda myths (cf. above) rather than to the bulk of the Umeda examples considered hitherto. On the other hand, they are clearly much more systematic and integrated into the language than is commonly the case.

Any such doubts are removed in connection with the Foi, who occupy (less mountainous) territory on the eastern edge of the plateau, near Lake Kutubu. Weiner (1991) is quite explicit in identifying phonological iconicity as a general feature of Foi language, much exploited in poetry. Weiner cites my 1979 paper and quotes certain of my comments, though I am sure he would have arrived at exactly the same conclusions had he lacked this particular stimulus. Weiner devotes whole sections of his book to exploring different types of iconisms in Foi, for example space/time deictics (ibid. 72 ff.), movement and rest, emotional qualities of tenseness and intimacy appertaining to kinship relations (81 ff.). However, he makes a very important point that has surfaced already, namely, that languages that are iconic are not necessarily iconic on the same basis; there is far from being any 'universal' system of iconisms. Thus he notes that Umeda has a 'k' sound in the first-person pronoun (*ka* = I) whereas in Foi, *ka* (for entirely different reasons) is 'woman'. The basis for the Umeda first person pronoun is the cultural postulate that 'bone' (*ke*) is the core of the person: the self is a hard, resistant, core of bone surrounded by flesh (*nih*). Hence the maximally hard consonant, 'k'. Whereas in Foi 'k' words all imply restraint, constraint, factors which inhere in affinal relationships, hence, '*ka*'.

Weiner concludes that one source of phonological iconism is the tendency of languages to develop sets of allied words on the basis of shared sound-associations (what I called 'a posteriori iconism', Gell 1979: 59; Weiner 1991: 84). That is to say, once a term is ensconced in the language, sound and meaning, even if arbitrarily conjoined initially, will henceforth be associated, so that new terms may accrete around the original one, exploiting the same established resonances. The reality of this phenomenon is not in doubt (Weiner cites English examples from Bolinger 1965) but I prefer to think that it is not the principle which is responsible for iconism in 'acoustic cultures' – or at least, not entirely. Even so, Weiner does not seem to discount 'a priori' iconism of the kind I was keen to demonstrate in Umeda. This question is obviously open to further debate.

But perhaps the most important theoretical development in Weiner's work, which I would like to take up in these closing remarks, is the analysis he provides of the relation between language and sensibility. Weiner takes a strongly Heideggerian stance in interpreting Foi sensibility (revealed particularly in their poetics) as an existential quest, to which he attaches absolute significance. Drawing on Heidegger's metaphor of language as the 'house of being' (1971: 132) he argues that poetic evocation of the world in language 'desevers the distances between us and things in their true being' (Weiner 1991: 200). Just as houses are not separate from their occupants but part of their personality, so languages are not a neutral tool, useful for describing a world 'out there' but are constitutive of the world itself. To have a house, a language, is to have a world. Foi poetic texts are journeys through this linguistic 'house', which are enacted inside a (long-) house which is itself metaphorically linked to the totality of the Foi territory and landscape (ibid. 64–70, 185–95). Running through all this is a critique of Cartesianism and 'western' rationalism. Weiner contrasts the home-grown pathos of Foi poetry, which arises directly from the experience of loss and abandonment, with the alienated character of western art, which is produced by virtuosi for an audience screened from the processes of art-making itself. Foi poetry abolishes the distance between subject and object, our art establishes and reinforces this distance (ibid. 202). He also cites Heidegger's claim that 'for speakers of modern European language, the existential link between poetry (art), life, and thinking has been lost' (ibid. 201). Among the Foi, this 'link' is still intact.

Weiner's commentary on Foi poetics raises a number of very interesting issues. The whole thrust of his book is to show a linkage between Foi poetics and a set of social attitudes, which may best be labelled 'sympathetic'. Foi culture, in its moments of self-revelation (when the songs of loss and abandonment are sung) culminates in the elicitation and display of sympathy for the dead, and sympathy for the survivors who remain behind to mourn their departure. The same can be said of the Kaluli, who express their sentiments in very similar poetic and institutional forms. 'Sociality', in Foi and Kaluli terms, is crucially bound up with the demonstration of sympathy, and given that (sung) poetry is the supreme instrument for the social communication of sympathy, there is reason enough to describe these as 'poetic' societies, invoking Heidegger, as Weiner does.

The interesting point for us, however, is that the culture of sympathy conducts itself in a tightly restricted code, a highly invariant musical idiom (well described by Feld) and an equally simplified poetic format. Claiming to discover in this restricted domain something amounting to the 'essence' of poetry, of art in general, seems to run the risk of romantic idealism. Weiner himself is forced to recognize that poetry, in this vein of artless truth, is only half of what Foi culture is about. Only women compose poetry (though men sing it) while male verbal art consists of spells whose efficacy reposes precisely in the fact that they subvert lived experience and impose a barrier between the apparent and the real (ibid. 16–17). Magic is not real poetry, says Weiner, but this is a question of critical dogma, and hardly consistent with the more commonly held view that verbal magic works through powerful metaphors, and is hence decidedly poetic, whether or not it is intended to be emotionally expressive. The same can be said of the poetics of political rhetoric, and other male verbal arts, in which dissimulation and concealment often play a marked role.

Weiner's conception of poetry as the spontaneous revelation of being, and nothing else, is too one-sided. The poetics of loss and abandonment which he and Feld describe so well is only one facet of Foi/Kaluli culture, for all that it is a facet they and their ethnographers choose to emphasize particularly. As such, it cannot be made into a touchstone for determining what ought to count as 'authentic' art, for them or for us. Rather than appeal to the universality of Heideggerian romantic notions of 'human nature' (ibid: 13) it seems better to construct theories which locate poetic practices, not in relation to 'being' but in relation to context, more narrowly understood. Because it is here, in the relation between landscape, personhood and language, that the factors that are responsible for the genesis of particular poetic forms are instituted.

The approach to ethno-poetics implied in this paper rests on this more local foundation. I agree with Merleau-Ponty (and oppose Heidegger) in emphasizing the crucial role of the body, perception, and the composite formed out of the body in its perceptual environment, in the grounding of language. Language is not the 'house of being', in any absolute sense; if anything, the body is that, and language is one function of the body. But there is no 'absolute' body, either; the body is a locality, an ambience, and a certain perceptual regime imposed by that ambience and inculcated over a lifetime. I trace the roots of Foi poetics not to language itself, therefore, but to this perceptual surround. The prevalence of iconisms is a diagnostic feature, not just of a style of life destined to culminate in a certain type of poetic expression, but also of a certain type of sociality which culminates in the expression of sympathy. The linguistic devices and predominating themes of this poetry share a common origin, that is, the contingencies, the characteristic instability (demographic, residential, political) of the marginal forest habitat.

Although I did not focus attention on it, the theme of 'sympathy' is equally prominent in Umeda culture, and the sung poetry of the Umeda is also comparable in style and tone. Like the Foi/Kaluli, the Umeda engaged in passionate, formalized, keening over the dead, the women sang dirges, and one whole night of the *ida* ceremony was entirely devoted to singing songs which, as far as I can reconstruct from wholly inadequate notes, very strongly resemble the kind of nostalgic, bird-infested songs described by Weiner and Feld (Gell 1975: 199–201). So, on the one hand, iconicity is peculiarly associated with marginal forest habitat and with the expression of the 'concrete' attitude of 'sympathy'; while on the other, the marginal forest habitat elicits 'sympathy' as a social necessity, since the vicissitudes of forest existence impose an inescapable instability on the collective institutions on which life depends.

This is a narrow, and, if you like, environmental-determinist theory of ethno-poetics. I insist on it only in so far as I believe cultural theories ought to be anchored in the specifics of physical localities, technologies, lifestyles, rather than seeking to appeal to absolutes and essences. It seems to me quite misguided to point to the languages of the Foi, Kaluli or Umeda as exemplary poetic languages, superior to our own (on Heideggerian grounds) since their poetic characteristics are strictly local, having no counterparts in the kinds of perceptual, social and linguistic experiences which are conducive to poetic expression hereabouts. The peculiar interest of these exotic poetic traditions and poetic languages lies in their rootedness in a certain landscape and a certain perceptual style, which we can appreciate (from afar) but in which we are debarred from full participation by virtue of the extraordinary gulf between our experience and theirs. But, even so, I admit that there is much we can learn from them when it comes to enlarging our conception of what is humanly possible. Even vicarious participation in alterity is subversive of the conceptual restrictions which motivate our own sense of the real, and, by derivation, our conceptions of the poetic.

REFERENCES

Bolinger, D. (1965) *Forms of English* (Tokyo: Hokouo).

Feld, S. (1982) *Sound and Sentiment: Birds, Weeping, Poetics and Song in Kaluli Expression* (Philadelphia: University of Pennsylvania Press).

Feld, S. (n.d.) 'Wept thoughts: the voicing of Kaluli memories', unpublished manuscript.

Fudge, E. (1970) 'Phonological structure and "expressiveness"', *Journal of Linguistics*, 6: 161–88.

Gell, A. (1975) *Metamorphosis of the Cassowaries*, LSE Monographs in Social Anthropology, 51 (London: Athlone).

Gell, A. (1977) 'Magic, perfume, dream', in I. Lewis (ed.), *Symbols and Sentiments* (London: Academic).

Gell, A. (1979) 'The Umeda language poem', *Canberra Anthropology*, 2(1): 44–62.

Goldstein, K., and Scheerer, M. (1971) 'Abstract and concrete behaviour', in Kurt Goldstein, *Collected Papers*, ed. A. Gurwitsch (The Hague: Martinus Nijhoff).

Haiman, J. (1985) *Natural Syntax: Iconicity and Erosion* (Cambridge: Cambridge University Press).

Heidegger, M. (1971) *Poetry, Language, Thought* (New York: Harper & Row).

Jakobson, R. (1965) 'In search of the essence of language', *Diogenes*, 51: 21–37.

Jakobson, R. and Waugh, L. (1979) *The Sound Shape of Language* (Brighton: Harvester).

Klima, E., and Bellugi, U. (1979) *The Signs of Language* (Cambridge, MA.: Harvard University Press).

Köhler, W. (1930) *Gestalt Psychology* (London: G. Bell).

Lévi-Strauss, C. (1985) *The View From Afar*, (London: Penguin).

Merleau-Ponty, M. (1962) *The Phenomenology of Perception* (London: Routledge & Kegan Paul).

Mimica, J. (1981) 'Omalyce: an ethnography of the Ikwaye view of the cosmos', unpublished PhD thesis, Australian National University.

Peterfalvi, J.-M. (1970) *Recherches Expérimentales sur le Symbolisme Phonétique* (Paris: Centre Nationale de la Recherche Scientifique).

Sacks, O. (1989) *Seeing Voices: A Journey into the World of the Deaf* (Berkeley, CA.: University of California Press).

Sapir, E. (1929) *Language* (New York: Harcourt, Brace & World).

Saussure, F. de (1966) *Course in General Linguistics* (New York: McGraw-Hill).

Schieffelin, E. (1976) *The Sorrow of the Lonely and the Burning of the Dancers* (New York: St Martin's Press).

Wagner, R. (1972) *Habu: The Innovation of Meaning in Daribi Religion* (Chicago: University of Chicago Press).

Weiner, J. (1988) *The Heart of the Pearl Shell: The Mythological Dimension of Foi Sociality* (Berkeley, CA.: University of California Press).

Weiner, J. (1991) *The Empty Place: Poetry, Space and Being among the Foi of Papua New Guinea* (Bloomington, IN.: Indiana University Press).

CHAPTER 9

EXALTING THE KING AND OBSTRUCTING THE STATE

A POLITICAL INTERPRETATION OF ROYAL RITUAL IN BASTAR DISTRICT, CENTRAL INDIA[1]

Why were there – why are there – 'tribal' societies in peninsular India? India's 'tribals' (or Adivasis) are not really tribes (i.e. ethnic groups) at all, but are numerically dominant agricultural castes which hold, or used to hold, land in clan-based village communities in the more remote, forested and hilly parts of the subcontinent. The puzzle exists because, except in tribal areas, Indian rural society has a characteristic layered caste/class structure which failed to develop fully in the statelets, or so-called 'jungle kingdoms' with tribal majorities (Schnepel 1996). Traditionally, Indian rural society was founded on the twin pillars of landlordism and officialdom; that is, the extraction of rents and land revenue from the peasant masses by high castes. In the 'jungle kingdoms', while they were able to maintain themselves intact, revenue extraction was under-developed. There were no layers of greater and lesser landlords between the 'tribal' cultivator and the Raja at the apex of the kingdom. In the tribal areas society was, so to speak, two-dimensionally hierarchical, founded on a stark opposition between the mass of ordinary subjects (the tribes) and the king and his court. By contrast, the more developed type of traditional kingdoms (known in the literature as 'little kingdoms') were three-dimensionally hierarchical in that a dense screen of social barriers and material relationships of clientship and extraction intervened between the very high and the very low, creating the minutely nuanced, infinitely graduated social hierarchy most students of Indian society recognize today.

The most common explanation advanced for the peculiar social features of 'tribal' areas in peninsular India or 'jungle kingdoms' – their hierarchical 'flatness' if I may phrase it so – has been historico-ecological. Three-dimensional hierarchy failed to develop in these areas because they were physically remote and unattractive, away from the major lines of communication, too poor and unproductive to be tempting to powerful kings who could have installed and protected a landlord/official class. The tribes are primitive folk who have simply never been given the historical opportunity to become an ordinary Hindu peasantry, as they would have under more 'favourable' circumstances. Either that or, due to centuries of neglect, they must have degenerated. But as anyone who has travelled in peninsular India knows, socially remote regions of the peninsula are not necessarily circumscribed by formidable geographic barriers. This is particularly true of the largest and most famous of the 'jungle kingdoms' of central India, the princely state of Bastar, the kingdom I wish to discuss in detail in this article.

Most of Bastar, an area the size of Belgium, is, in fact, relatively flat, and such hilly areas as exist there are no more formidable than in other regions of the subcontinent which have been under the sway of fully developed state systems for millennia. Something more than a reflex explanation based on geography seems called for. In Bastar some additional ideological or structural restraint on the consolidation of landlordism and clientage seems to have inhibited the internal differentiation of the state over a long period. In this article I am going to canvass a political and ideological explanation for the development of the kingdom of Bastar in its particularly hypertrophied 'tribal' form.[2]

Bastar State, now a mere district (*zilla*) of the post-Independence state of Madhya Pradesh, was, until 1947, the largest of the princely states predominantly populated by offshoots of the great 'Gond' tribe, of which there are a cluster in southeastern Madhya Pradesh and highland Orissa. My thesis is that the political characteristics of the kingdom of Bastar were the result of a distinct political strategy effected by the tribal Gond people of Bastar. It was the tribal people who kept the state 'two-dimensional'; and the means through which they achieved this (for them) desirable political outcome was, paradoxically, the cult of the Raja of Bastar as a divine ruler. I am going to argue that the ritual relations between Raja and people constituted a bulwark against the rationalization of the polity in Bastar. Moreover, as I will describe, the people of Bastar periodically rebelled against the government when their ritual relationship with the raja was deemed to be under threat. During the most recent of these rebellions, in 1966, Pravir, the last ruler of Bastar, died in a gun battle with police at the royal palace in Jagdalpur, thus finally bringing to an end the history of Bastar State.

An appearance of poverty and primitiveness is an important weapon in the peasants' battle to keep exploitation by overlords at bay. Bastar has always appeared to be one of the poorest places in India, and is still believed to be so mostly by those who have never been there and especially who have not drunk and feasted regularly in tribal houses, as I have. Perhaps the time has come to ask whether 'tribal society' in India, in Bastar particularly, is not so much a relic of bygone centuries as rent- and tax-minimization on a huge, indeed civilizational, scale. While the kingdom of Bastar was in existence, the tribal population enjoyed the benefit of their extensive lands and forests with a degree of non-exploitation from outside which would hardly be matched anywhere else in peninsular India.[3] The capacity of the Bastar ruler and members of the Hindu elite around him to extract land revenue, even from areas relatively close to the capital, was a fraction of the extractive capacity of even a third-rate raja in more civilized parts of India (Sunder 1997).

Let me insert a few facts and figures here just to show what I mean. Even in the 1940s, when British power in India was at its height, the total revenues of Bastar State, from all sources, only amounted to about two rupees per head per year, a very low figure indeed. A similar picture of wholesale under-extraction of revenue by the state in Bastar can be traced back to the nineteenth century (see Sunder 1997).

From the 1860s, under British tutelage, the Raja of Bastar, whose finances were notoriously chaotic, embarked on a series of taxation reforms designed to increase his income. From 1868, tax farmers (*malguzars*) were allocated blocs of villages from which tax was to be raised at a notional rate of two and a quarter rupees per plough. Some revenue was raised from village headmen by sending parties of soldiers and an elephant to the villages nearer the capital, but revenue-raising was very sporadic at the best of times because of the wildness of the country. Even the official figures for expected state revenue reveal that in the period around 1906 land revenue ranged between one-half and one-quarter of a rupee per head per annum, much of which probably remained uncollected. Let us just contrast this picture with that prevailing in 'modernized' parts of India at the same time. On the basis of some figures provided for 1905–6 by Jayati Ghosh (pers. comm., 1996) the per capita revenue (or rent) payments of peasants in Uttar Pradesh, on the same basis, would have been about three rupees per head per annum, which was collected more or less in full – i.e. six or twelve times as much. It seems reasonable to conclude that turn-of-the-century Bastar peasants worked very much less hard, and kept very much more of the fruits of their labour, than was typical of the peasants elsewhere in India at the time.

Bastar State evidently lacked the leverage over the ordinary cultivators to raise levels of revenue extraction significantly, despite official attempts to do so. The Bastar rural power-vacuum was the consequence of the social characteristics of the indigenous population, who long preserved an image of 'wildness' totally at odds with their lack of military organization or political leadership. It was not that the wild tribes could resist the imposition of power – they were in fact generally very docile – but that they seemed to slip through the meshes of power, a protean mass motivated by unpredictable impulses inaccessible to civilized reason. Too primitive to be governed, they could only be preyed upon by small men (grubby *malguzars*, traders, moneylenders), but not by an established ruling class.

The main royal ritual of the Bastar State, Dasara, was part of the process through which the Bastar power-vacuum was created and sustained. The ritual created the public impression (a true impression, though partial) that the Raja of Bastar was fanatically worshipped by his subjects and that he was a powerful ruler who could not be politically challenged. Dasara was a massive ritual event which played a key role in preserving Bastar as a large, unified, kingdom. Despite the size of the kingdom and the lack of roads, tribal people from all over the state regularly made their way on foot to the capital for the annual event, where they encamped for the duration, forming a great multitude who were both armed (with axes and bows and arrows) and in a very excitable condition. These multitudes attending Dasara, which was a religious festival celebrating many tribal gods as well as the 'state' mother-goddess, Danteshwari, were, from one point of view, only the Raja's most loyal subjects, unanimously demonstrating their subservience and worship to their lord. But from another point of view they were 'the people' assembled and unified, demonstrating their potential political muscle.[4]

We have here, I think, an instance on a mass scale of what Appadurai (1990) has recently identified as a basic strategy in Indian interpersonal relations between superiors and subordinates. I am referring to what he calls 'coercive subordination' (1990: 97 sqq.) in the context of his brilliant analysis of the use of praise as a means of social control in Indian civilization. Coercive subordination, or ritualized coercive deference, are techniques through which the subordinate so flatters the superior that the superior must accede to the inferior's demands or risk loss of status. In the course of Dasara, the people of Bastar imprisoned their Raja (literally, as we will see) in a close embrace of worship which both exalted and neutralized him and which made the power-vacuum possible, in that the whole mechanism of state was made to revolve around the divine ruler, yet the divine ruler himself was made 'by acclamation' of the people, by their praise.

Besides looking at the politico-religious implications of Dasara there is another angle of approach to the Bastar power-vacuum which I want to take simultaneously. When Bastar State is written about, two themes dominate: one is Dasara, the other the periodic eruption of 'tribal rebellions', of which the last was the one in 1966 which saw the state finally collapse. Previous tribal rebellions took place in Bastar in the years 1876, 1910 and 1961. The usual approach taken to these rebellions is to try to interpret them as popular uprisings by 'the poor' against abuses committed by the rich and powerful: that is, to assimilate them as far as possible to revolutionary mass-action as understood in the west (see Anderson and Huber 1988; Sunder 1997). But if it is true, as I would steadfastly maintain, that the people of Bastar had less to complain about in terms of restrictions on access to land, water and forest than almost any rural population in India, and were less taxed, why should these popular uprisings have occurred? Rather than seeing these uprisings in the way in which they were seen by anxious British political agents, and are still seen today by historians, as tribal reactions to state oppression, I prefer to see them instead as a parallel mechanism, along with Dasara and the religious cult of the Raja, to ensure that oppression was actually minimal because the country was thought to be filled with ungovernable primitive tribes. They were all, in other words, pre-emptive, designed to head off a feared outcome rather than protest about actual abuses. In each case the 'feared outcome' was the disruption of the all-important relationship between the Raja and his subjects by an over-mighty prime minister (*Diwan*), or later the Indian government. The symbolic mechanism in all of these uprisings was the same: that is, the assertion of tribal control over the Raja's person and, through him, the capacity to resist the extension of the power of the state. As I will show the rebellions of 1876, 1910 and 1961 actually succeeded to some extent in securing the position of the tribal population of Bastar, even if they did not achieve their ostensible aims at the time, and only the unrest of 1966 must be judged a failure.

I argue that 'pre-emptive unrest' has the same logical structure as calendrical ritual, which is also pre-emptive in the sense that calendrical rites assure a 'happy normality' against the possibility of adverse alterations in the order of things prescribed by God. Ritual is conservative, against change; so too were the Bastar rebellions. In fact, just as I have suggested that the Dasara celebrations had a political side to them in representing the unity of the people in a most unambiguous way, so, from the opposite side, I want to suggest that the notorious Bastar rebellions were enactments of the ritual relationships expressed in Dasara, but in an ostensibly secular-political mode.

However, let me turn to some of the ethnography and history which supports these assertions. The first matter to be dealt with is the format of the Bastar rites of Dasara and the status of the state goddess, Danteshwari.

According to legend, the Rajas of Bastar owe their position to their possession of the sword of Danteshwari, which was brought to Bastar by the first of the line, Annam Deo, in the fourteenth century from the kingdom of Warangal, whence they came in flight from Muslim invaders. They were accepted by the wild tribes of Bastar as rulers, and the sword gives them the status of sacrificers and priests of Danteshwari, whom Hindus generally see as a form of the Hindu goddess Durga. They established the temple of Danteshwari at Dantewara and founded their capital at Bastar village, and later at Jagdalpur.

However, although the ruling family can claim to have introduced the cult of Durga/Danteshwari into Bastar, the legitimacy of their rule depends on the fact that Danteshwari has been assimilated to the generic tribal mother goddess, of whom there is a wide variety of local forms. It was (and is) taken for granted by tribal people that in sacrificing to Danteshwari the rulers were sacrificing to the autochthonous forms of the goddess, to whom local village priests (Pujaris) also sacrifice at seasonal festivals. The process of the Hinduization of 'tribal' divinities as part of the legitimacy-creating ideology of rulers has been subjected to much study in neighbouring Orissa, particularly in relation to the cult of Jaganath in Puri but also in relation, more recently, to the smaller divinities of the 'jungle kingdoms' of the Orissa Ghats (Kulke 1984; Schnepel 1994). The Bastar kingdom fits the pattern established in the jungle kingdoms of Orissa in every respect. It seems to me, though, that interpreting the cult of Danteshwari/Durga as the Hinduization of local divinities is only half the story. It is equally valid to interpret Durga, as Danteshwari, as being subjected to 'tribalization' so as to lose her Hindu attributes and gain tribal ones, particularly the attribute of being represented, not as an image but 'in person' through possessing a human 'vehicle'. There is scope for changes in perspective when viewing the state goddess: for the Raja, and especially the Brahmins he patronized, she may indeed have been Durga, but for the masses Danteshwari was a magnified but still recognizable version of every local village goddess.[5]

The Dasara ritual was inaugurated by the lowest caste, the Mahars (weavers), who selected a young girl of seven or so to act as the medium through which the goddess spoke, in the Raja's presence, sanctioning the performance of the ritual and enjoining that it proceed smoothly. The child-shaman uttered the goddess's words while being swung on a ritual swing, as the Raja would be very much later on; though her swing seat was decked with thorns, his with cushions.

A notable point is that during Dasara the Raja had to abdicate and formally hand over his power, for the liminal period, to his prime minister, to resume it again (with the blessing of the goddess) once Dasara was over. In this ritual of state, during which the Raja performed his quintessential functions of honouring the divinities and performing sacrifices, he was not a ruler at all but a renouncer. He could not wear rich attire, or shoes, or eat meat, and he had to sleep on the floor. He could not greet or be greeted by anyone during this period, as if he were a non-person. He could not ride in any vehicle except, of course, the *rath* (chariot) on which he was seated on certain days to be paraded around the town.

Not only did the Raja abdicate temporal power, he was also substituted for, in his temporary role as renouncer, by a stand-in who performed austerities on his behalf. The role of stand-in Raja was taken by a Halba of the 'Jogi' subcaste. For this man, a pit was dug in the *durbar* (court-assembly) hall, 6 ft long, 3 ft wide and 1 ft deep. The stand-in was seated on a heap of ashes, covered by a cloth, at one end of the pit, while at the other were placed a pot of water, a heap of grain and a sword (auspicious objects). The Jogi had to remain fasting in the pit for the whole of the nine nights (*navratri*) of Dasara, without moving, and to ensure this a plank was secured over his thighs while another plank was placed vertically behind his back, against which he could lean.

From the third day of Dasara the Raja began daily rides around the capital on his chariot, derived from those in use in Puri for the cult of Jaganath, though only having eight wheels rather than sixteen, the streets of Jagdalpur being too small to accommodate anything bigger.[6] The massive (20 ft tall) chariot, with its solid wheels, adorned with banners, canopies and carved horsemen, was dragged around a set route by large teams of Gond and Dhurwa tribals who pulled on the ropes, urged on by the crowds of spectators. From the third to the ninth day of Dasara the programme essentially was the same: that is, daily rounds by the Raja to perform worship (*puja*) at the Danteshwari shrine in the Jagdalpur palace compound and the shrines of other local gods situated in the immediate vicinity plus chariot processions through the town. The eighth night was occupied with the religiously most significant ceremonies to appease Danteshwari, in the palace and, later on, in a garden where the Raja remained until dawn. On the following day, nine unmarried women were worshipped, being given food and clothing (*Kumari puja*), after which the Brahmins who had assisted at the ceremonies were given presents and the Raja himself ate a dish of rice supposedly from the new season's crop.

In the evening Dasara 'proper' came to an end with the arrival at the palace of the *doli* (palanquin) in which the image of Danteshwari was contained, from her temple at Dantewara 60km. distant. The Raja proceeded to the edge of town (not far, as Jagdalpur was no metropolis) where he shouldered one end of the pole on which the *doli* of the goddess was suspended, the other being taken by the chief priest from Dantewara. Together, they bore the goddess to the palace. Meanwhile, the Halba stand-in was released from his pit, and in former times he was at this point allowed to loot the bazaar with impunity, before making himself scarce, since it was imperative that he and the Raja should never set eyes on one another. (Later it became customary to reward him with ornaments or money.) The Raja at this point resumed his royal attire and was enthroned as secular ruler once more in the durbar hall, beside Danteshwari whose *doli* was placed on a separate throne. He received tribute and presents from his court and officials. That night, the Raja was paraded through the town on the chariot before a huge crowd, eventually returning to his private apartments.

In any properly conducted little kingdom, one would have thought, that would have been the end of Dasara, but not in Bastar; for on this and the ensuing night there took place what seem to me the most interesting events of this already quite interesting series. During the eleventh night it was customary for the Raja to be 'abducted' by tribals and to be borne off in a palanquin (i.e. a large *doli*) to a spot two miles to the southeast of Jagdalpur, where the multitudes of Gonds (Maria and Muria) customarily encamped. Here he remained over the next night, being entertained by his tribal subjects who undertook a ritual hunt and who plied him with wild meats (and I suspect, though the sources do not confirm this, liquor). He was offered grain and money. Finally, on the following afternoon, he was brought back in triumph on his chariot before a massive and exceptionally excited crowd. Here is a contemporary description from the 1911 Census of India:

> In the evening amidst a huge concourse of people the chief seated on the big Rath [chariot] is dragged slowly towards the town. He is dressed in a yellow robe and carries a bow and arrows and is seated on a swing chair suspended from the roof of the Rath. Buffaloes are sacrificed in front of the Rath. Till fifteen years ago, buffaloes were thrown in front of the Rath and crushed to death, but this was stopped by the Administrator of that time. On this day all the people congregate on the large *maidan* [common ground] to the east of the town, to view the Rath. The place is crowded with villagers and their children all dressed in their brightest colours. Bands of Murias armed with bows and arrows rush about amidst the crowd shrieking out their war cries and every now and then capturing men to help drag the Rath along. A small cannon is dragged along and fired at intervals and hundreds of dhols, or tomtoms, and native musical instruments complete the Babel of sound. By the time the Rath enters the town it is dark and the houses and road are all illuminated with lamps, and fireworks are let off at intervals.
>
> (Census of India 1911: 86)

Upon arrival, the Raja prostrated himself before Danteshwari. After this he was seated on his throne and salt and mustard were scattered around him to drive off evil spirits. The following day the ceremony ended.

It will be apparent that Bastar Dasara falls into two distinct segments: the first ten days (and nights) conform to the conventional temporal organization of Dasara. The second segment, occurring once the Raja has ostensibly resumed both secular and religious authority over the state, consists of the abduction of the Raja from his capital by the people and his triumphant return thither on the chariot. Let me begin by offering some remarks about the first segment of Bastar Dasara, the period of the Raja's 'abdication'.

During this period the kingship goes into temporary eclipse. Let us recall that Dasara takes place after harvest-time, at the point of transition between the Old (agricultural) Year and the New Year. Old enterprises must come to an end before Dasara and new enterprises may commence once Dasara is over. Dasara marks a liminal period, time out of time. Even in Hindu terms, the Raja's abdication and assumption of the role of a renouncer signify a little death, in that renouncers are classically 'dead' in shedding worldly attachments. However, the point is much more graphically underscored through the institution of the stand-in renouncer-king, the Halba Jogi.

This man is clearly dead, seated on his heap of ashes. However, from the tribal point of view it would be the pit rather than the ashes which would convey the message, since the Gond people bury, rather than cremate, their dead. The pit in the durbar hall is a grave. The objects in the stand-in Raja's grave are symbolic of the death/rebirth cycle of agricultural operations which bring together four factors: seed, water, ashes and iron. The sword is the ploughshare (or steel-tipped digging stick) and the harvester's sickle; the seed is seed, the pot of water is rain, and the ashes are the ashes which fertilize fields (produced by firing the bush in the making of swidden fields).

Here I may make my bow to Frazer, if only in passing. The most tentative Frazerian can appreciate the symbolism of the Bastar Raja's death and rebirth, mirroring the cycle of natural fertility. However, there is another, no less Frazerian, aspect of the situation which demands mention. Initially, British interest in the affairs of Bastar were partly motivated by the desire to stamp out the human sacrifices of which the Raja of Bastar was believed to be guilty in large numbers. Since Grigson (1938), no serious student of Bastar has given any credence to these rumoured human sacrifices, which were no more than politically motivated slurs on the ruling family. Nonetheless, although there is no evidence for the actual practice of human sacrifice in Bastar, it would be wrong, I think, to imagine that the 'idea' of human sacrifice is not part of the indigenous repertoire of symbolic forms, a mere red herring introduced by the British to justify sweeping Bastar into the colonial embrace. We are, I think, entitled to interpret the stand-in Raja as a sacrificial victim, though there is not the least suggestion that he would be sacrificed. One telling point, here, is the way in which his reward for undertaking the Raja's austerities was to be permitted to loot the bazaar with impunity once he was released. As a 'dead' non-person, he could not commit any crime; it was as if he had passed out of existence.

More evidence for this line of thought was assembled by the Indologist Crooke, who, not surprisingly gave the Bastar ceremonies pride of place in his comparative essay on the subject of Dasara (1915: 28–59). He points out the similarity between the Bastar substitute Raja and the equivalent personage in the Dasara rites of the neighbouring 'jungle kingdom' of Jeypore (Orissa).[7] F. Fawcett provided Crooke with a description of the role of 'sacrificial victim' in Jeypore:

> A man representing the victim for the sacrifice was, from the day of the new moon, immured in a cage-like box in a shed especially erected for this purpose during the nine days of the festival. In front of this was kept a lamp, which was kept alight without intermission, and beside it was placed a sword daubed with sandalwood paste and decorated with flowers. While in the cage, the man neither ate nor drank, nor might he sneeze; it was said that even the ordinary functions of nature were denied him during his confinement.
>
> (Crooke 1915: 34–5)

On the ninth day a sheep was sacrificed in the man's stead, after having its head shaved and being marked on the forehead with a red spot 'as used to be done in the case of human victims'. Once the sheep had been beheaded, its blood was offered to the goddess (Kali). The surrogate sacrifice once completed, the man was given money and told to depart at once (Crooke 1915: 35).

It will be seen that the substitute Raja in the Bastar ceremonies can plausibly be interpreted in a number of different frames of reference: he is both an ascetic renouncer, an embodiment of the natural-cum-agricultural cycle of death and rebirth, a human sacrifice (implicitly of the Raja himself) for the benefit of the realm, and a scapegoat who does penance for the Raja's sins and who receives loot or presents and money to bear them away. It does not seem exaggerated to interpret all this in terms of 'the Dying God' as Frazer's contemporary and colleague, Crooke, did. I would certainly endorse a Frazerian interpretation myself.

If this is acceptable, then one can identify the basic scenario of Bastar Dasara as the ritual death and rebirth of the Raja, at the moment of the renewal of the year. The person of the Raja is identified with the cycle of natural regeneration which dominates the agricultural year. But the naturalization of the Raja itself involves a marked derogation of the kingly way of life, in the sense that it is no business of kings, normally speaking, to die and be reborn: their role is to make war, rule kingdoms and perform sacrifices. The Bastar Raja, as we saw, abandoned secular power for the period of his little death; but at the same time he performed kingly sacrificial functions during Dasara proper, in his own person.

In effect, what happens during this time is a splitting of the Raja into two persons: a sacrificed king (the stand-in), and a sacrificing king, who rides around the town on the chariot and worships at the various temples in the capital, including those shrines dedicated to tribal divinities who demanded blood sacrifices in which he assisted. At the same time the cross-identity between these two *personae* is underlined by the fact that the stand-in Raja occupies the assembly hall to exclusion of the real Raja for this period, while the real Raja maintains the dress and lifestyle of a renouncer.

The net result is that the Raja sacrifices himself, as ascetics do, but is revived and reinstalled in his true role as secular Raja, 'clad in purple and red, decked with all jewels and ornaments' (Majumdar 1939:164) by the agency of Danteshwari, his personal deity, on her arrival from Dantewara. If, as modern scholarship suggests, Danteshwari as state goddess is a 'Hinduized' version of the local mother goddess, the implication would naturally be that it is by the grace of this local goddess that the Raja of Bastar is able to rule over his kingdom. The ruler's authority rests on the support, if not of 'the people' then of their goddess, which really amounts to the same thing. At the same time, if Danteshwari is a foreign (high, Hindu) goddess, who, like the Raja's ancestors, has come from afar and settled in the country (becoming naturalized and tribalized in the process), then the implication is that the prosperity of the ruler and the kingdom depends on the capacity of the Raja, as sacrificer, to mediate with 'the outside' (beyond, above, outside the compass of the Raja's ordinary subjects). The Raja is a 'stranger king', as indeed is made explicit in the legendary foreign origins of the royal house. My own contention would be that both of the above interpretations are simultaneously made, and indeed it is precisely the function of ritual to obviate the contradiction between them. Danteshwari is both foreign and local, the Raja is both a mediator with the outside and the vehicle of the goddess of the *bhum*, the land and the people. As Bloch (1991) has noted, the very essence of ritual thought is to be able to play both ends against the middle.

However, the revival or regeneration of the kingship which occurs on the tenth night of Bastar Dasara, via the agency of Danteshwari, is, as we have already noted, not definitive. The second segment of Dasara (which in a sense is not part of Dasara at all but an add- itional rite) consists of the abduction of the Raja on the eleventh night, his overnight sojourn in the tribal encampment, his feasting on wild food and his triumphal return.

This sequence enacts the appropriation by the tribes of their Raja, whose power is derived from 'outside', and his own deity Danteshwari, and their tribalization of him, through commensality. During the return journey he is Danteshwari in person, now a tribal deity. Thus the abduction of the Raja in a palanquin makes an explicit reference, I think, to the fact that the image of Danteshwari makes its way from Dantewara to Jagdalpur in a similar palanquin. The confinement of the Raja in a palanquin and his carrying-off in this manner, thus begins a sequence in which the Raja himself ceases to figure either as a renouncer or a sacrificer, but as an incarnation of the goddess.

However, equally important was the 'domestication' of the Raja by the tribals through his eating of their food, especially the wild game they hunted. Of course, the Raja, as a Rajput, was in no way forbidden by caste from eating meat. But a certain derogation seems to be implied in a Rajput taking cooked food from Shudras, which is what the Bastar Gonds technically are, despite their beef-eating. The key symbolic act was not the Raja's meat-eating as such, but the provision of the meat by the tribal people who fed their ruler as 'hosts' and thus implicitly established a lien on him.

In offering meat (and liquor) to the Raja the tribals were doing two things: first of all the Raja was being brought down to the tribal level through a shared meal, being anchored to the middle world (*nadum bhum*) through sharing in the basic experience of this world which, in the estimation of tribals, is *girda* (enjoyment). At the same time, the Raja was being turned into a god(-dess) because offering meat, liquor and money (silver) is exactly what the tribals do to the *pen* (gods and goddesses) during the visitations of the divinities to the villages during *pen karsana* (village festival honouring the local deities). After the offerings, the villagers start to wrangle with the gods, explaining their grievances to them, just as I am sure they did to the Raja at this time.

But let us pause for a moment here and ask why the Raja submitted to these proceedings (abduction, feasting) given that he had just been resoundingly confirmed, by the goddess, as ruler? Was this the price he had to pay to secure the political support of the tribal people? But support against whom? And what support might he expect from a rabble who would, in a short while, disperse to their villages? However much *a posteriori* analysis might suggest that these transactions established a political pact between ruler and people, it would be quite incorrect to suppose that the Raja was consciously submitting to being placed on his throne by the excited tribal mob, even if such may appear to be the case objectively.

The Raja and his circle could only sanction these proceedings by mythologizing them in a way which secured their conformity to a Rajput model. May, the writer of the report on Bastar Dasara published in the 1911 Census, says that the episode of the abduction of the Raja, and his triumphal return, enacts 'the abduction of Rama and his return after fourteen years' sojourn in the jungles to his capital of Ajodhya' (Census of India 1911: 86). It was quite common in India for festivals for Durga to be followed immediately by ceremonies in which the king assumed the identity of the Hindu god Rama, as was evidently the case in Bastar. Fuller (1992: 108 sqq.), in a recent comparative discussion, has emphasized the centrality of military and warlike symbolism in these ceremonies of kingship. Commonly, the Raja worshipped his weapons at this time (as did the Bastar Raja on his return from the final procession) and ceremonially embarked on a campaign. Dasara does indeed mark the season, after the monsoons, during which kings might initiate military operations to expand their kingdoms, though we have no record of the Raja of Bastar having done so – his kingdom was, if anything, already too big. But, comparing Bastar with Fuller's 'military-expansionist' model of Dasara, one encounters an odd discrepancy between Bastar Dasara and the Dasara ceremonies of the more 'advanced' kingdoms (Mewar, Mysore, Dewas Senior, etc.) Fuller describes. In every case (except Bastar) what was ritually enacted in Dasara was the Raja's 'departure' for war; and this is logical because following Dasara is the time for beginning enterprises, not concluding them, as we have already seen. Bastar Dasara, as 'Rama's return to Ayodhya' was Dasara-in-reverse. Politically and historically, this corresponds to the fact that, far from being an 'expansionist' kingdom ruled by an ambitious monarch, Bastar was not a military power of any consequence. Rather, the kingdom was a place of sanctuary for a refugee king protected by Danteshwari's sword from outside interference, but not one to wield it outside Bastar's borders. The political 'introversion' of Bastar State was subtly encoded in the inversion of the normally expansive symbolism of Dasara, even though the Raja projects, at one level, the identity of Rama, the great warrior-king. Nothing could be less warlike than the Bastar Raja's abduction from the palace on the eleventh night; for he was, supposedly, fast asleep in the cradle-like palanquin as he was conveyed by the tribals to their jungle encampment. He was not departing for war but snoozing in his palanquin. Nor, subsequently did he 'defeat' any identifiable enemy, fire arrows, or perform warlike acts. He simply 'returned in triumph' to his palace, at the head of an 'army' of tribals who were plainly his supporters, not his defeated enemies.

In other words, the Rajput model was inverted in Bastar so that, while remaining a 'warrior king', the Bastar Raja merely regained his *own* kingdom, rather than divesting rival kings of theirs. In this way, an accommodation was achieved between the 'courtly' perspective on Dasara, in which the Raja must figure as an autonomously powerful warrior king, and the demotic perspective in which the Raja was placed on his throne by his subjects, while impersonating 'their' goddess. I do not think that the identity between the Raja and Rama played an important part in tribal perceptions of the culmination of Bastar Dasara. From the tribal point of view, the primary identification of the Raja at this time was with his own personal goddess, Danteshwari, who, even as Durga, belongs in a quite separate category from Rama.[8]

The most important physical symbol of the Raja's ritual status during the culminating episode of Dasara (the return to the capital on the chariot) was the placement of the Raja on a swing – the swing which was suspended from the roof of the chariot on this occasion only. It will be recalled that the very *first* episode of Bastar Dasara was the possession of the juvenile Mahar girl by Danteshwari. This girl-shaman, from the very lowest caste, was swung, to induce possession, on a bed of thorns. The very *last* episode is the swinging of the Raja himself on the swing mounted on the chariot, a luxury swing rather than a thorny one.

I suggest the following interpretation of the contrast between the thorny swing and the luxurious one. Being seated on swings is both the means of becoming identified with divinities (especially the mother goddess) and a sign of this identity – the divinities are represented in this way, for instance, in the lost-wax sculptures for which Bastar is famous. The swing participates in the mechanics of trance-induction, as I have discussed elsewhere (Gell 1980). Mortals become the 'horses' of the divinities by losing their normal sense of physical selfhood, and through succumbing to religious vertigo. Insensibility to pain and fatigue demonstrate possession; tribal and lower-caste shamans swing on seats of thorn or nails, beat themselves with ropes and chains, and so on. This self-torture applies only to the 'horse' or vehicle of the divinity, and indicates the hierarchical gulf between the low-status shaman and the high-status divinity 'riding' him or her, comparable to the thrashings administered by humans to animal beasts of burden.

The divinities riding on swings do so because vertiginous pleasures are intrinsic to divine sensibility as imagined by the tribals. Riding on horses, or elephants, or tigers, or Rath-chariots, or swings, involves elevation from the unmoving earth, to which ordinary mortals remain firmly attached, and a giddy, swaying motion. This is not torture, but pleasure and ease (rocking in the cradle) though in a form which cancels the secure rootedness from which the tribals draw their sense of security in the middle world, and which in their station they may experience only vicariously. We may therefore draw a contrast between the girl-shaman, who is possessed as the vehicle of Danteshwari, on a swing of thorns and the Raja who, more nearly 'is' Danteshwari, on her swing of unmixed (but inaccessible) pleasure. The doubling-up of the mechanisms of divine vertigo exhibits the redundancy of the code; the Raja's swing, inducing vertigo, was itself mounted on the vertiginous tottering chariot, 20ft tall, borne along by a teeming multitude over which the rider in the chariot exercised no direct control. The Raja, during his apotheosis, had no need to enter a trance state, as lower-status shamans must. He was enraptured, transported, divinized, through the mechanism of vertigo, which allowed him to embody divine sensibility unmediatedly rather than vicariously, like a shaman.

I see a parallelism therefore between the culminating phase of the first segment of Bastar Dasara, namely, the arrival of Danteshwari in her palanquin, borne on the shoulders of her chief priest and the Raja, and the culminating phase of the second segment of Bastar Dasara, also a great 'entry into the capital', but on this occasion the role of 'bearers of the palanquin' is taken by the great mass of tribal people, and the role of Danteshwari in her swaying receptacle is taken by the Raja. In effect, the first segment of Dasara, in which the Raja enacts the role of devotee, is being replayed with the Raja in the 'goddess' position, and the people in the 'devotee' position. According to the logic of these substitutions, the implication arises that at this critical moment 'the people' are 'the Raja'. And it is on these slippages, between goddess and Raja, and between Raja and people, that the structure of the kingdom of Bastar ultimately rested.

I break off the analysis of Bastar Dasara at this point in order to look at the situation from a different angle, the political one. May's account of Bastar Dasara in the 1911 Census communicates in its subtext a certain sense of political crisis. Here was a kingdom with a notoriously ramshackle administration and no established military elite or well organized policing mechanisms, which every year subjected its capital to a vast influx of excitable, armed, tribal people in the grip of politico-religious effervescence motivated by forces well beyond the scope of civilized rationality. May mentions the Murias 'armed with bows and arrows who rush about amidst the crowd shrieking out their war cries', the vast numbers, the noise, the firing of the cannon and so forth. Speaking of 'war cries' in this connection is, in fact, a significant misperception in that the Muria and the other tribes were not organized for 'war', did not recognize 'warrior' as a social role, and never did engage in 'tribal warfare' in any meaningful sense. Their 'arms' were hunting weapons and axes, rather than special-purpose man-killing weapons.

There was no real threat of civil disorder during the scenes in which Dasara culminated. Yet the mere numerousness, unity and exuberant self-confidence of the tribal people at this time surely impressed those charged with attempting to govern them. Suppose we occlude, for a moment, the Raja in his chariot and focus only upon the great stream of persons converging, amid thunderous noise, upon the capital: is there not something menacingly like a riot or rebellion here? And even if one allows the Raja to reappear, does it not seem equally like an uprising, though a loyalist one, in that the great mass of people, led by their ruler, are pressing forward against some countervailing power which they will overcome? This counterrailing power, evoked yet largely effaced in the ritual, was 'the government', that is, the Raja's prime minister, the British authorities who assumed the prime minister's function and title more and more completely and latterly the governments in Bhopal and Delhi.

I would argue that the political significance of Dasara was that by elevating the Raja, the people of the state indirectly intimidated his government and checked the political will to rationalize the collection of revenue and the extension of state power. Needless to add, I cannot offer historical proof of this contention, but in support of this idea I would like briefly to draw out certain parallels between Dasara as a political ritual and the Bastar 'rebellions' of 1876, 1910, 1961 and 1966 (Sunder 1997). All these rebellions shared a common feature: they were ostensibly in support of the ruler (or a claimant, in the case of the 1910 rebellion) against the government, or, after Independence, the state and national governments. These great assemblies (i.e. 'rebellions') were called, by the tribals, *bhumkal* (Singh 1985: 146). Assemblies called *bhumkal* occur routinely in villages whenever collective issues have to be thrashed out. They are not intrinsically military affairs, but expressions of the solidarity of the *nar* (the autonomous village unit) presided over by the *siyan* (the elders, wise persons).

The unrest of 1876 was occasioned by the decision of the then ruler, Bhairondeo, accompanied by the Prime Minister, to meet the Prince of Wales, then paying a state visit to Agra. The tribal perception of this was that the (unpopular) Prime Minister was attempting to carry off the Raja. Large numbers of tribals congregated on the southern route out of the state, preventing the departure from Bastar soil of the Raja on whom its prosperity depended. Some were killed by the Prime Minister's soldiers, but the Raja was captured and confined within the palace for some weeks. The British political agent made haste to the scene and listened to the grievances against the Prime Minister voiced by the tribal spokesmen. There was no further bloodshed. He caused the unpopular ministers to be dismissed, and the Raja was allowed to resume his duties, without meeting the Prince of Wales. In these events, one is surely entitled to see a kind of mirroring of the 'capture' and 'restoration' of the Raja which took place during the culmination of Dasara; only here played out as a secular struggle over the person of the Raja and his confinement to the bosom of his people, rather than a ritual one.

The 1876 rebellion set a pattern whereby the British, who now had effective control of the Raja's government, tried to impress on his ministers the need to govern the country in a philanthropic spirit. However, trouble broke out again in 1910. Once again, the scenario consisted of the formation of an encampment around the capital. Only in this instance the trouble had been fomented not by the ruling Raja (who was controlled by the British) but by a would-be usurper, the Lal, the ruler's uncle, who promised the tribes that if he were placed on the throne he would remove the Prime Minister and the government. Following Grigson (1938), historians of these events have believed that at the root of the 1910 rebellion lay the problem of forest reservation by the crown, which restricted the access of the tribals to their traditional resource-base. One should not imagine that the tribals were, in 1910 or later, actually interested in making money out of forestry operations, a capitalist enterprise completely foreign to their way of life. In practice, reservation threatened their practice of unrestricted shifting agriculture, which was itself a defensive adaptation to the state system, in that it is near-impossible to raise land revenue from cultivators whose fields look like wastelands and which are abandoned after one or two seasons.

My presumption is that the tribals' worries about crown forest reservation in 1910 was that it involved the prospect of harsher taxation and more effective landlordism, which cannot take hold when shifting agriculture is permitted to take place freely. The rebellion of 1910 was a pre-emptive strike against administration as such, rather than because the tribes 'needed' their forest land in order to subsist.

Once again, the 1910 rebellion seems to echo the format of Dasara, though perhaps less closely than before. The key elements were nevertheless in place, namely the besieging of Jagdalpur by thousands of tribals, headed by one whom they regarded as their divine ruler, in opposition to the Prime Minister's government. The unpopular Prime Minister was removed from office in the aftermath of the rebellion, which was quickly crushed once government forces arrived from Raipur. The schoolmasters, whose abrupt appearance in many villages (demanding material support and school attendance) had precipitated much tribal hostility, were also withdrawn and soon calm was restored.

This calm lasted a long time and from the pages of Grigson (1938) and Elwin (1947), Bastar's pre-war ethnographers, one can see that a *modus vivendi* was established between the ruler, the British government and the tribal people, which allowed the latter to flourish and do what they had always done best, that is, avoid creating surplus value for the state or any ruling class. The minimal bloodshed of 1876 and 1910 purchased for the tribal population the privileges of backwardness; in other words the enjoyment of under-productive leisure, local autonomy and sensuality. Of course, this resistance of the tribes against the forces of modernity was only relatively successful since gradual encroachment of the state over the tribal hinterland was an irresistible trend. But I like to think that the shock to the administrative system produced by the rebellions of 1876 and 1910, tending to make the government adopt a gently-as-she-goes approach, was annually reinforced at Dasara, since each performance, involving as it did a besieging of the capital by the multitude in the sway of evidently irrational passions, must have given notice to the government that they were dealing with combustible material.

Under British control, Bastar remained a power-vacuum, relatively speaking, just as it had been before. After Independence this state of affairs began to break down. Bastar was not among the princely states recognized by the union, and became merged with Madhya Pradesh, an alteration incomprehensible to most of its citizens but deeply offensive to the ruler, Pravir. In 1953 the ex-ruler was deprived of his property on the grounds of mental instability. To recover his property from the Court of Wards, Pravir turned Congressman and was elected in the 1950s as a Congress parliamentarian, with massive tribal support. But he was disappointed, and became a bitter opponent of the Nehru regime. He was arrested, imprisoned and formally deposed as Raja in 1961. But so far as the people were concerned, Pravir was still their Raja. Tribal dissatisfaction with the incarceration of the Raja led to the rebellion of March 1961, during which an armed mob attacked police who were supposedly holding the Raja in the police lock-up at Lohandiguda (in South Bastar) though he was actually being held hundreds of miles away, at Narsinghpur. There were echoes of the 1876 rebellion in the unrest of 1961 in that both centred on 'releasing the Raja from captivity', or, to put it another way, recapturing him for the people. In this respect, too, the 1961 events recapitulated the Dasara scenario.

Shortly after the 1961 events, the ex-ruler was indeed released from jail and returned to Jagdalpur, where he uneasily shared the palace with his brother, no longer ruler even in name and not able to ride on the *rath* chariot (where his place was symbolically taken by the umbrella of Danteshwari) but still in position in the mystical sense. More demonstrations on his behalf continued intermittently for the next few years, and were successful in the sense that eventually control of his property was restored to him by the Court of Wards.

However, by this time the Raja (who firmly believed in his own divinity) was becoming fatally ambitious, having been resoundingly victorious in the elections as an independent candidate on a platform of support for tribal interests. The crunch came in 1966 when, as a result of famine in other parts of India, the government proposed to make a levy of rice from the Bastar cultivators (whose harvests had been satisfactory). The plan of the government to levy rice in Bastar reflects the fact that, despite its reputation for extreme poverty, Bastar district produces rice surpluses year after year and can more than feed its own people. However, there is extreme local resistance, especially among tribals, to allowing rice produced in the village to go to market or be subjected to a levy in the way the government proposed. This attitude is founded on the idea that if rice leaves the village the divinities responsible for the fertility and productivity of the village land will be angered, and future harvests will diminish. In a way, this conservationist attitude to rice is only another aspect of the proprietary attitude of the tribals towards their ruler (who should not leave the kingdom, just as rice should not leave the village). The Raja's campaign against the rice levy was therefore symbolically over-determined from the tribals' point of view, and their resentment became greatly inflamed.

The Raja made inflammatory speeches on this subject, and large numbers of people congregated at the palace and refused to disperse. Two clashes occurred at the palace between tribal demonstrators and police. During the second of these, the Raja, who may actually have been attempting to restrain his supporters, was shot and killed. According to the official report, twelve tribals died as the police swept the palace compound with rifle fire, though tribals and local residents believe that the number was vastly greater than this. Thus perished the Raja of Bastar amidst his people, and the Bastar power-vacuum was finally eliminated by the armed might of a modern state.

In conclusion, I would like to suggest that Bastar Dasara was that anthropological staple, a 'ritual of rebellion', but of a strange and paradoxical kind, in that its ostensible objective was the celestialization of royal power. But this paradoxical strategy, exalting the king in order to weaken the state, was perhaps the only one really open to the people of Bastar for whom, like the rest of India, a state *of some kind* was an ontological given, like food, light and air, not an arbitrary historical imposition. By co-opting royal ritual and enmeshing the ruler in coercive subordination, the people had, first of all, a sanctioned occasion for annual demonstrations, within sight of the capital and the government, of their unity and armed strength, and secondly a basis for 'loyal' anti-government agitation. The peace of Bastar, during the British period, rested on the willingness of the government to align itself with the Raja, who in turn aligned himself with the tribal people, to the detriment of political and social modernization, which was kept at bay for a long time. When this triadic relationship was disturbed, there would be 'loyalist' rebellions which converted the Dasara scheme into popular expressions of intransigence of a more transparent kind. But I hope that I have demonstrated that Bastar Dasara was indeed subversive in that it tended to mitigate the possibility of rational state administration and the development of a rural ruling class for a prolonged period, to the substantial benefit of the mass of rural Bastarians. In other words, royal ritual is not necessarily about enhancing the power of rulers and elites to the detriment of the ruled. In the case of Bastar, I believe that it was precisely the opposite.

NOTES

1 The Frazer Memorial Lecture, delivered at Cambridge on 22 November 1996.
2 The best general account of tribal society in India is provided by Singh (1985), to whom this article owes far more than may be superficially apparent. The discussion by Beteille (1991) is also very important.
3 The untrammelled lifestyle of the north Bastar Gonds in their pre-Independence heyday is described in the work of Elwin (1947). In the 1970s and early 1980s, when, with Simeran Gell, I worked in north-central Bastar myself, the situation was in many respects unchanged.
4 The best descriptions of Bastar Dasara are the one in the 1911 Census of India and, secondly, a detailed account tucked away in an article by Majumdar (1939) of Dasara as performed in the 1930s, before the storm broke over the head of the last ruler, Pravir.
5 Currently, it seems that tribal people are not prepared to accept that the goddess 'Danteshwari' is the Hindus' Durga, since this proposition was explicitly denied by Jaidev Baghel, celebrated artist and spokesman of contemporary tribal opinion, in conversation with Gregory, who has written most interestingly on this subject. Gregory, in his unpublished manuscript (Gregory n.d.) cites Baghel's version of the story of Danteshwari in which the goddess appears as a tribal girl born to a human couple, but supernatural in possessing, from birth, a full set of teeth (a mytheme based on the association between Danteshwari and *dant*, meaning 'tooth' in Hindi/Halbi). Danteshwari in Baghel's 'tribal' perspective is Durga-like in having a special affinity for tigers (replacing Durga's lion) and in being of a violent disposition, protective of her followers and banishing illness and inauspiciousness generally. The tribal Danteshwari is clearly not Durga, the standard Indian goddess. On the other hand, I do not think that the crowds at Dasara thought that the Raja (never considered to be a tribal by the tribals themselves) was sacrificing to a deified tribal girl rather than his own deity; our own conversations with Murias on the subject of Danteshwari suggested that

she was thought of as like the local goddess, but much bigger and more powerful, and that only a Raja, nearer to her in social status, could conduct sacrifices to her. Did the Raja undertake the 'Hinduization' of the local goddess(es) in order to legitimate his rule, or did the tribal people 'tribalize' Durga, or rather the cult of Durga in her Danteshwari form, in order to bind the ruler to them, and thus create the power-vacuum of which I have spoken? These are complementary, rather than alternative, propositions and one is in no way obliged to choose between them. However, the second proposition is perhaps the more novel, and this is the line I will pursue in describing the cult.

6 There were actually two chariots, one big one and one smaller one, used on alternate days. The chariots were made for each annual performance of wood contributed by specific villages, which was later auctioned off.

7 Schnepel (1996) provides an excellent account of Jeypore Dasara. He examines the subject from the Raja's and the court's point of view, rather than the tribals'. He, like me, places great stress on the very large and turbulent crowds which attended Dasara in this neighbouring state, though he does not draw the implication that the authorities were actually subject to intimidation at this time, as I do. He cites a number of descriptions of Jeypore Dasara, but does not mention the data from Fawcett published by Crooke (1915) which I cite above.

8 I owe the ideas expressed in these paragraphs to Fuller (1992 and pers. comm. 1996). He is not, of course, responsible for any remaining misconceptions on my part.

REFERENCES

Anderson, R.S. and W. Huber (1988) *The Hour of the Fox* (Seattle: University of Washington Press).

Appadurai, A. (1990) 'Topographies of the self: praise and emotion in Hindu India' in C. Lutz and L. Abu-Lughod (eds) *Language and the Politics of Emotion* (Cambridge: Cambridge University Press).

Beteille, A. (1991) 'The concept of tribe with special reference to India', in *Society and Politics in India* (London: Athlone).

Bloch, M. (1991) *Prey into Hunter* (Cambridge: Cambridge University Press).

Census of India (1911) *The Central Provinces* (ch. 4, Religion) (Nagpur: Govt Printer).

Crooke, W. (1915) 'The Dasahra: an autumn festival of the Hindus', *Folklore*, 26, 28–59.

Elwin, V. (1947) *The Muria and their Ghotul* (Bombay: Oxford University Press).

Fuller, C. (1992) *The Camphor Flame* (Princeton: Princeton University Press).

Gell, A. (1980) 'The gods at play: vertigo and possession in Muria religion', *Man*, (n.s.) 15: 219–48.

Gregory, C. (n.d.) 'Danteswari: images of an Indian goddess', unpublished draft.

Grigson, W. (1938) *The Maria Gonds of Bastar* (Oxford: Oxford University Press).

Kulke, H. (1984) 'Tribal deities at princely courts: the feudatory rajas of central Orissa and their tutelary deities' in S. Mahapatra (ed.) *Folk ways in Religion: Gods, Spirits and Men* (Cuttack: Institute of Oriental & Orissan Studies).

Majumdar, D.M. (1939) 'Tribal cultures and acculturation', *Man in India*, **2/3**: 99–173.

Schnepel, B. (1994) 'Durga and the king: ethnohistorical aspects of politico-ritual life in a south Orissan jungle kingdom' *J. Roy Anthrop. Inst.*, (n.s.) **1**: 145–66.

—— (1996) 'The Hindu king's authority reconsidered: Durga-*puja* and Dassrà in a South Orissan jungle Kingdom', in À. Boholm (ed.) *Political Rituals* (Göteborg: Institute for Advanced Studies in Social Anthropology).

Singh, K.S. (1985) *Tribal Society in India* (Delhi: Vikas).

Sunder, N. (1997) *Subalterns and Sovereigns: An Anthropological History of Bastar 1854–1996* (Delhi: Oxford University Press).

The Published Work of Alfred Gell (1971–1998)[1]

1971   'Penis sheathing and ritual status in a West Sepik village', *Man*, 6: 165–81.

1974   'Understanding the occult', *Radical Philosophy*, 9: 17–26.

1975   *Metamorphosis of the Cassowaries: Umeda Society, Language and Ritual* (London: Athlone).

1977   'Magic, perfume, dream', in I.M. Lewis (ed.) *Symbols and Sentiments: Cross-Cultural Studies in Symbolism* (London: Academic).

1978   'The Umeda language-poem', *Canberra Anthropology*, 2: 44–62.

1979a   'Reflections on a cut finger: taboo in the Umeda conception of self', in R.H. Hook (ed.) *Fantasy and Symbol: Studies in Anthropological Interpretation* (New York: Academic).

1979b   'On dance structures', *Journal of Human Movement Studies*, 5: 18–31.

1980   'The Gods at play: vertigo and possession in Muria religion' (Curl Prize essay for 1978), *Man*, 15: 219–48.

1982   'The market wheel: symbolic aspects of an Indian tribal market', *Man*, 17: 470–91. [Chapter 3].

1985a   'How to read a map: remarks on the practical logic of navigation', *Man*, 20: 271–86.

1985b   'Style and meaning in Umeda dance', in P Spencer (ed.) *Society and the Dance: the Social Anthropology of Process and Performance* (Cambridge: Cambridge University Press) [Chapter 4].

1987   'Newcomers to the world of goods: consumption among the Muria Gonds', in A. Appadurai (ed.) *The Social Life of Things: Commodities in Cultural Perspective* (Cambridge: Cambridge University Press.

1988a   'Technology and magic', *Anthropology Today*, 4: 6–9.

1988b   'Anthropology, material culture and consumerism' (review article), *Journal of the Anthropological Society of Oxford*, 9: 43–8.

1992a   *The Anthropology of Time: Cultural Constructions of Temporal Maps and Images* (Oxford: Berg).

1992b   'The technology of enchantment and the enchantment of technology', in J. Coote and A. Shelton (eds) *Anthropology, Art and Aesthetics* (Oxford: Clarendon) [Chapter 5].

1992c   'Inter-tribal commodity barter and reproductive gift-exchange in old Melanesia', in C. Humphrey and S. Hugh-Jones (eds) *Barter, Exchange and Value* (Cambridge: Cambridge University Press) [Chapter 2].

1992d   'Under the sign of the cassowary', in B. Juillerat (ed.) *Shooting the Sun: Ritual and Meaning in the West Sepik* (Washington, DC: Smithsonian Institution Press).

1993   *Wrapping in Images: Tattooing in Polynesia* (Oxford: Clarendon).

1994   '1991 Debate – "Language is the essence of culture: against the motion (1)"', in: J. Weiner (ed.) *Language is the Essence of Culture*, Group for Debates in Anthropological

THE ART OF ANTHROPOLOGY

Theory, University of Manchester, Department of Social Anthropology. [Reprinted in T. Ingold (ed.) *Key Debates in Anthropology* (London: Routledge, 1996).]

1995a   'The language of the forest: landscape and phonological iconism in Umeda', in E. Hirsch and M. O'Hanlon (eds) *The Anthropology of Landscape: Perspectives on Place and Space* (Oxford: Clarendon). [Chapter 8].

1995b   'On Coote's "Marvels of everyday vision"', in J. Weiner (ed.) ' "Too many meanings": a critique of the anthropology of aesthetics', *Social Analysis* (special issue), 38: 18–31. [Chapter 7].

1995c   'Closure and multiplication: an essay on Polynesian cosmology and ritual', in D. de Coppet and A. Iteanu (eds) *Society and Cosmos in Oceania* (Oxford: Berg).

1996   'Vogel's net: traps as artworks and artworks as traps', *Journal of Material Culture*, 1: 15–38 [Chapter 6].

1997   'Exalting the king and obstructing the state: a political interpretation of royal ritual in Bastar District, Central India' (Frazer Lecture, 1996), *Journal of the Royal Anthropological Institute*, 3: 433–50. [Chapter 9].

1998   'Time and social anthropology', in Y. Nagano (ed.) *Time, Language and Cognition*, Senri Ethnological Studies, 45 Osaka, Japan: National Museum of Ethnology.

1998   *Art and Agency: An Anthropological Theory*, (Oxford: Clarendon).

Notes

1. This is not a comprehensive bibliography as it does not include the numerous book reviews Alfred published during his career. Alfred was a frequent and often brilliant reviewer for the journal *Man* (and later [1995] when it became the *Journal of the Royal Anthropological Institute*), and most of his best reviews are to be found in that journal.

INDEX

London School of Economics Monographs on Social Anthropology series
Series Editor: Charles Stafford

With over 70 volumes published since 1949, including classic work by Gell, Barth, Leach and Firth, the LSE Monographs now form one of the most prestigious series in the discipline of Anthropology. Presenting scholarly work from all branches of Social Anthropology the series continues to build on its history with both theoretical and ethnographic studies of the contemporary world.

CPSIA information can be obtained at www.ICGtesting.com
Printed in the USA
LVOW11s1801141015

458264LV00001B/31/P